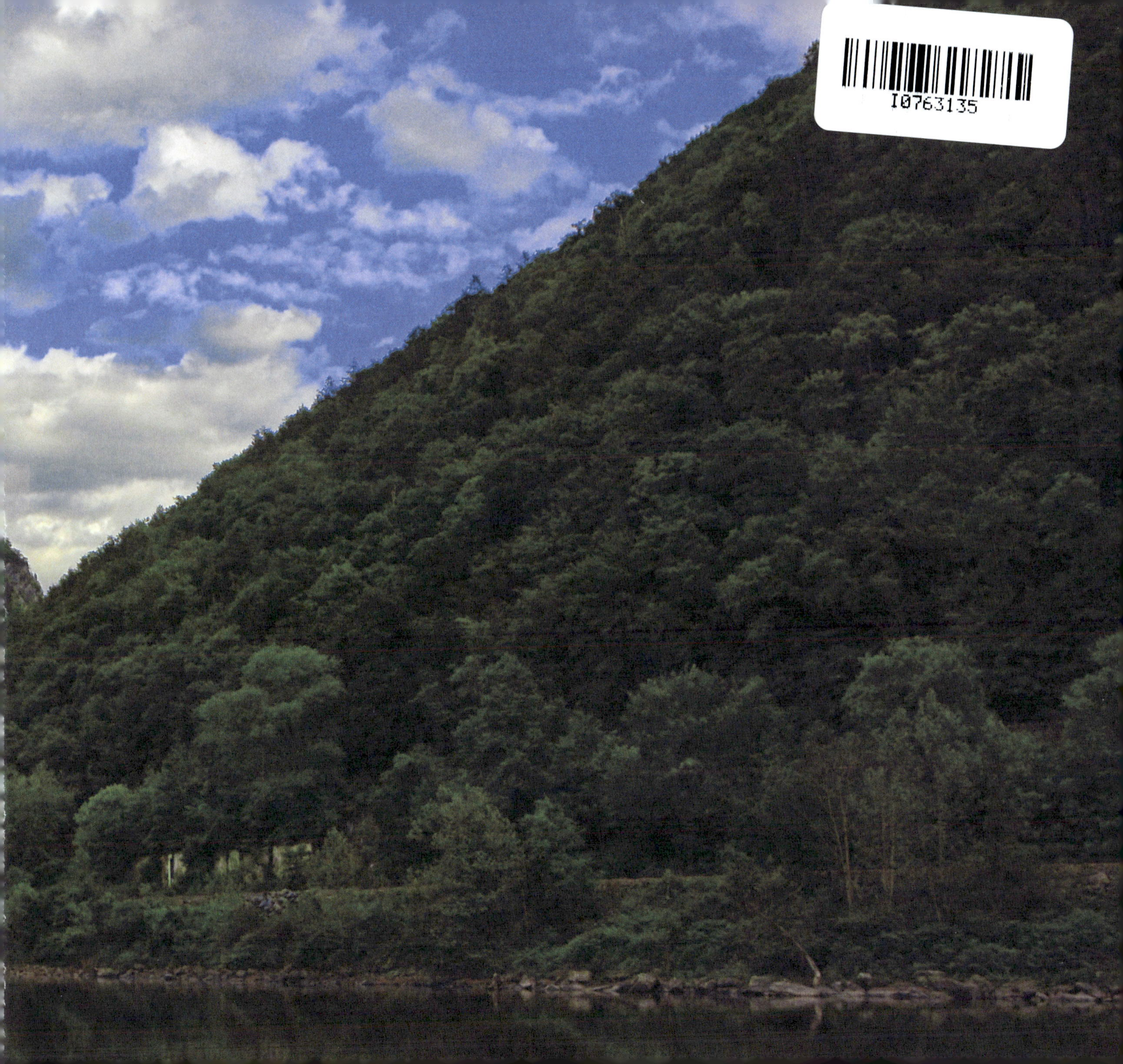
I0763135

I WISH TO DEDICATE THIS BOOK TO MY FAMILY AND FRIENDS.

Library of Congress Control Number: 2025936758

Cover photo is of Jeremy's Run Overlook in Shenandoah National Park

Designed by Alexa Harris
Type set in Aviano / Greycliff CF

ISBN: 978-0-7643-7036-6
ePub: 978-1-5073-0619-2
Printed in China
10 9 8 7 6 5 4 3 2 1

Published by Schiffer Publishing, Ltd.
4880 Lower Valley Road
Atglen, PA 19310
Phone: (610) 593-1777; Fax: (610) 593-2002
Email: info@schifferbooks.com
Web: www.schifferbooks.com

For our complete selection of fine books on this and related subjects, please visit our website at www.schifferbooks.com. You may also write for a free catalog.

Schiffer Publishing's titles are available at special discounts for bulk purchases for sales promotions or premiums. Special editions, including personalized covers, corporate imprints, and excerpts, can be created in large quantities for special needs. For more information, contact the publisher.

Introduction

I am an outdoor photographer who focuses on the United States of America's national parks, national forests, and national trails. I have section-hiked over half the Appalachian Trail. I am known as a photographer who goes the extra mile for his photographs. I love to spend time with family and friends in the great outdoors.

I was captivated by the outdoors at a young age. I learned to ski early in life in the Tetons. I learned more than just skiing; I developed an appreciation of the mountains and the great outdoors. The hiking lightbulb was turned on in the summer going into sixth grade, on a family trip to Yosemite National Park, California. The Appalachian Trail bug caught me during a cross-country preseason day hike on Pennsylvania's section of the Appalachian Trail, which included the highlight called the Pinnacle.

My photography interest started as a stress-reduction hobby of taking photographs of the sunsets while in a master of arts program in economics at the University of Connecticut. The hobby grew even more after finishing graduate school. I was most inspired by my father's interest in photography, particularly his *Crescent Moon Double Exposure*. Ansel Adams's dreamlike Yosemite National Park and Snake River Overlook iconic photographs also played an important role in developing my sensibilities for my own art.

The official start of hiking and taking photographs of the Appalachian Trail started about seven years later, while hiking on New Year's Day with a friend to New Jersey's Sunfish Pond and on the Appalachian Trail in Worthington State Forest and the Delaware Water Gap National Recreation Area. This inspired me to become a leader for the Appalachian Mountain Club and to take others on the Appalachian Trail as day-hike adventures. As of this printing, I have led day hikes along the Appalachian Trail from the James River, George Washington National Forest, Virginia, through Route 16 in New Hampshire, and also hikes on other trails.

The scope and breath of awe-inspiring beauty and variety that Mother Nature offers can be captivating in the moment and offer the pleasant lingering of a special memory that can last a lifetime. It may be an amazing vista with a spectacular cloud formation, lit to perfection with a brilliant sunrise or sunset. Sometimes nature presents itself in more-subtle ways with a scenic undulating woodland trail where trees, rock, groundcover plants, and light remind us that Mother Nature is the true master landscape architect.

It is always a pleasant experience when we get to hike on a beautiful sunny day, but sometimes things don't work out as we plan. Even those moments when there is a storm approaching and the clouds look harsh and ominous offer a unique apprehensive exhilaration. The stark contrast between the presentation of a calm sunny day and a storm of rolling clouds moving in is intense, to say the least.

Experiencing some of these special places in different seasons adds so much to their palette. The colors of fall in places where overlooking vistas offer one of nature's most amazing spectacles. For the more adventurous, hiking in the winter months with snow on the ground or even in a winter storm (of course with the appropriate safety precautions) can be an amazing memory you will never forget. Whenever you come across a field of wildflowers in the spring or the summer, it will put a smile on your face for sure.

Some destinations, such as Harpers Ferry National Historical Park on the Appalachian Trail, offer a unique blend of the rustic wilds of nature with a hint of civilization. Views of a small town along a scenic waterway nestled between towering palisades offer a special heartwarming presentation. This can make you feel both connected to the vast, wild beauty of nature and, at the same time, appreciate how small we are in nature's landscape.

On any given day, most of these hikes will offer scenes of contrast between spaces that evoke a sense of calm and relaxation and others that present a rustic beauty and the challenge of the trail, keeping us on high alert. The ebb and flow of how gradually or, at times, how abruptly things can change from one to the other is unique to each of these special places.

Collectively, there are so many emotional states that are evoked by the dynamic nature of a beautiful and scenic landscape. It certainly can be a different experience for each individual and at the same time can be a memorable, special experience for everyone fortunate enough to be there.

The diverse and breathtaking landscapes along the Appalachian Trail, ranging from verdant forests to rugged mountain vistas, each had their own part in inspiring me to write this book. I would say that the views of approaching, hiking on, and then looking back at Mount Greylock, the highest peak in Massachusetts, were very memorable to me. The Green Mountains in Vermont were also special because I was able to enjoy them in all seasons and got to combine my outdoor loves (photography, hiking, and skiing) to bring this book to you.

Also, my quest was to capture those special moments the Appalachian Trail has to offer and to share them in such a manner that can evoke some of the truly special feelings I experienced while taking each given photograph, and to inspire many to make plans to visit some of these awe-inspiring and accessible places themselves, ideally with friends and family.

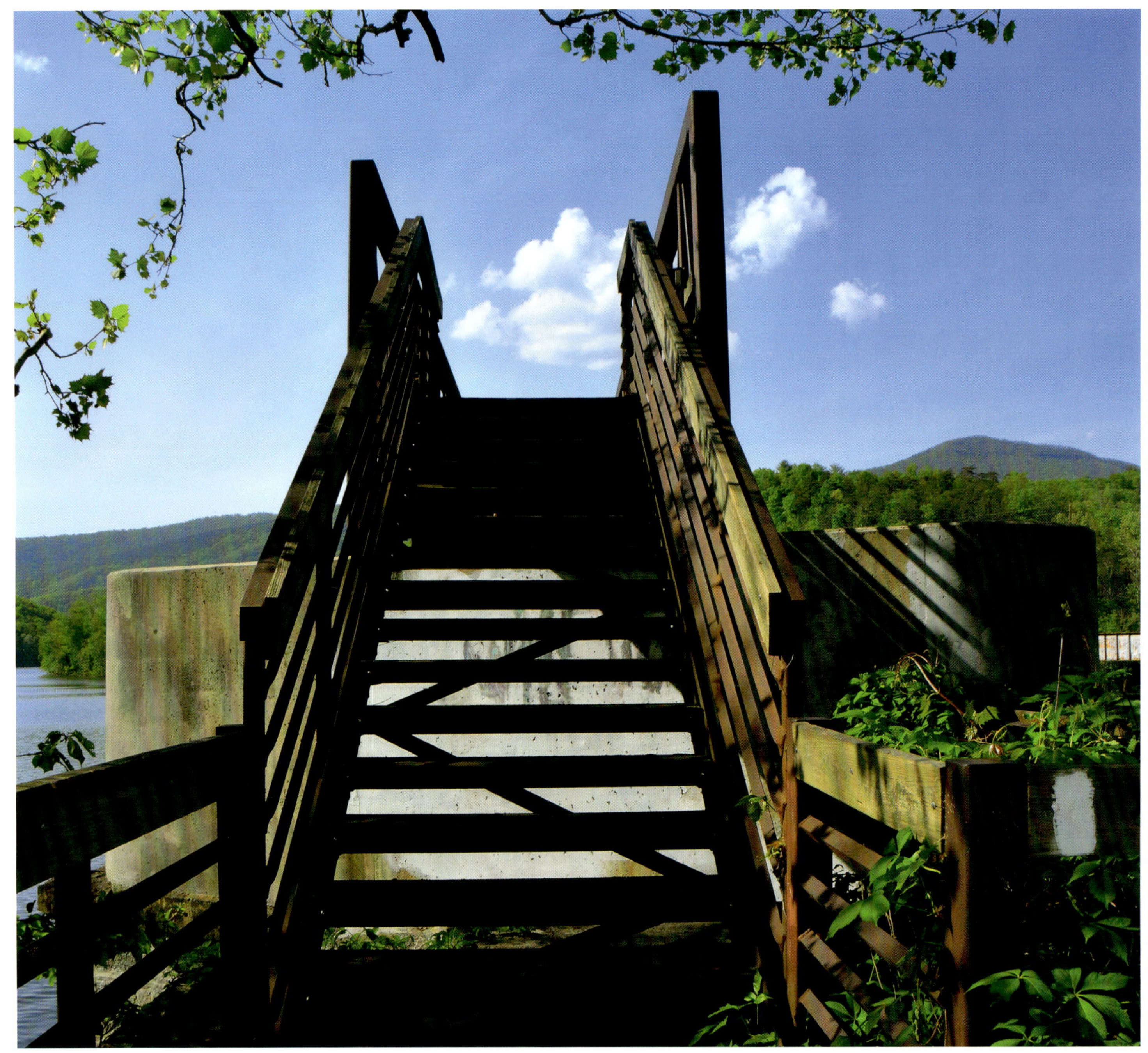

South side of James River Foot Bridge

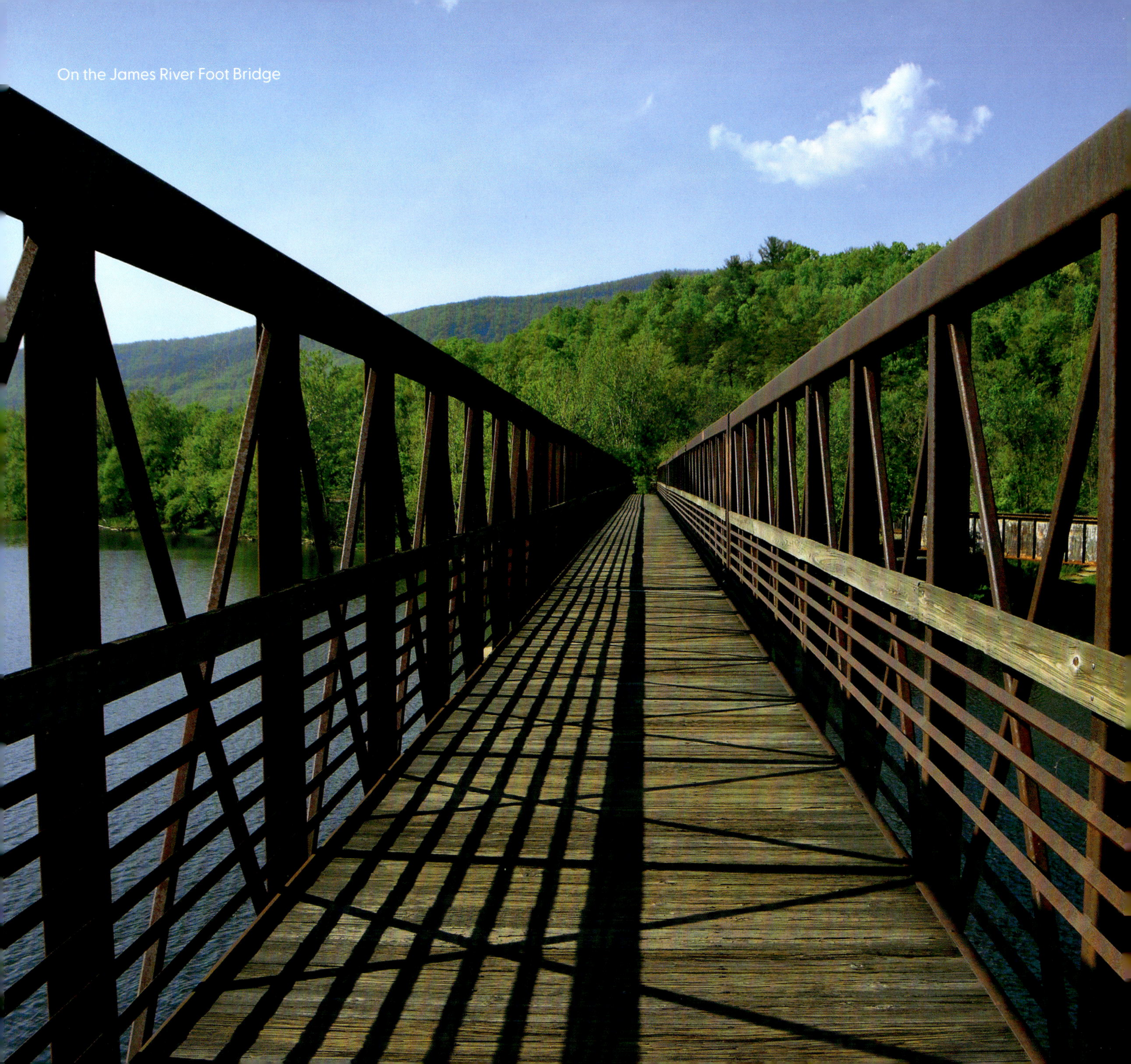
On the James River Foot Bridge

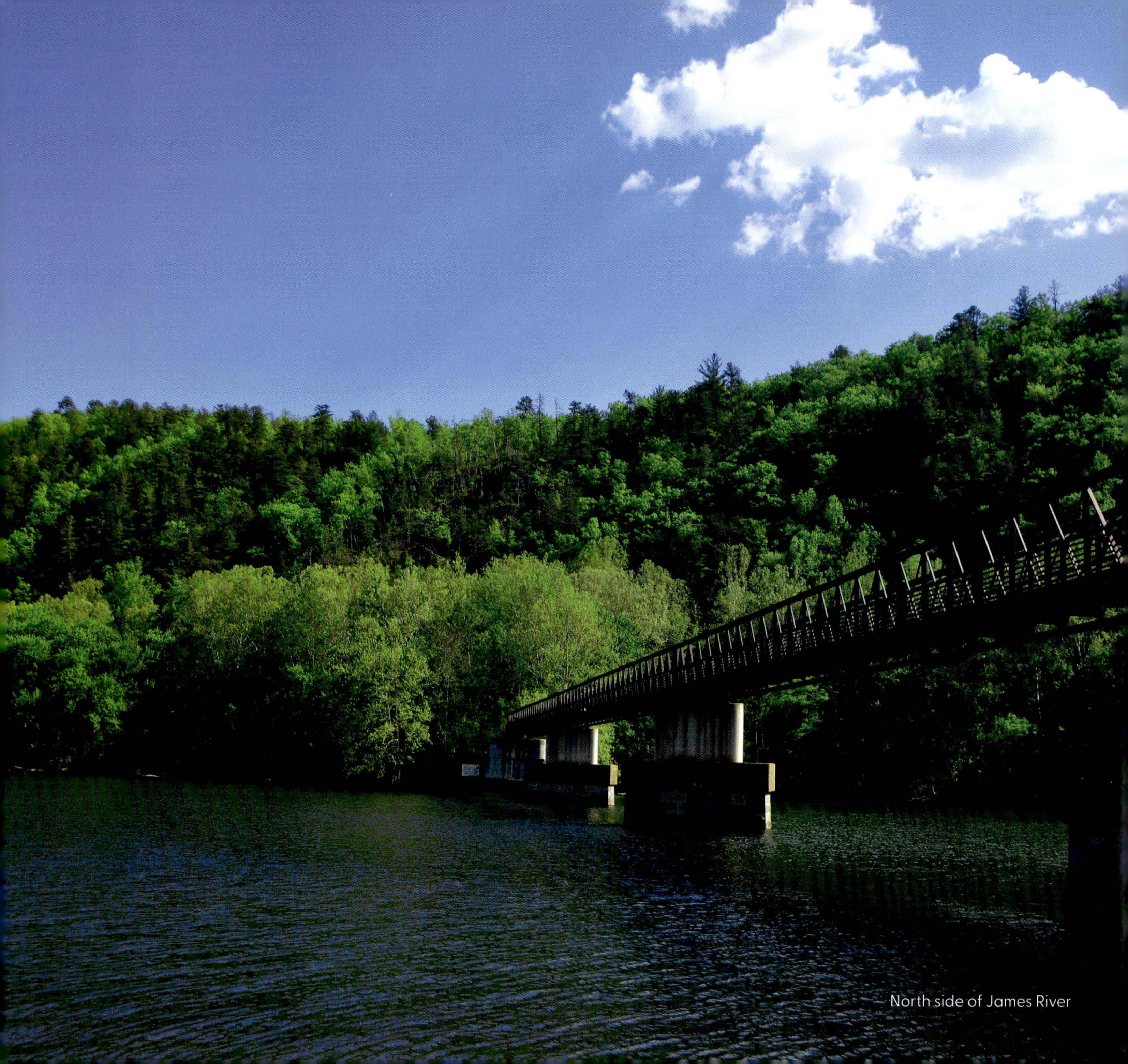

North side of James River

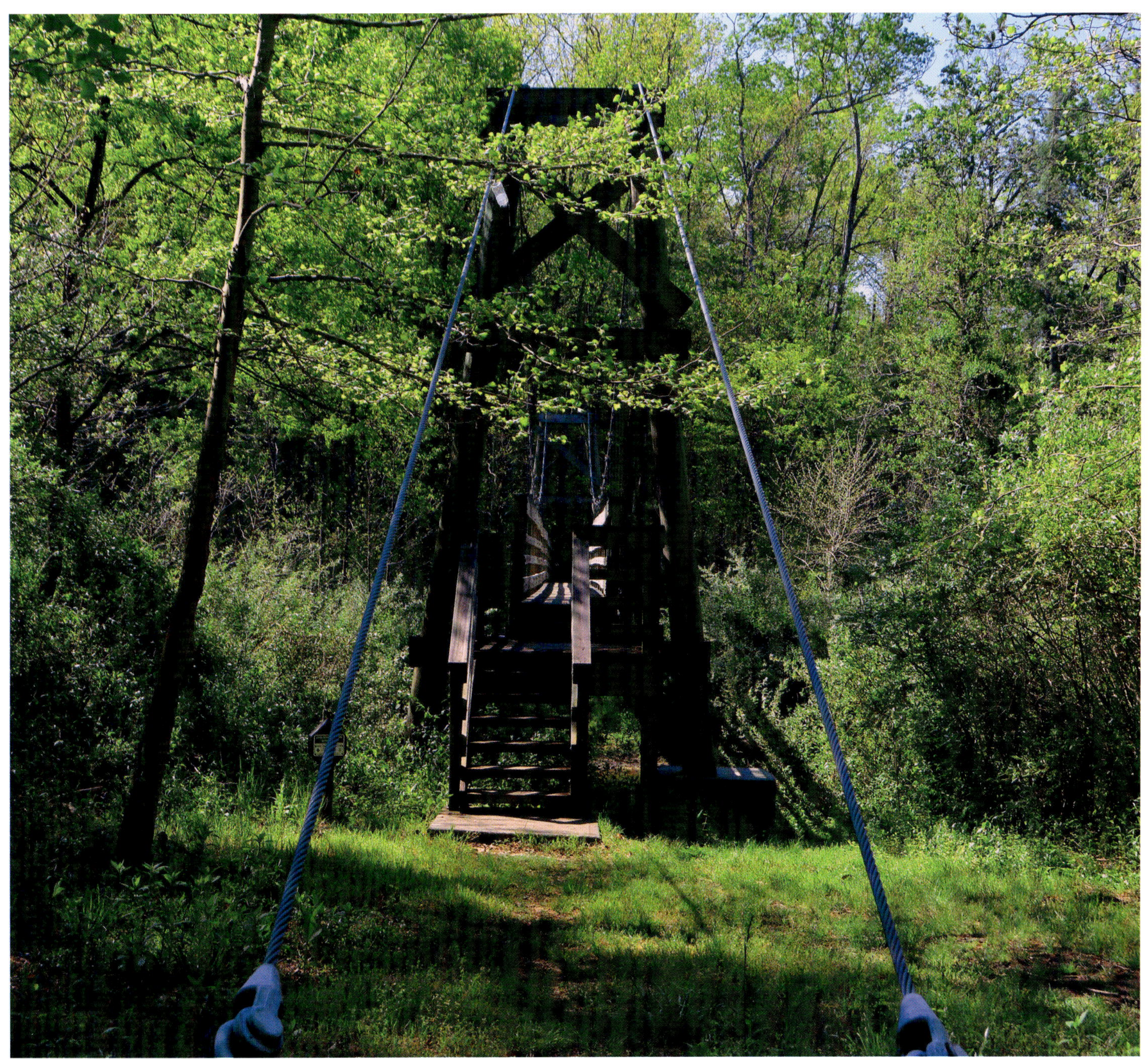

Pedlar Creek Bridge

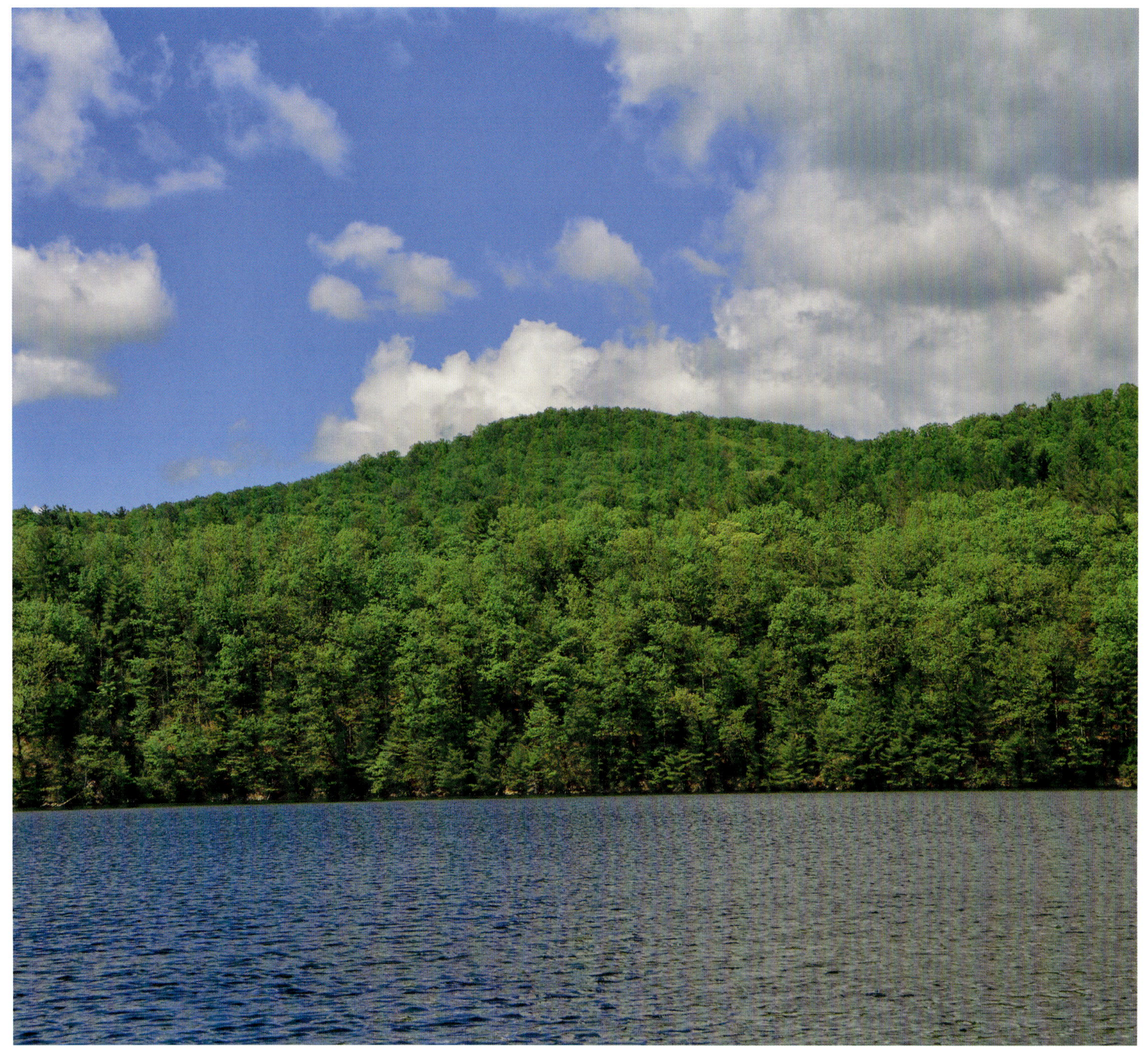

Pedlar Reservoir, Virginia

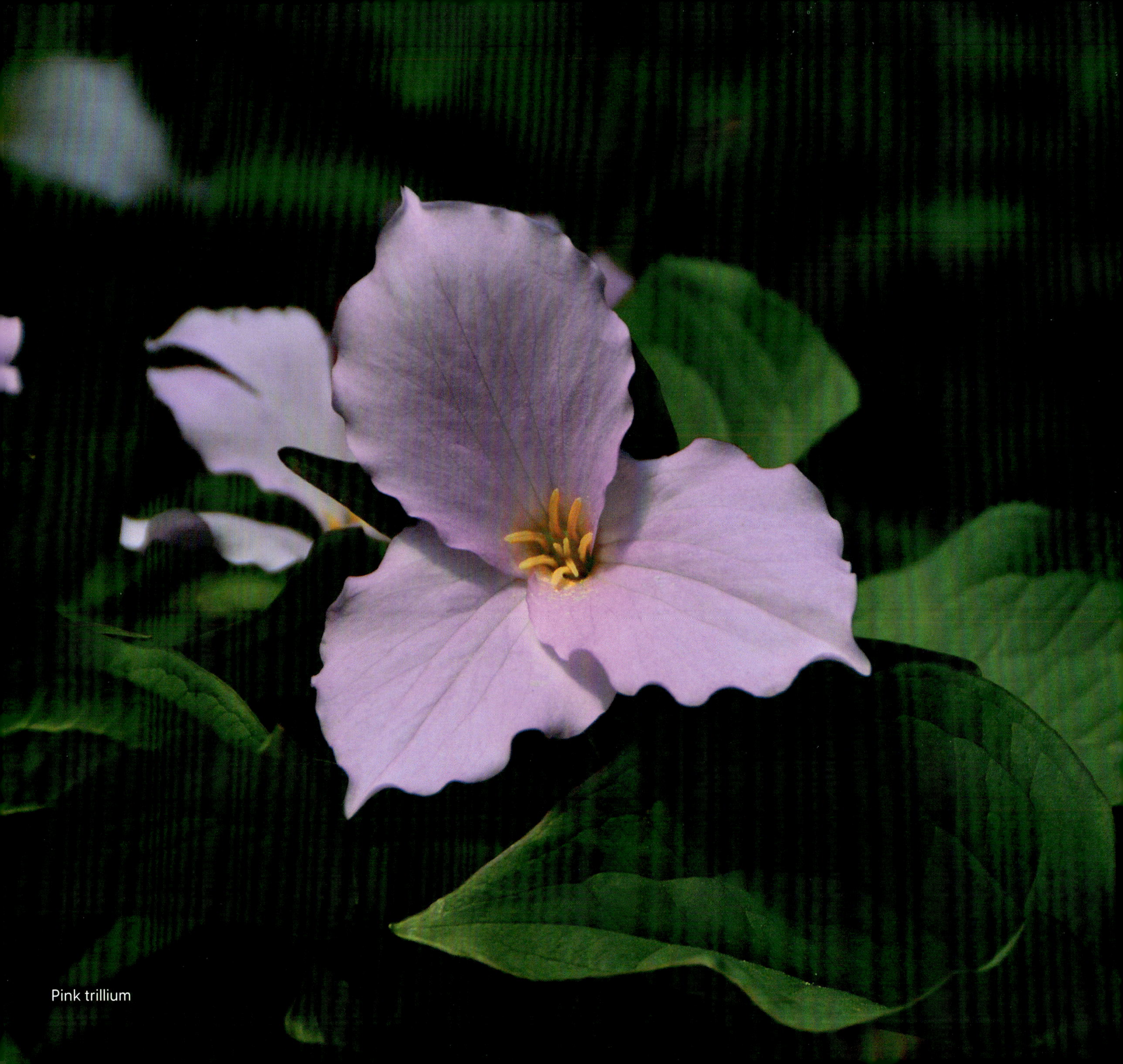
Pink trillium

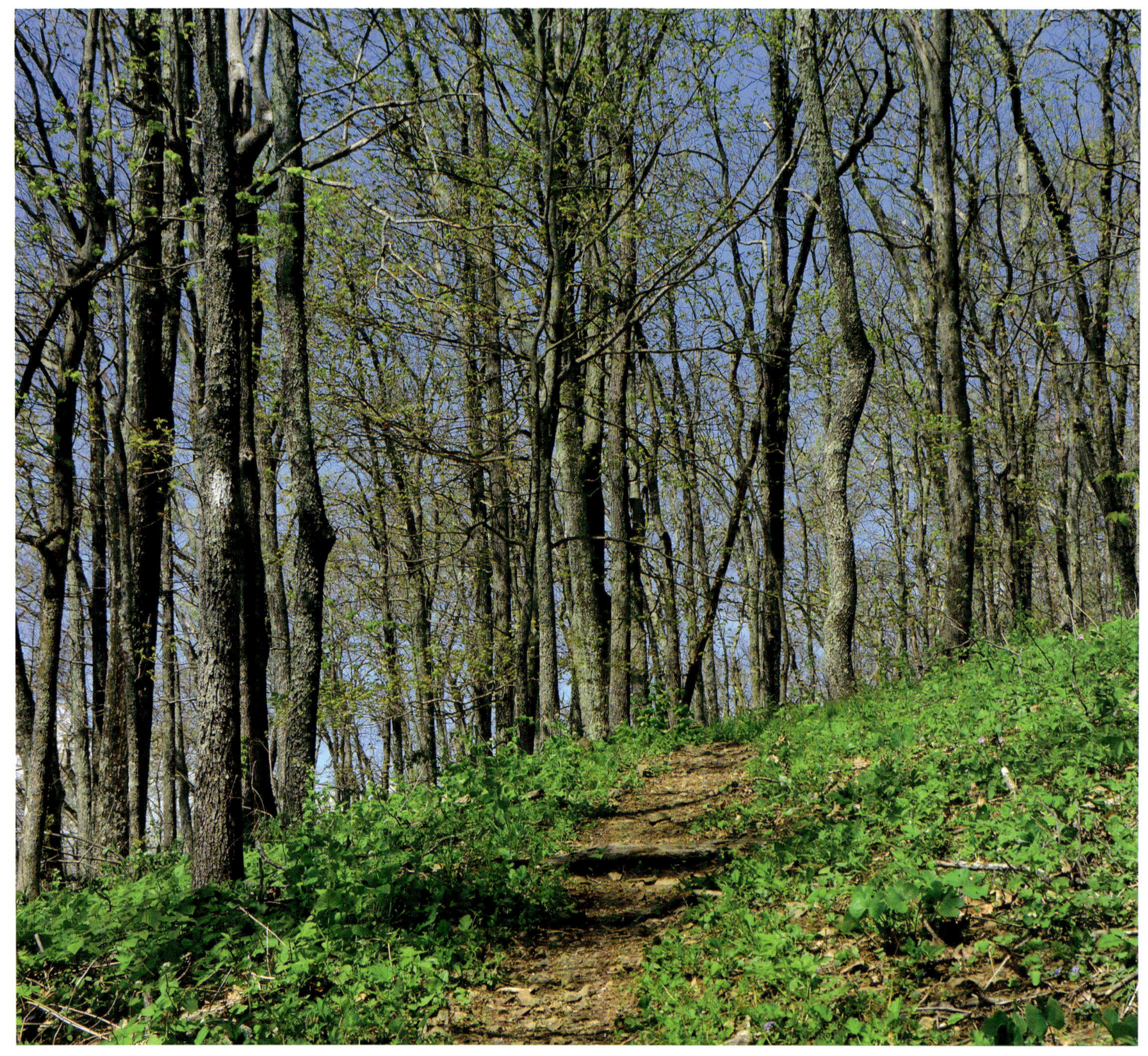

Heading north on the Virginia portion of the Appalachian Trail

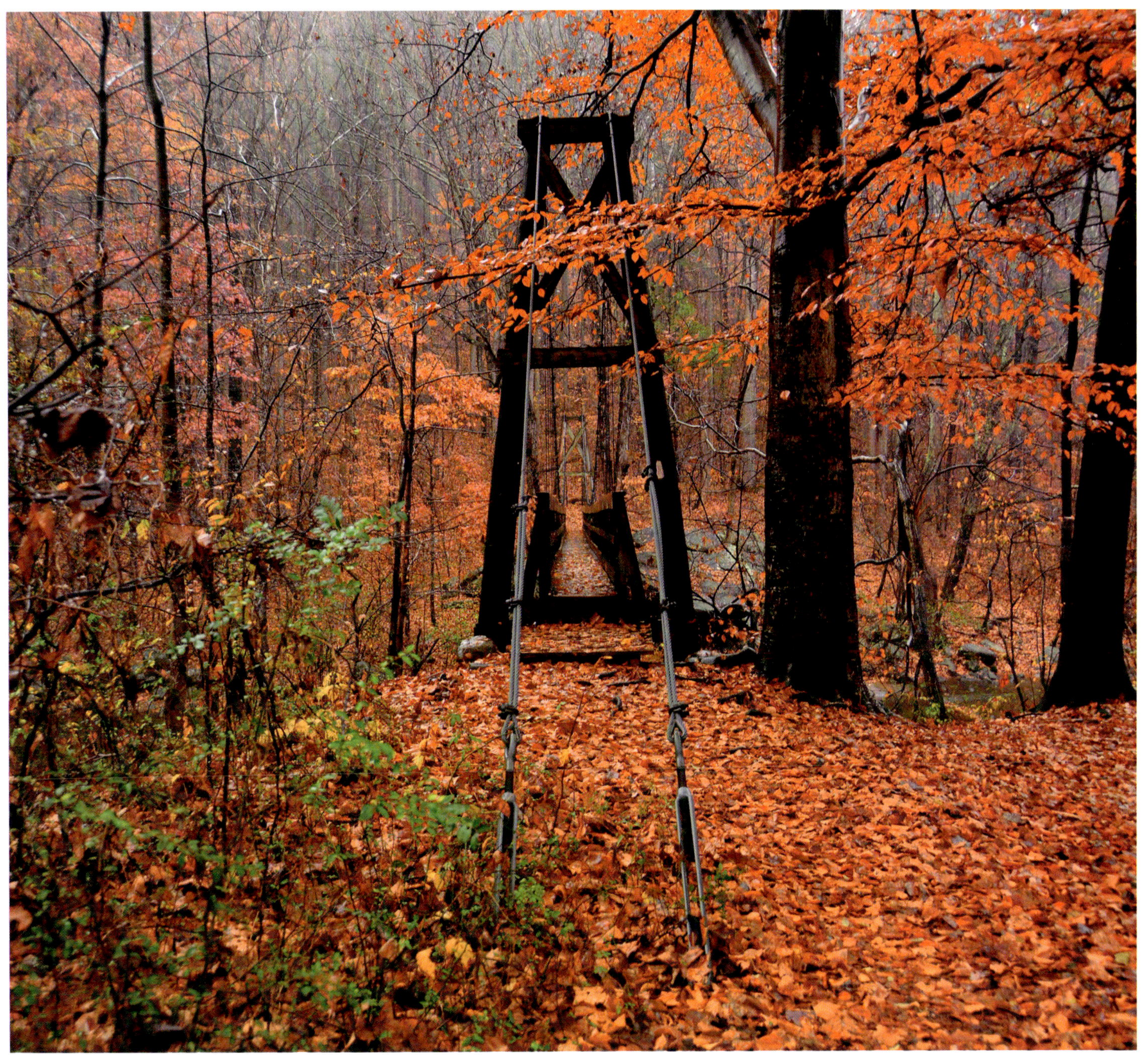

Washington-Jefferson National Forest's Tye River Bridge

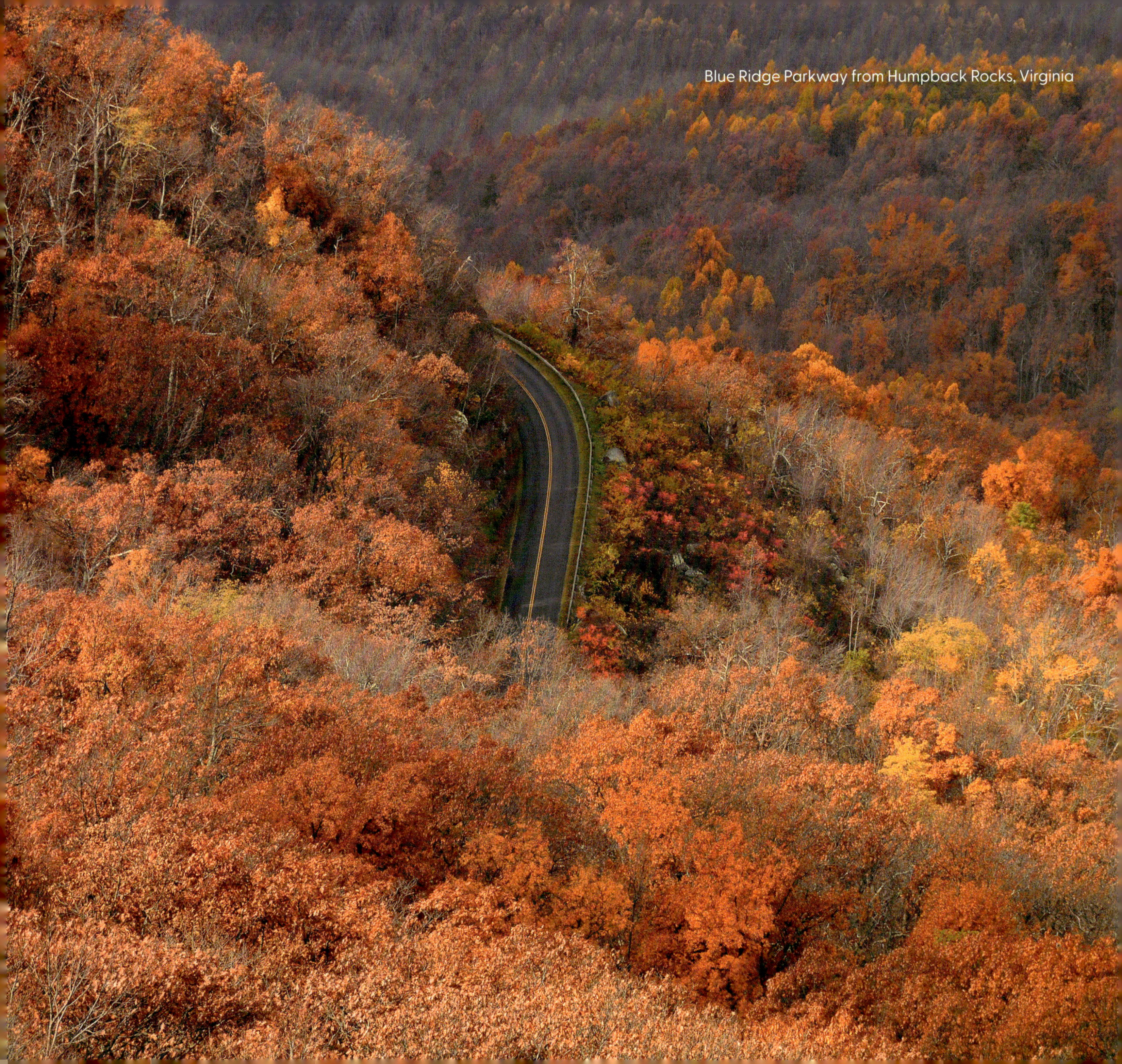

Blue Ridge Parkway from Humpback Rocks, Virginia

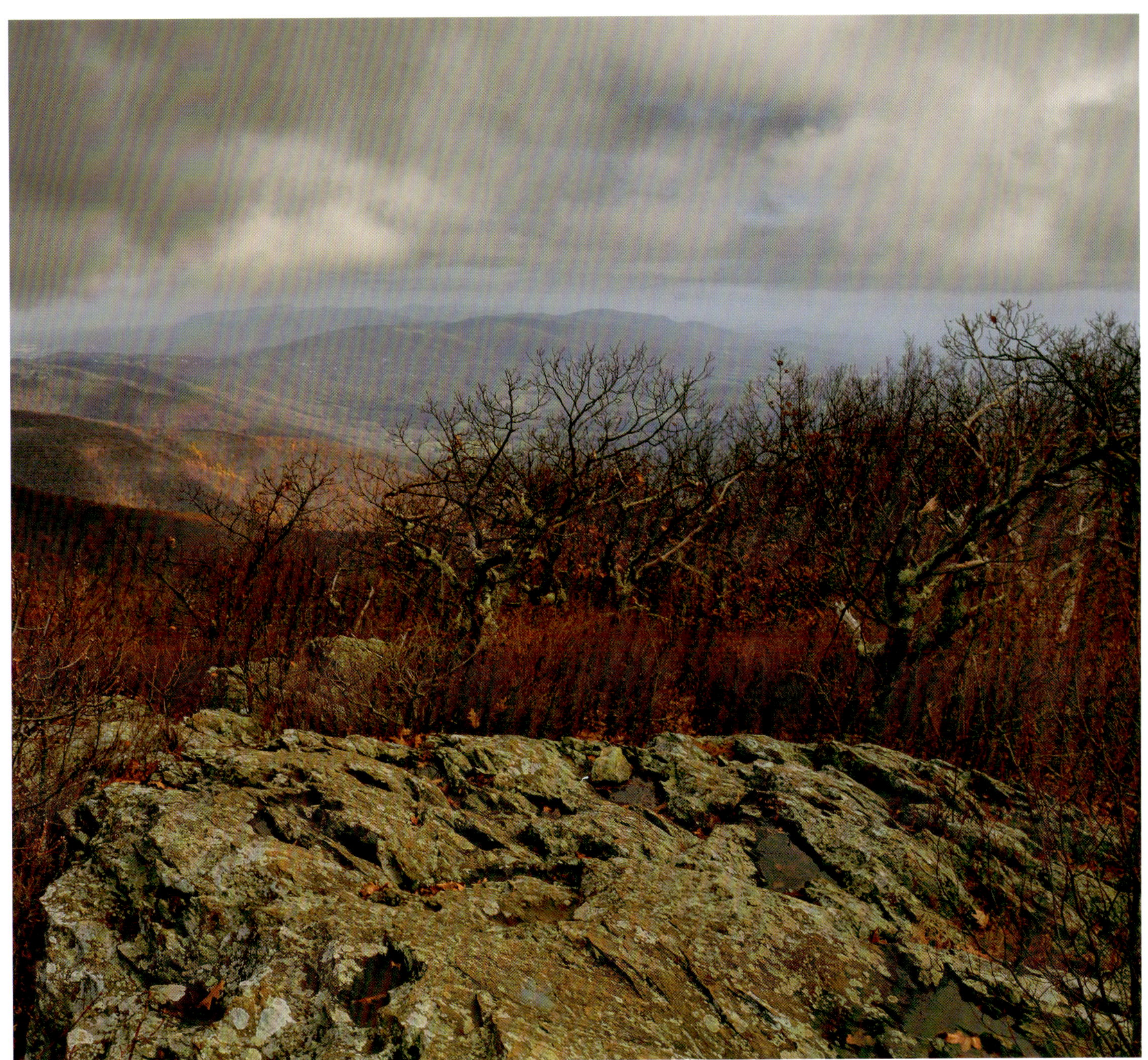

Blue Ridge Mountains approaching Shenandoah National Park, Virginia

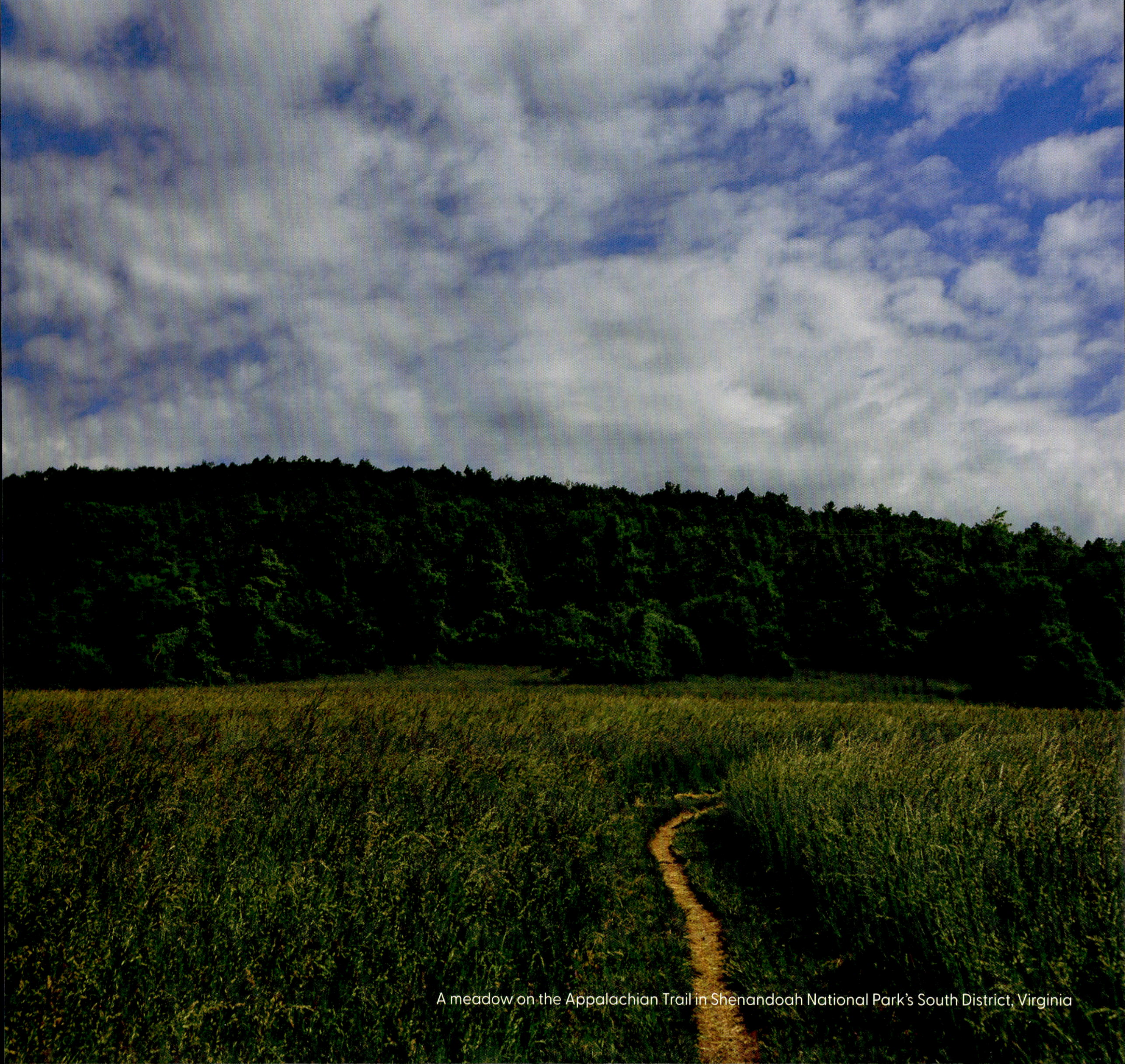

A meadow on the Appalachian Trail in Shenandoah National Park's South District, Virginia

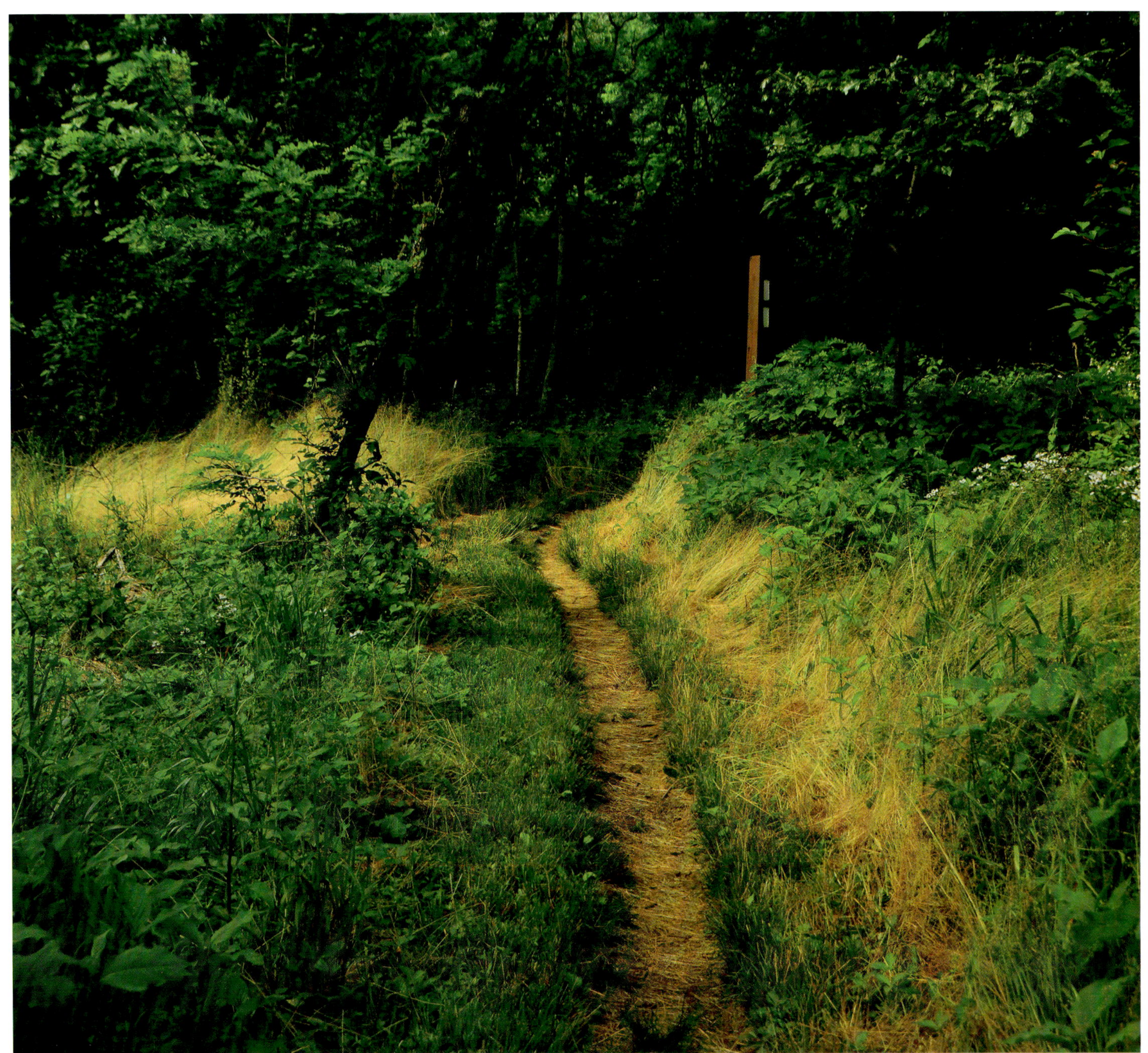

The Appalachian Trail turning right in Shenandoah South District, Virginia

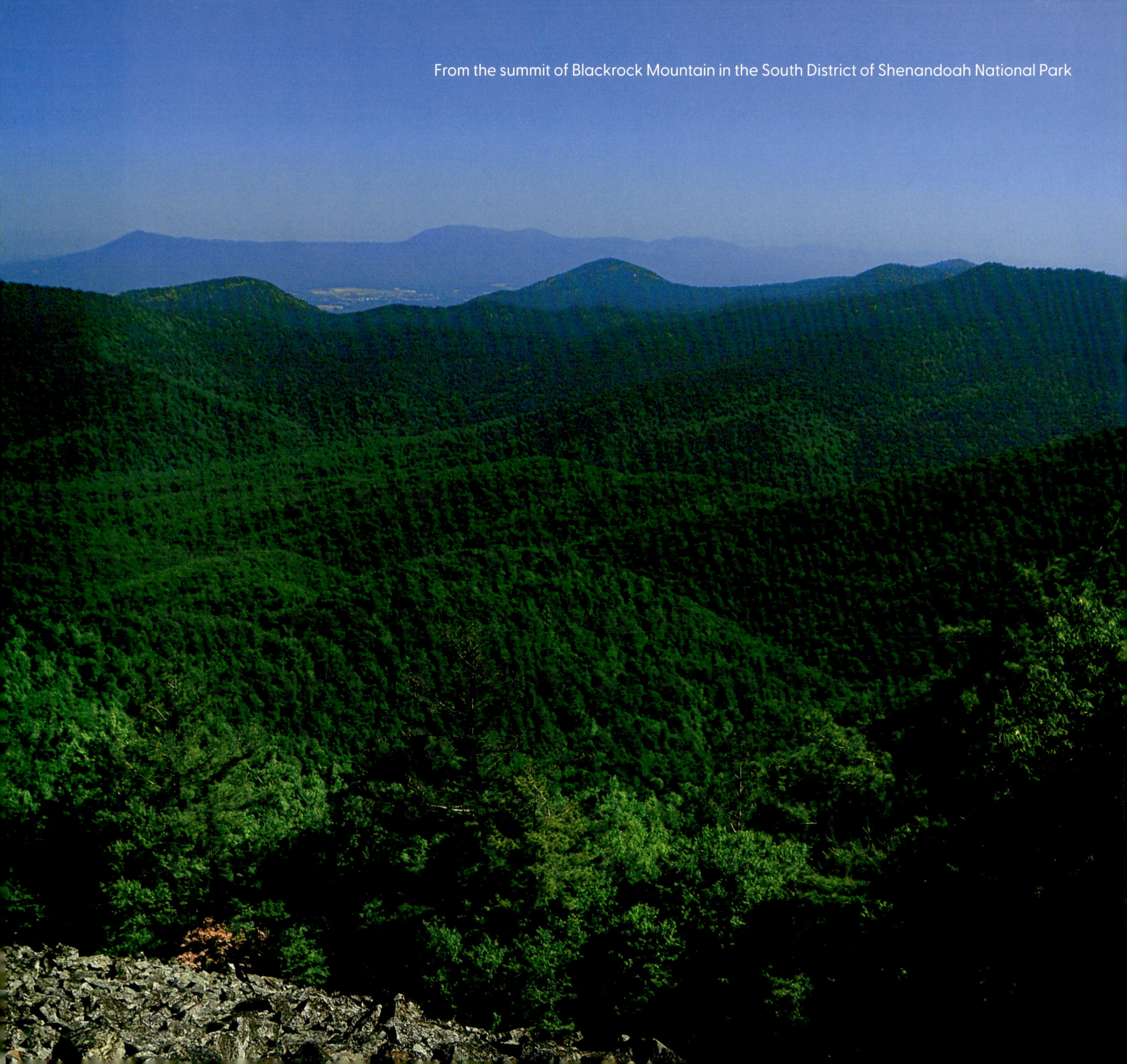

From the summit of Blackrock Mountain in the South District of Shenandoah National Park

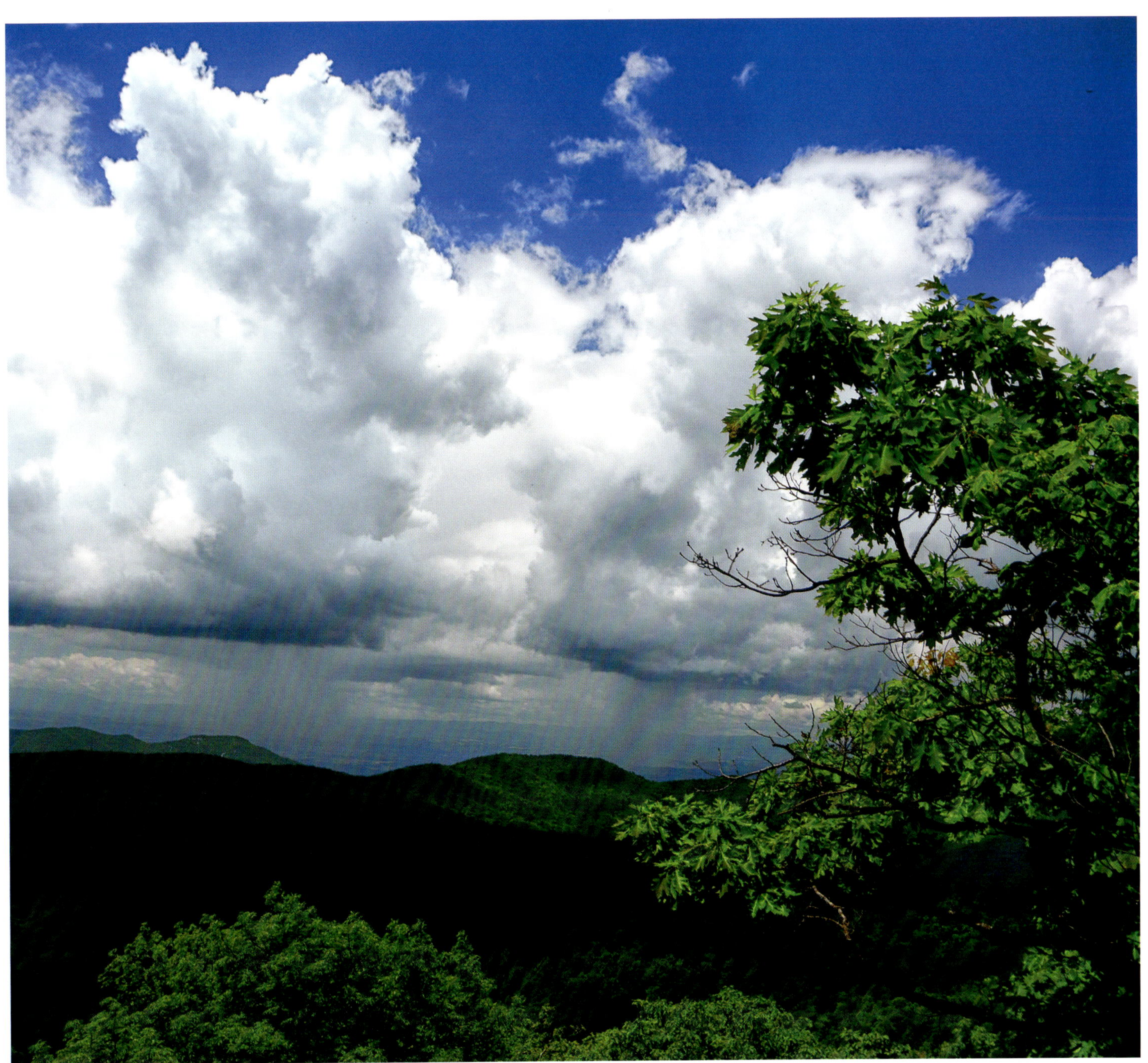

Thunderheads approaching the Appalachian Trail in Virginia

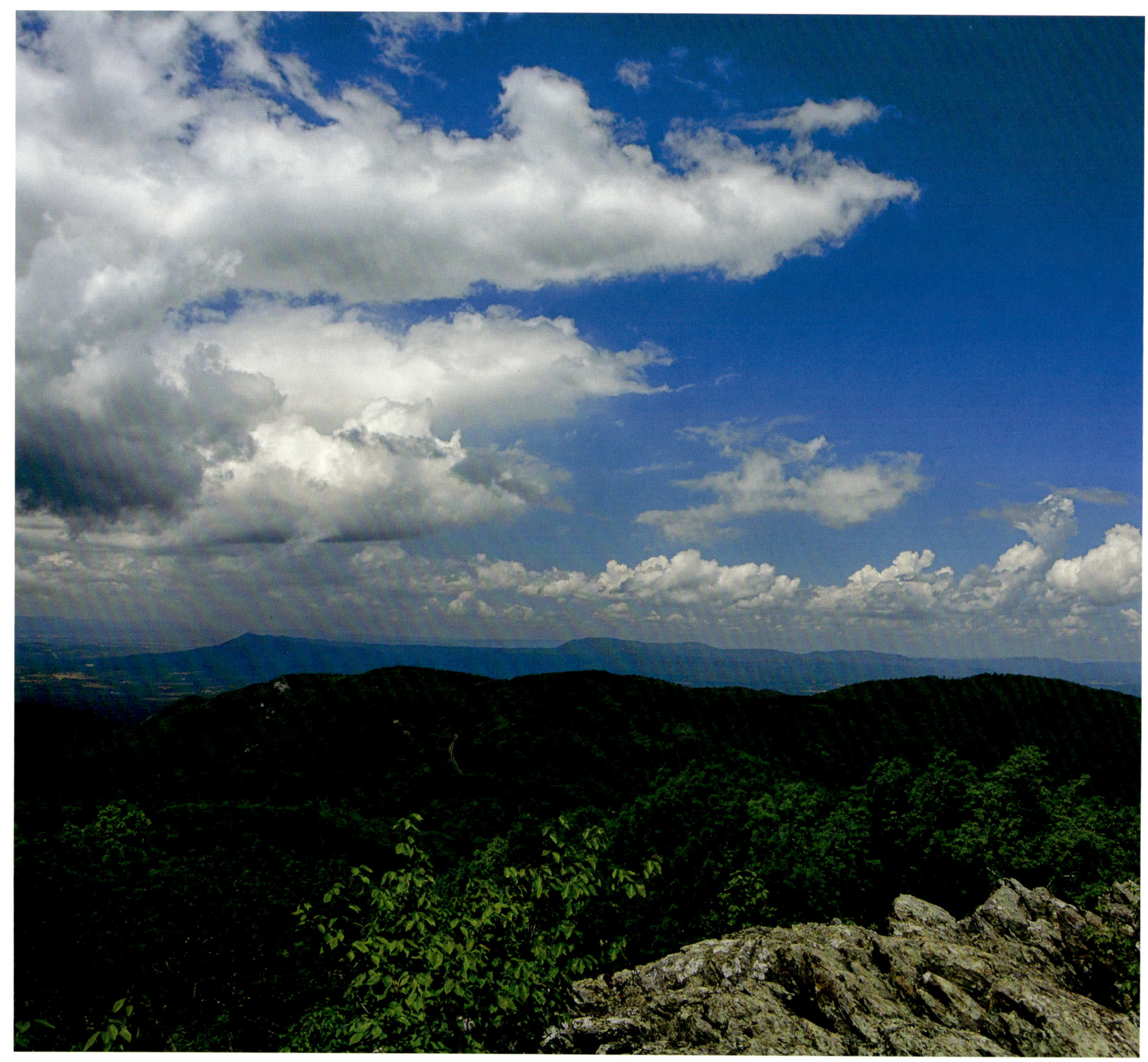

Massanutten Mountain and other Blue Ridges

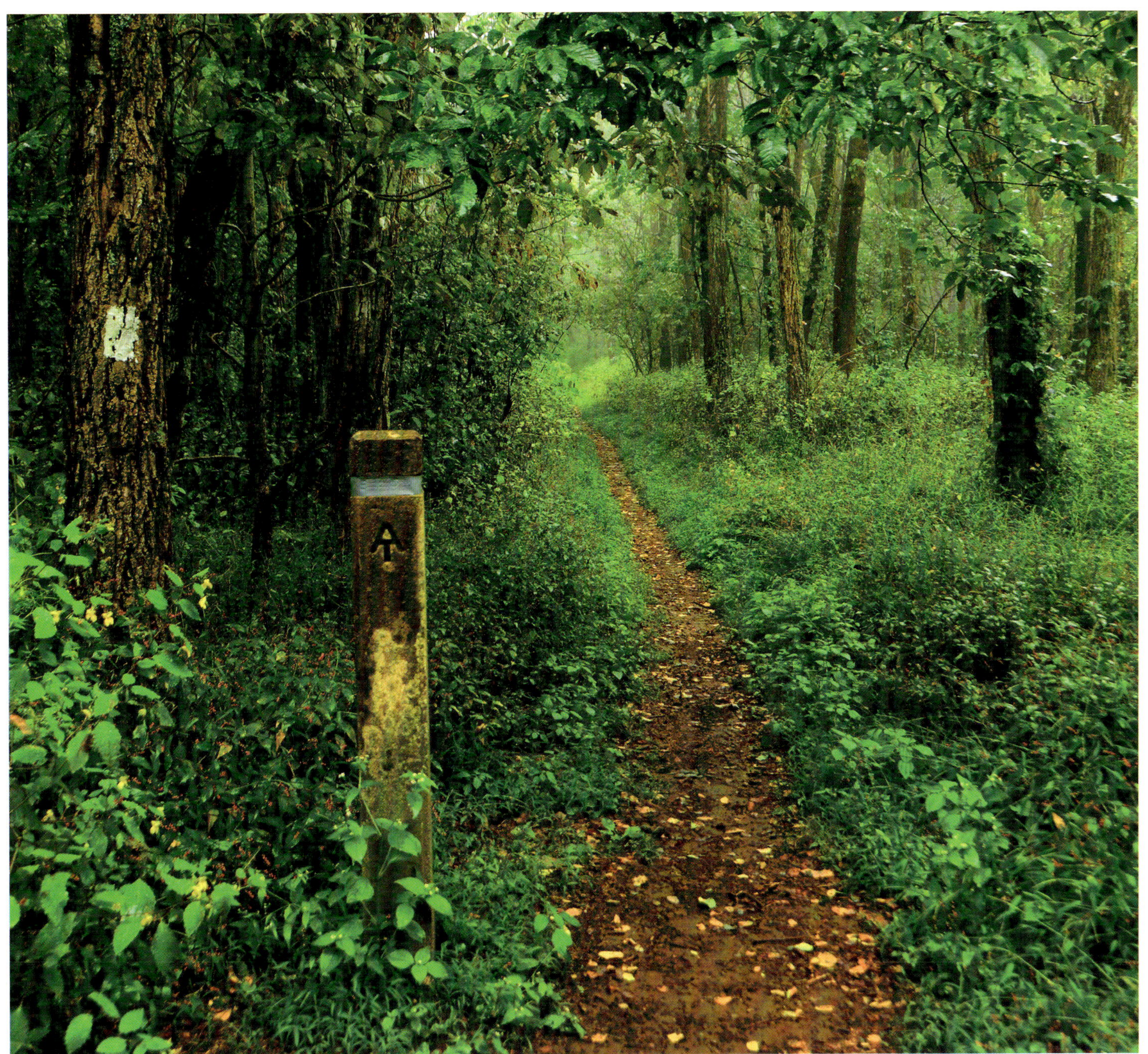

The lush green Shenandoah National Park, the Appalachian Trail

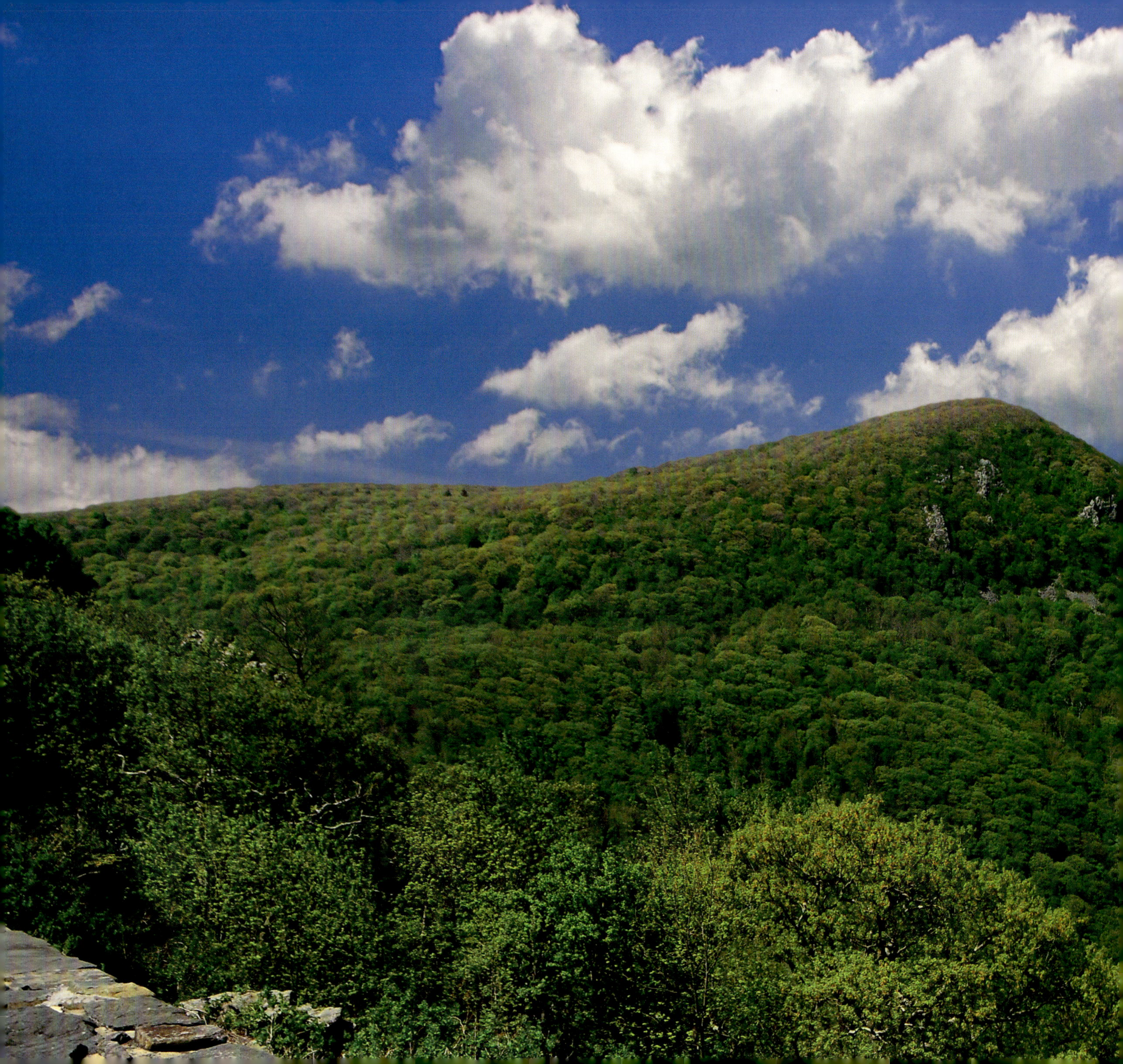

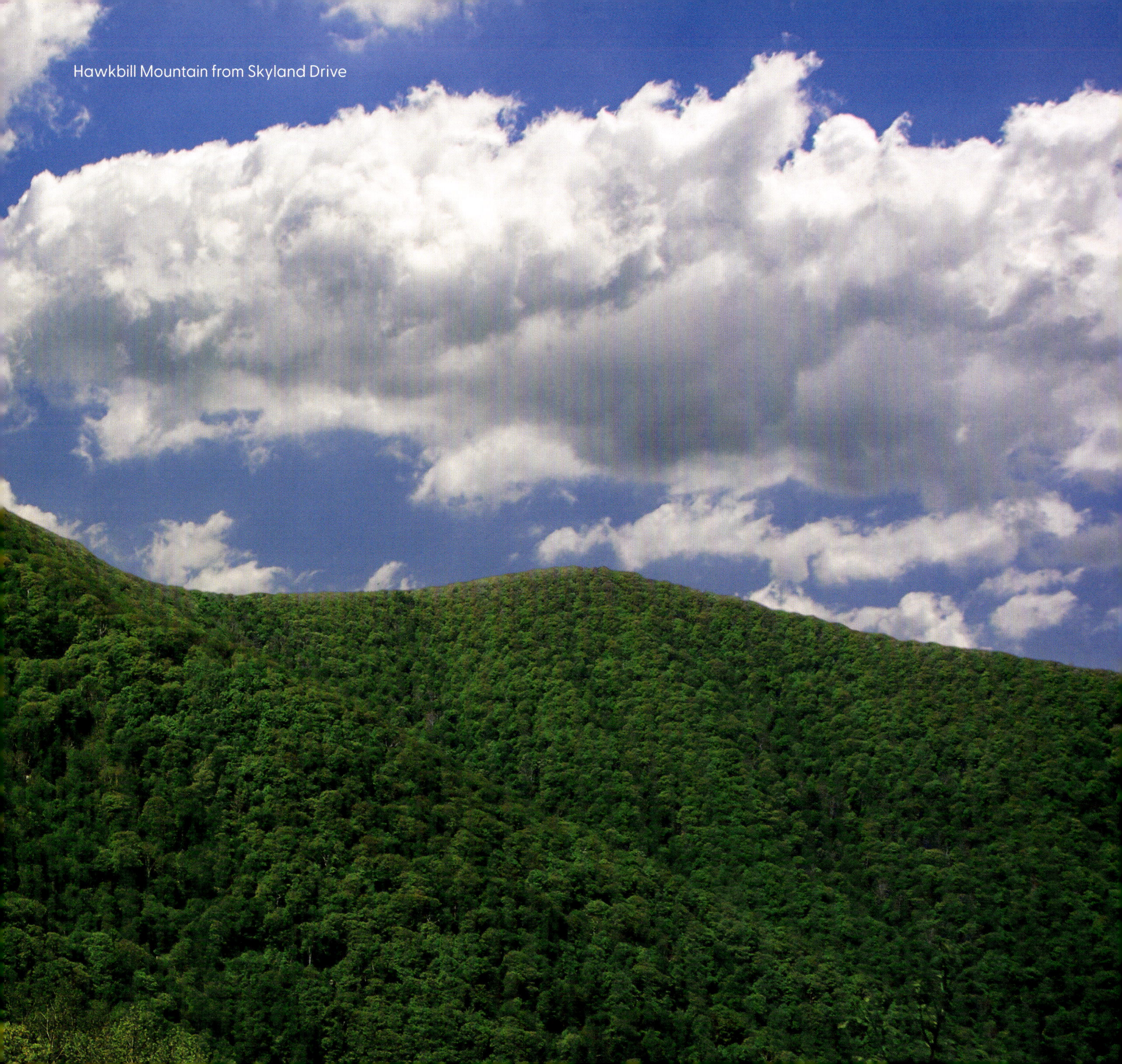
Hawkbill Mountain from Skyland Drive

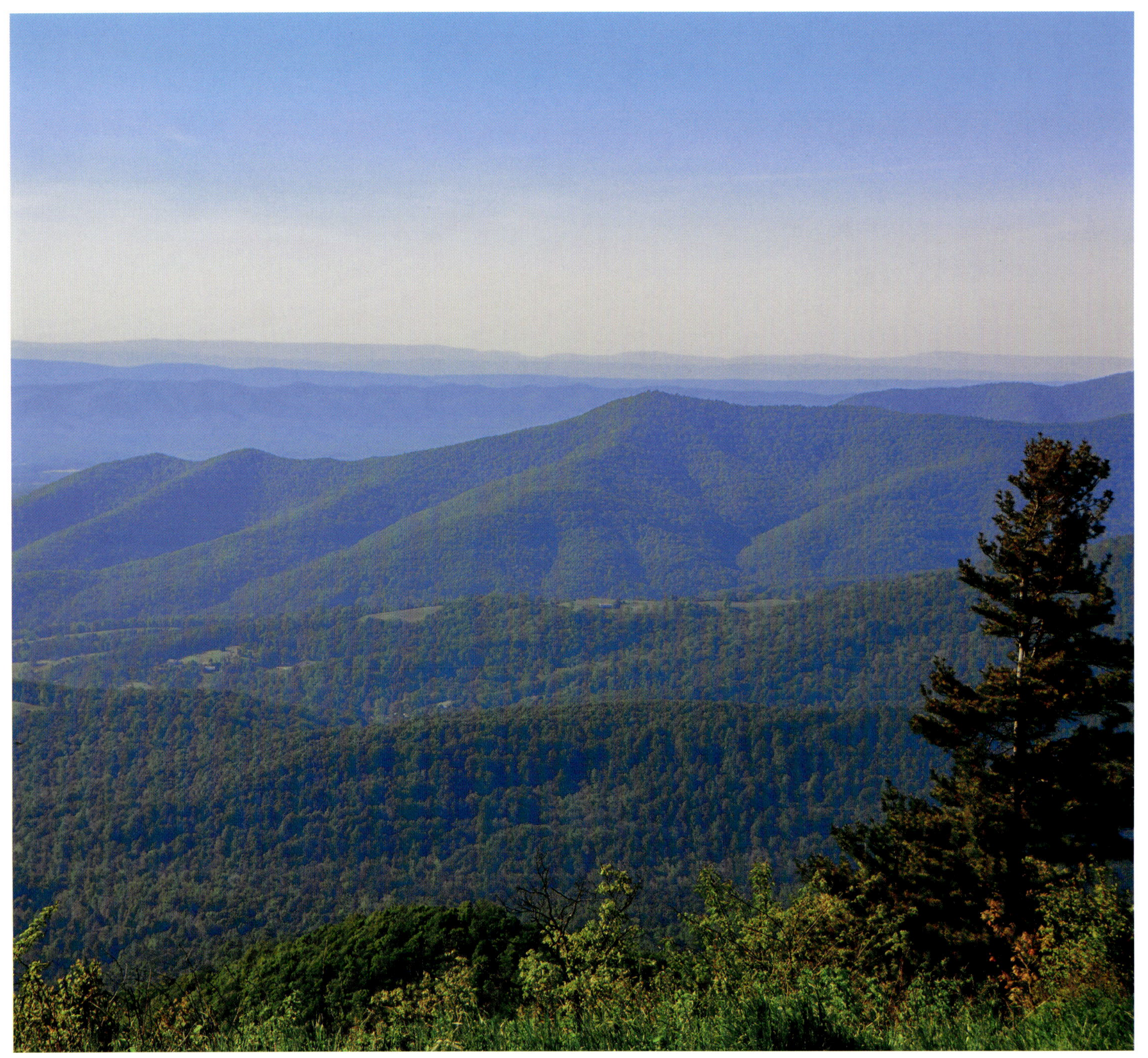

From near Stony Man Overlook in Shenandoah National Park

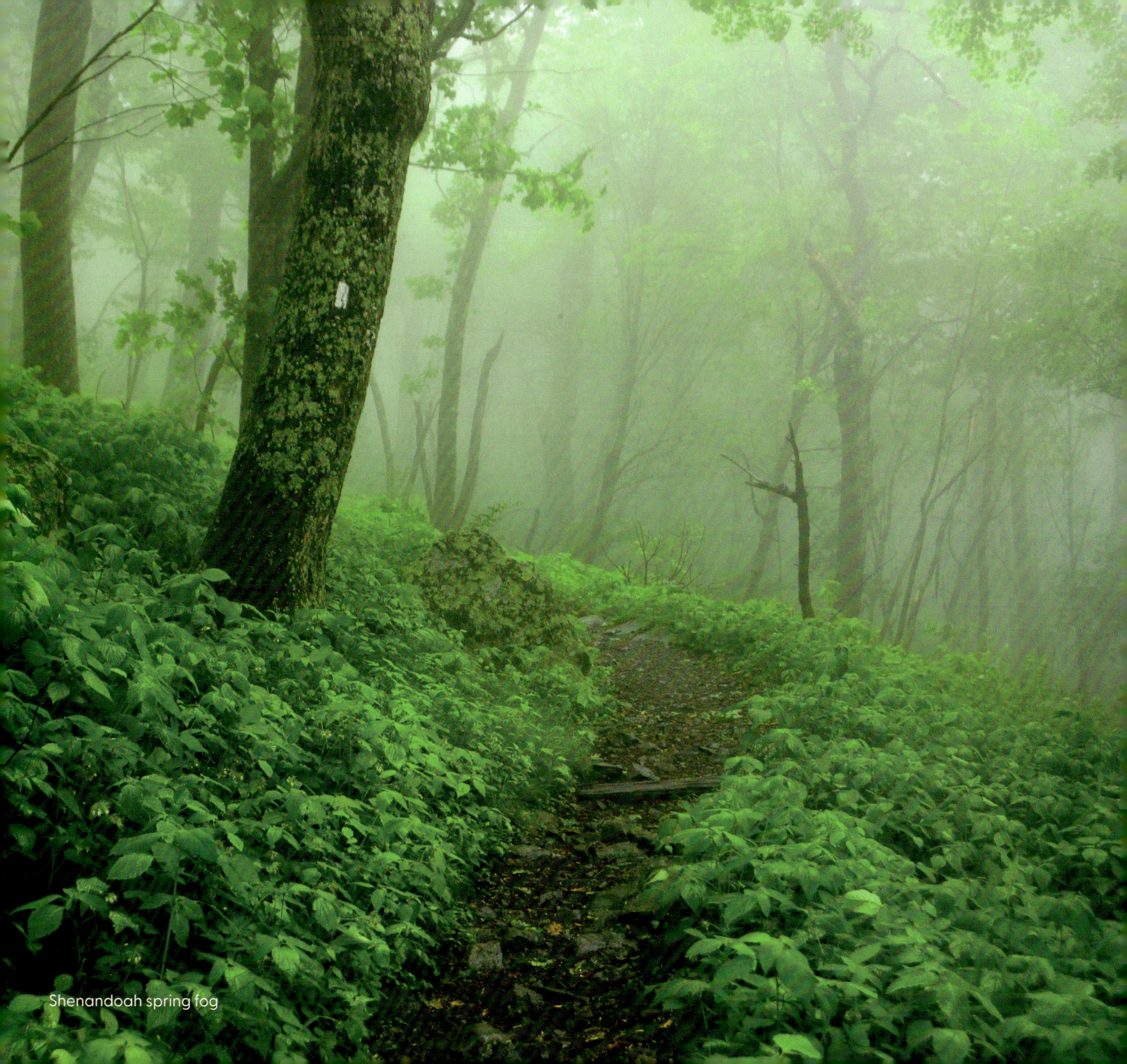

Shenandoah spring fog

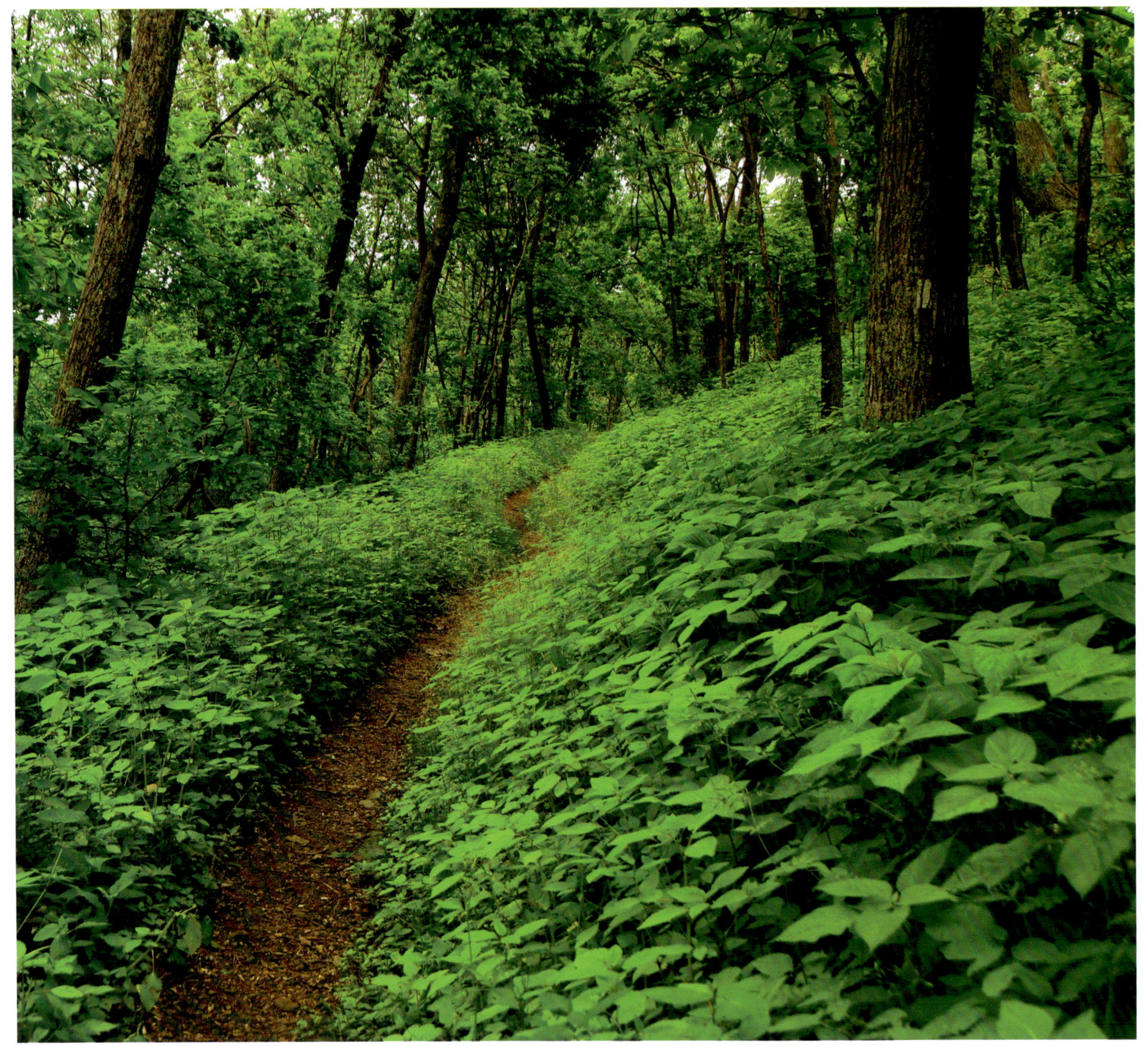

North District of Shenandoah National Park, lush green

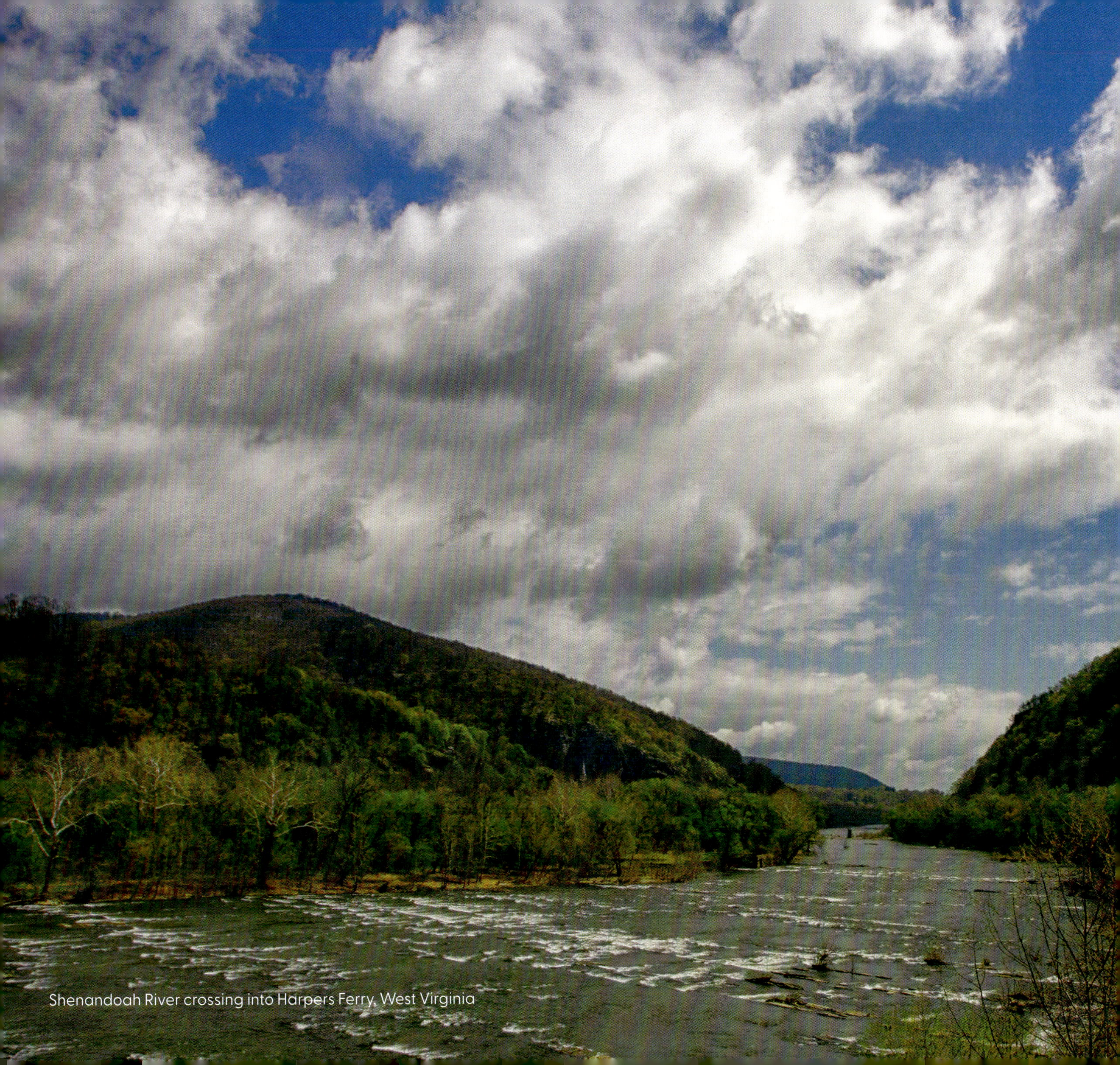

Shenandoah River crossing into Harpers Ferry, West Virginia

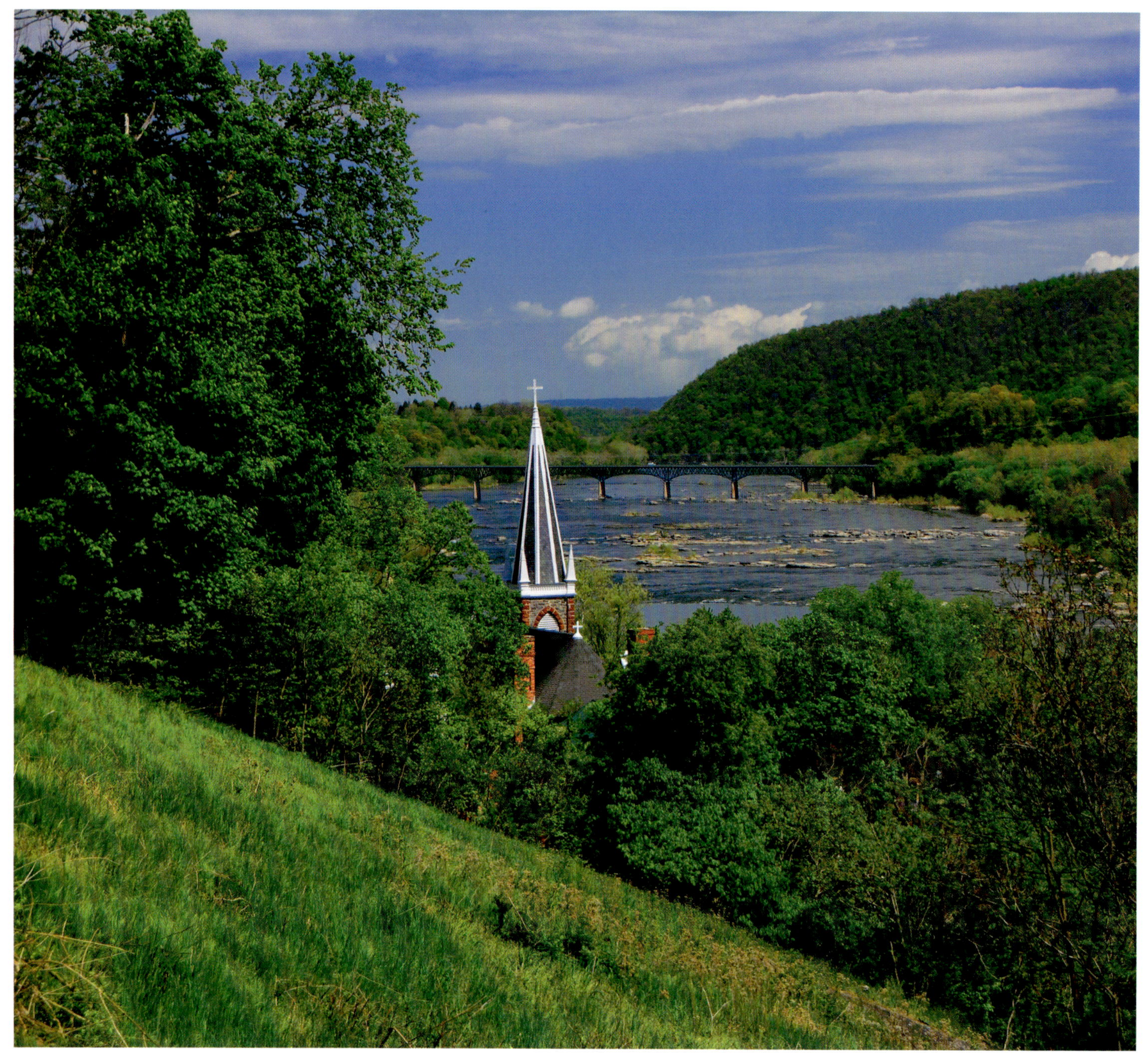

Saint Peters Roman Catholic Church overlooks the Shenandoah River

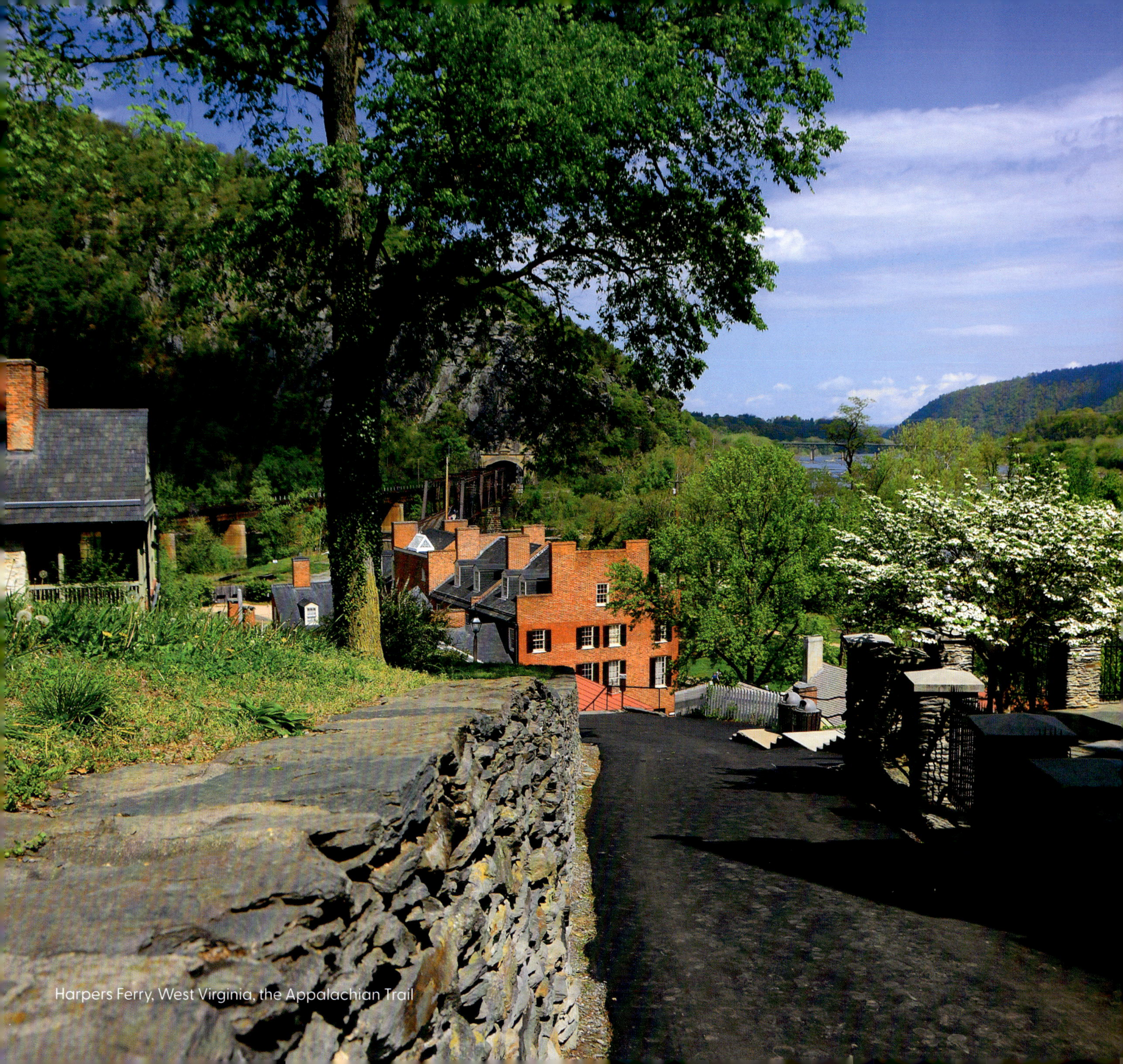

Harpers Ferry, West Virginia, the Appalachian Trail

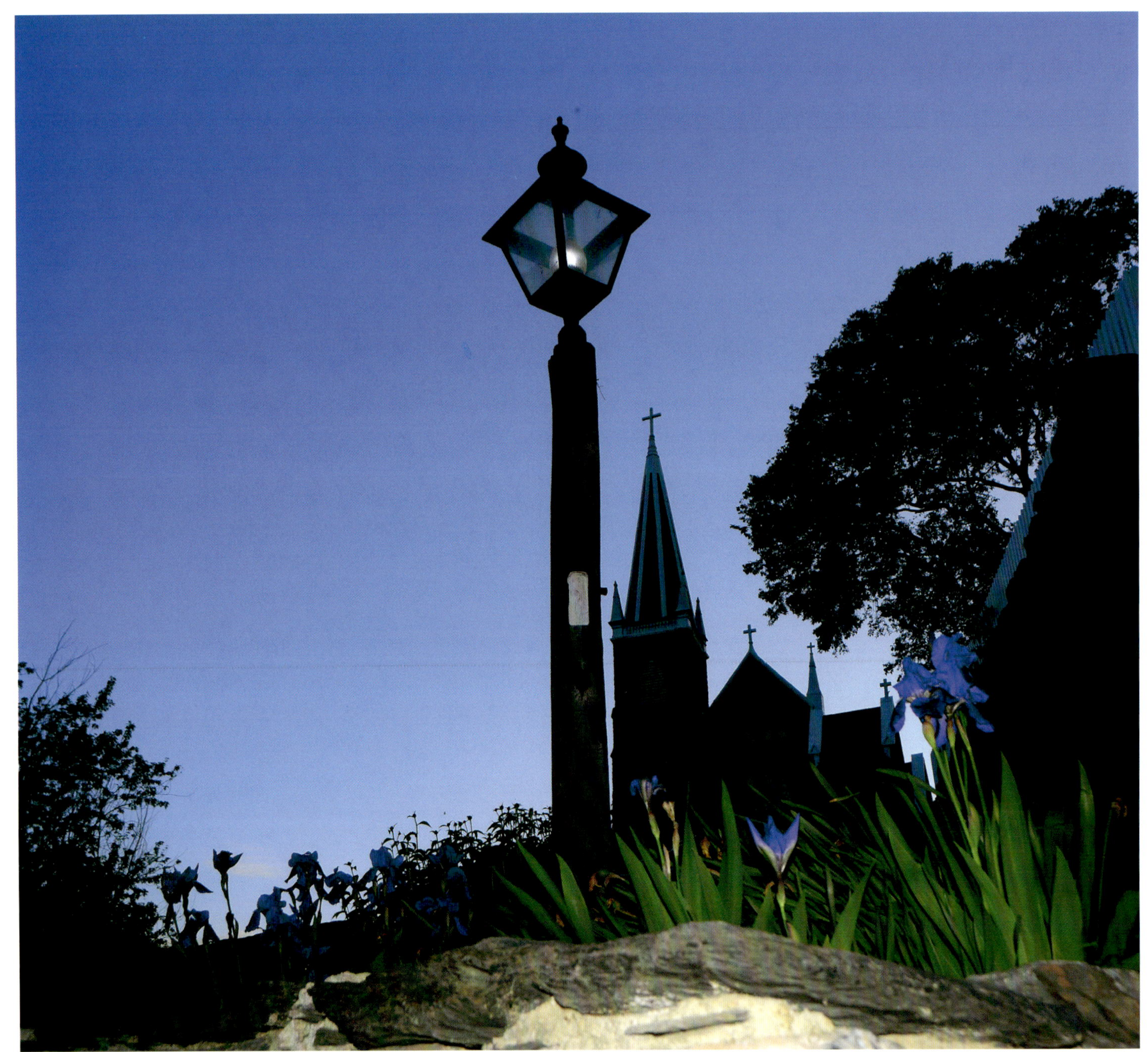

Spring flowers and the town of Harpers Ferry in spring

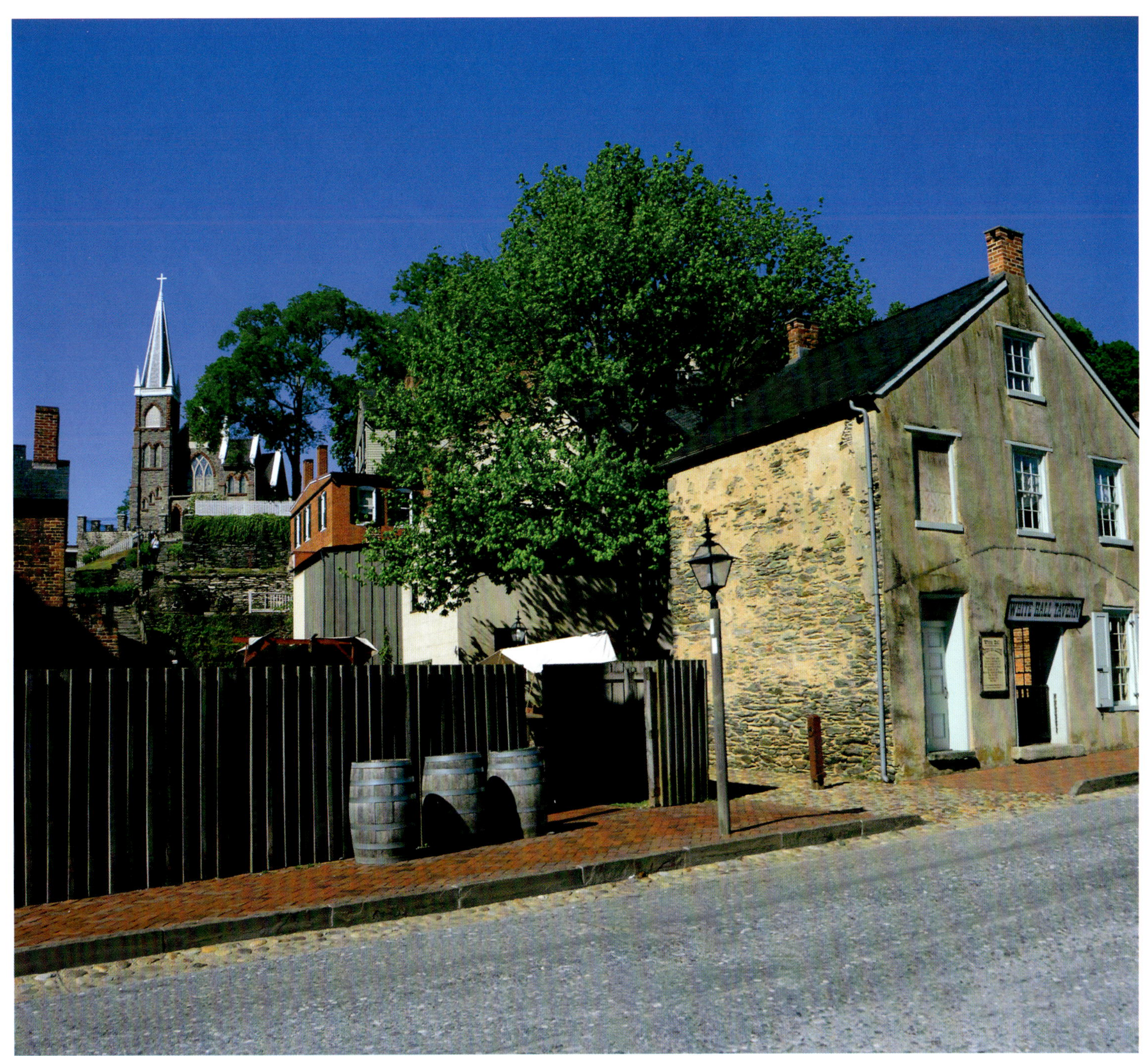

Lower town of Harpers Ferry, West Virginia

The Point (convergence of the Shenandoah and Potomac Rivers)

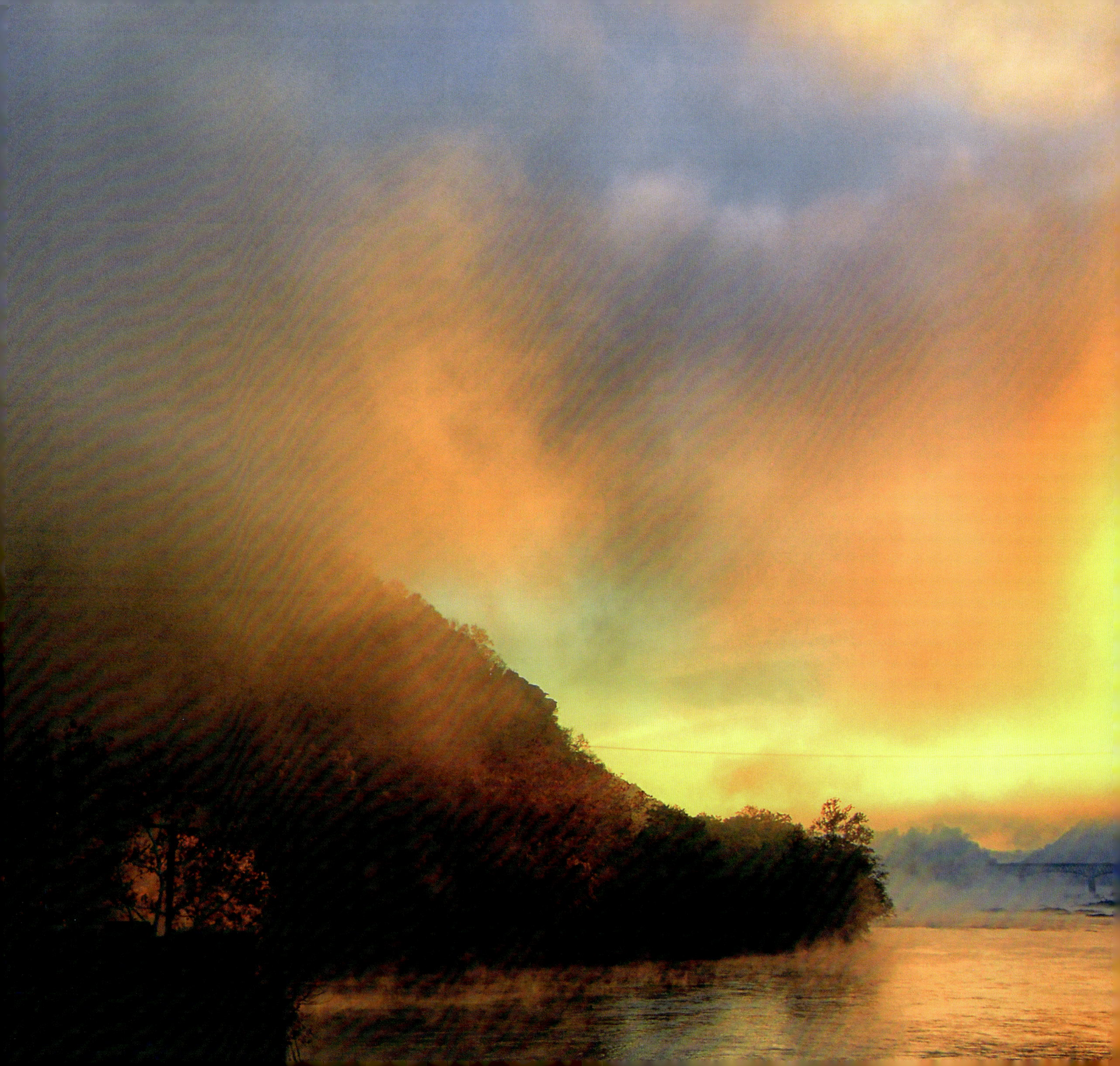

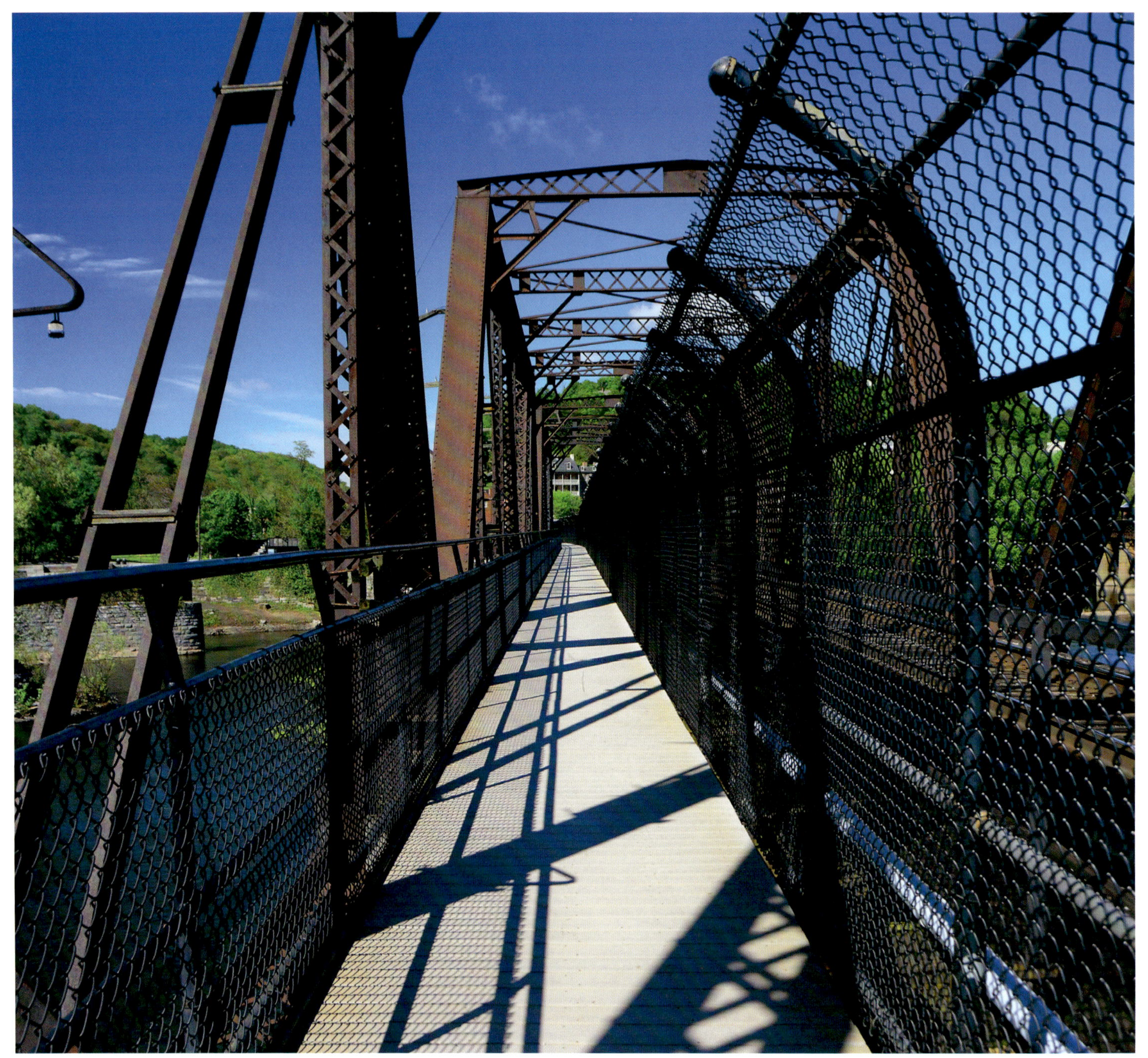

Crossing the Potomac River into West Virginia / Maryland

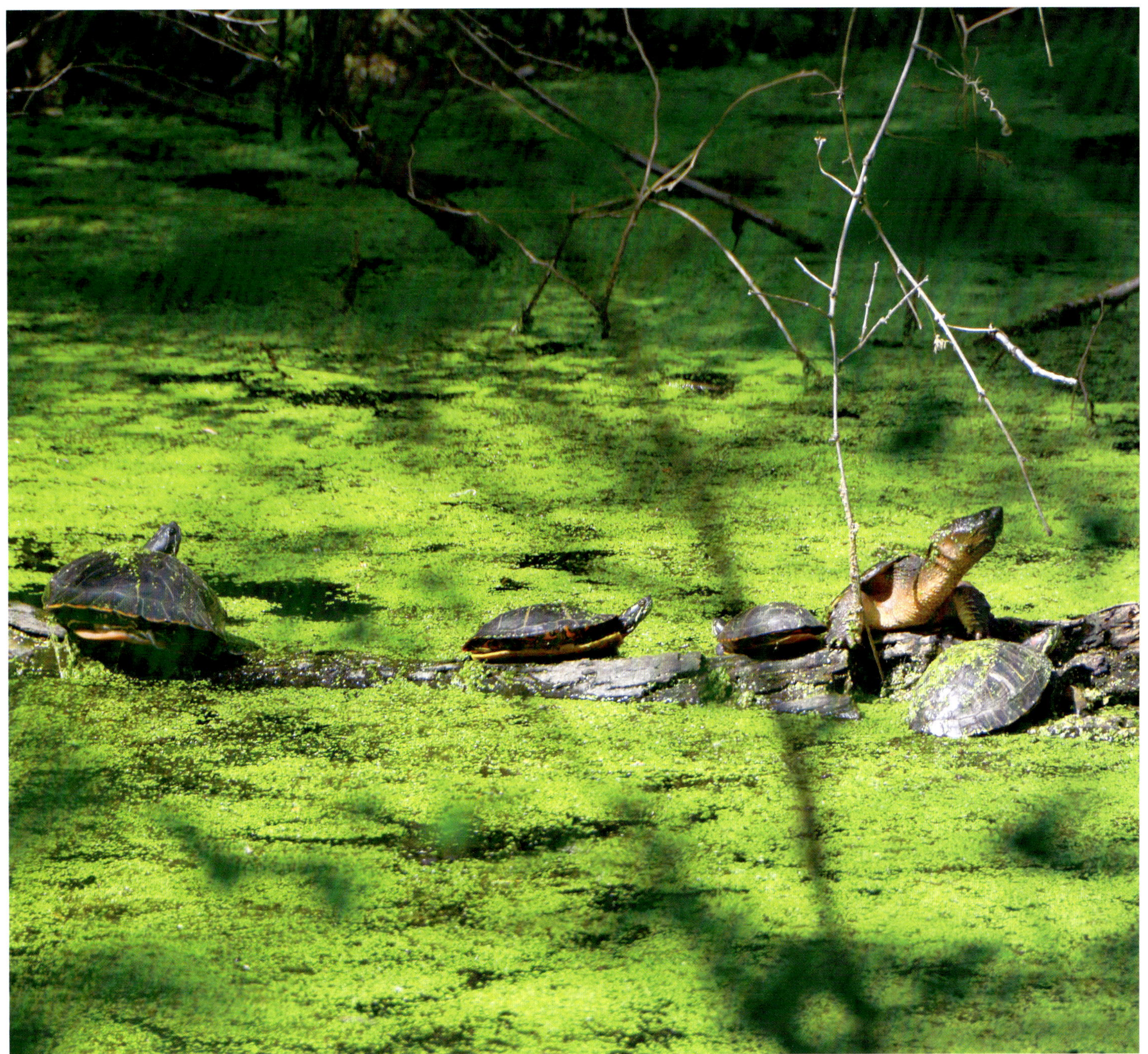

Turtles on the Appalachian Trail in Maryland

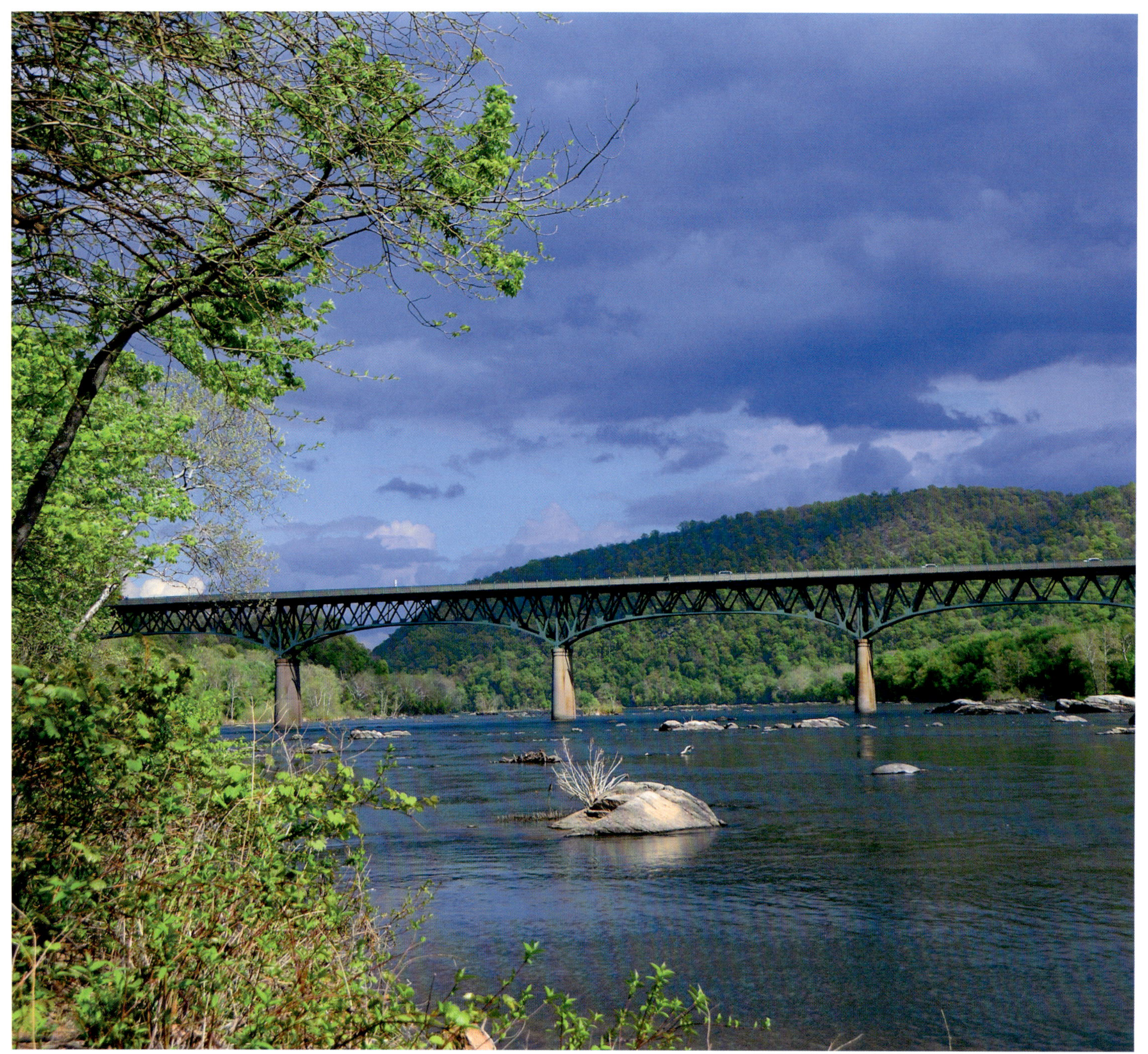

Potomac River from the Appalachian Trail in Maryland

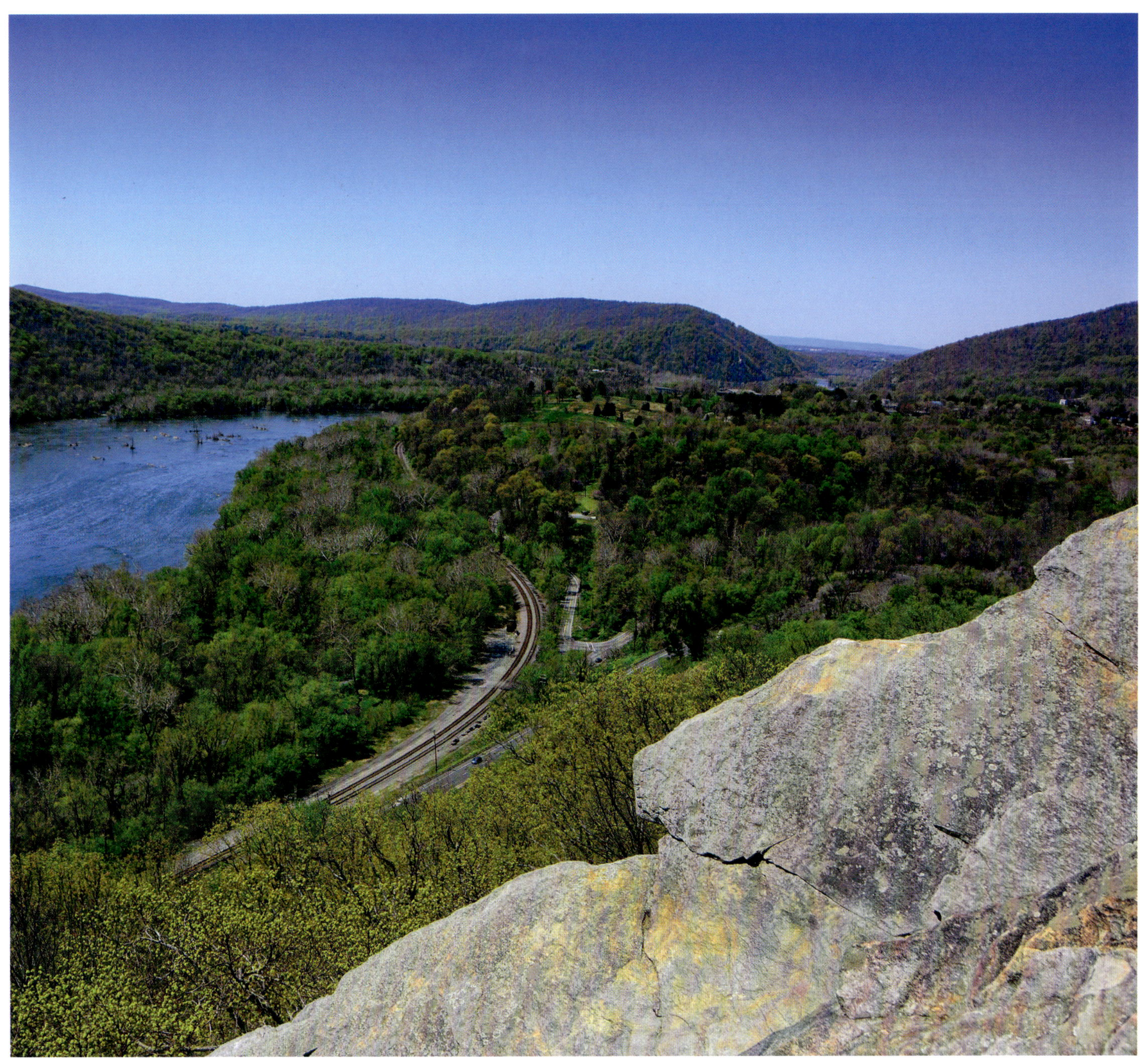

Looking back toward Harpers Ferry, West Virginia, from Weverton Cliffs, Maryland

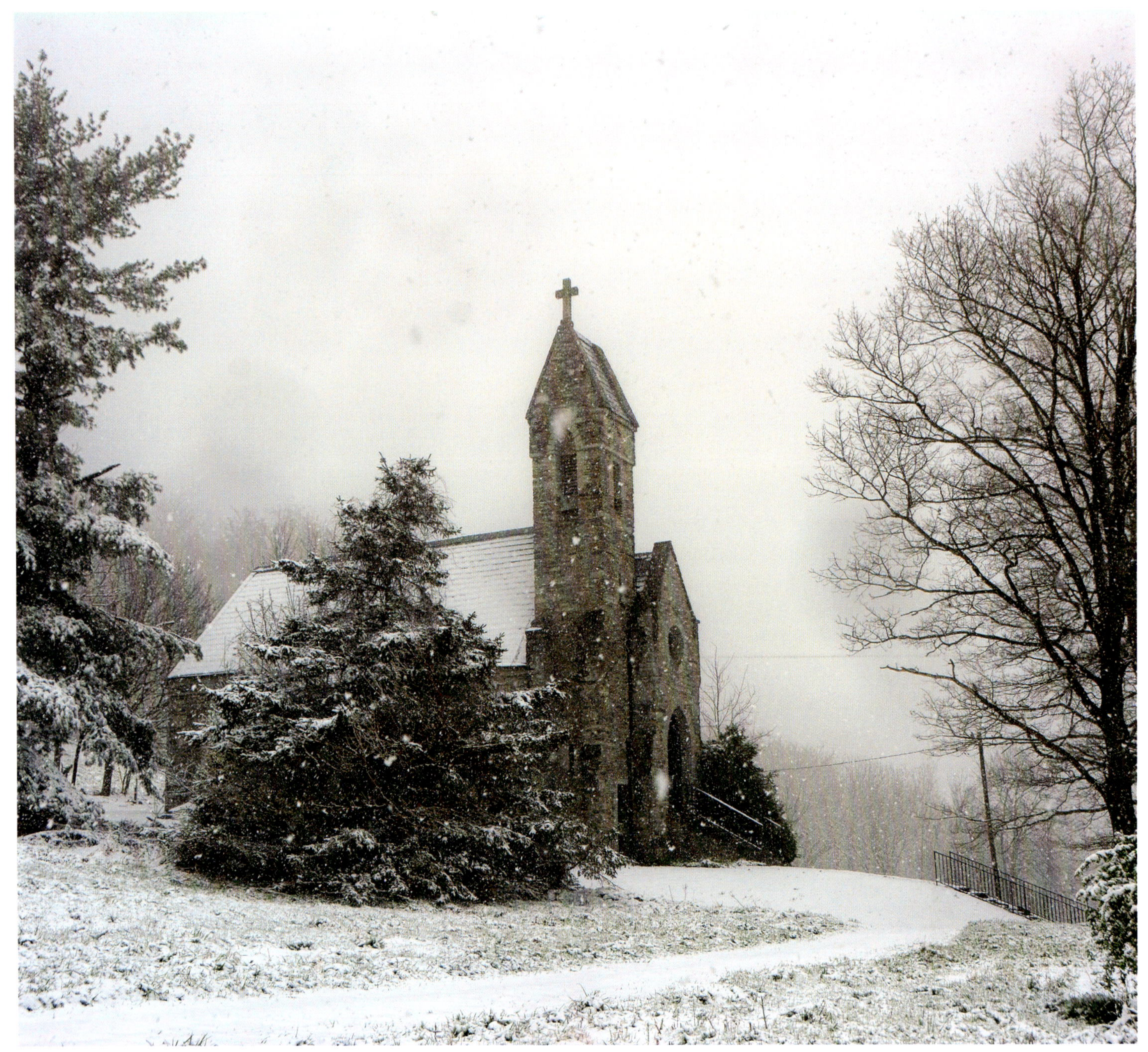

Dahlgren's Chapel in Maryland

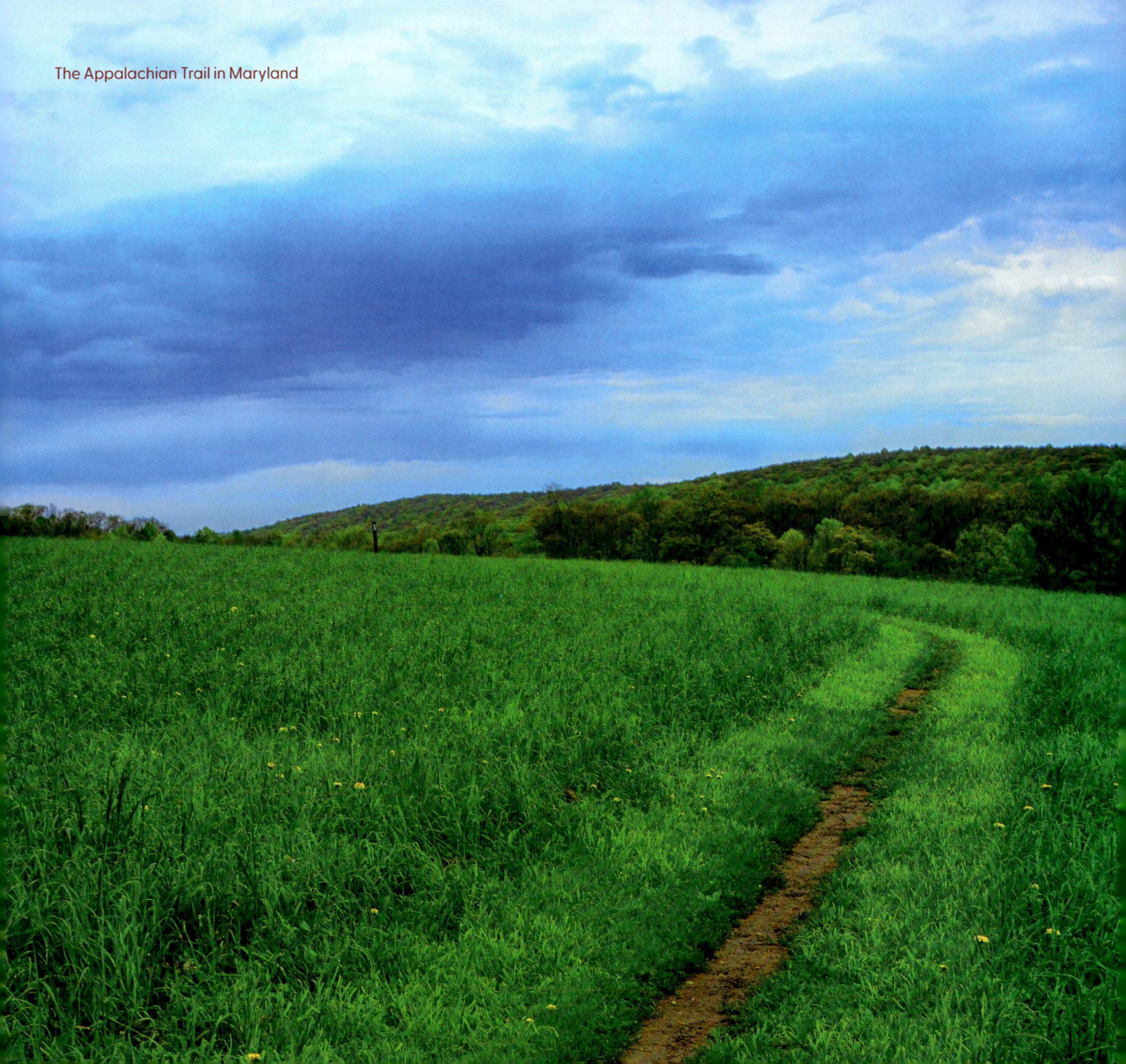
The Appalachian Trail in Maryland

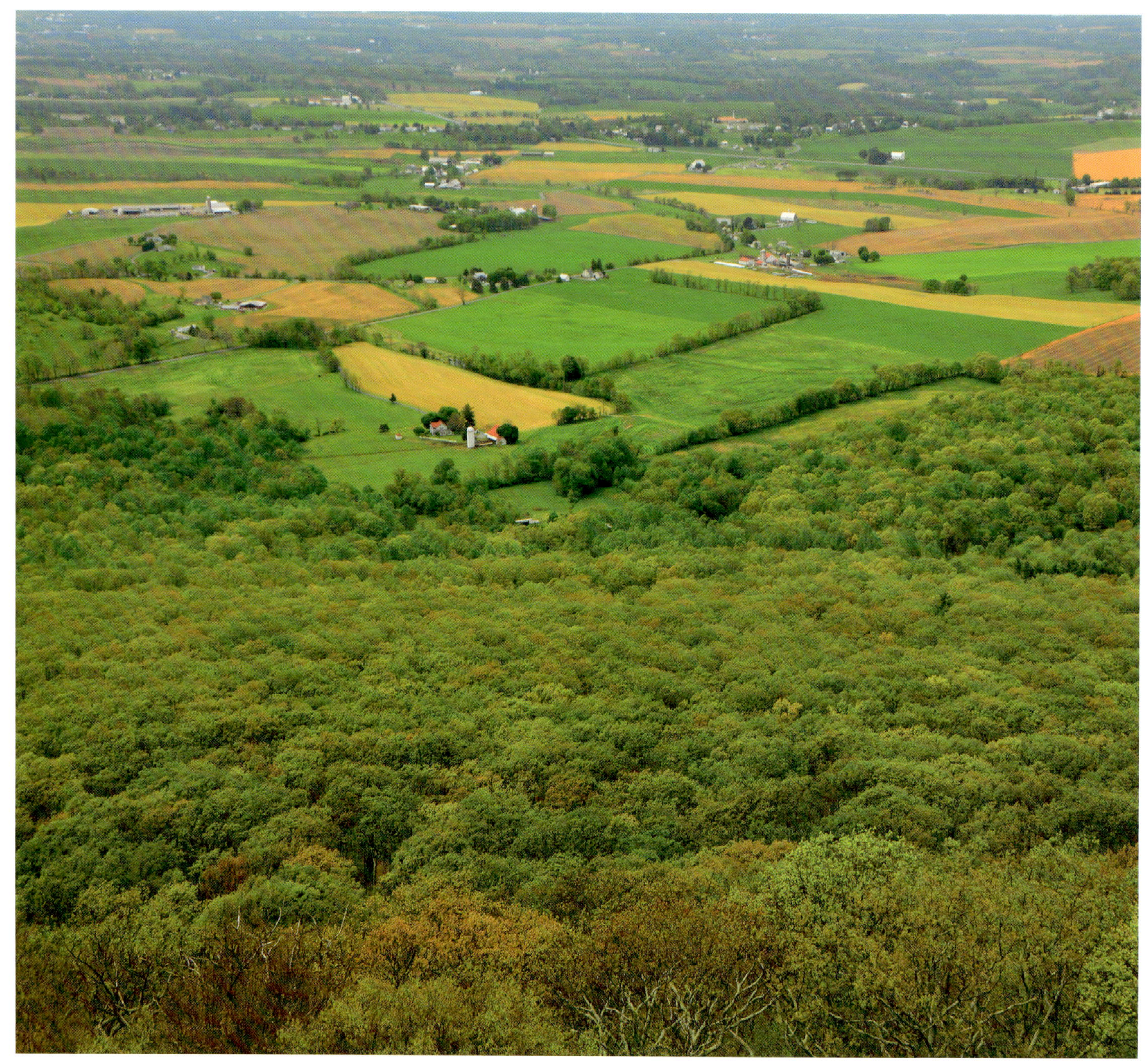

Farmland from the Appalachian Trail in Maryland

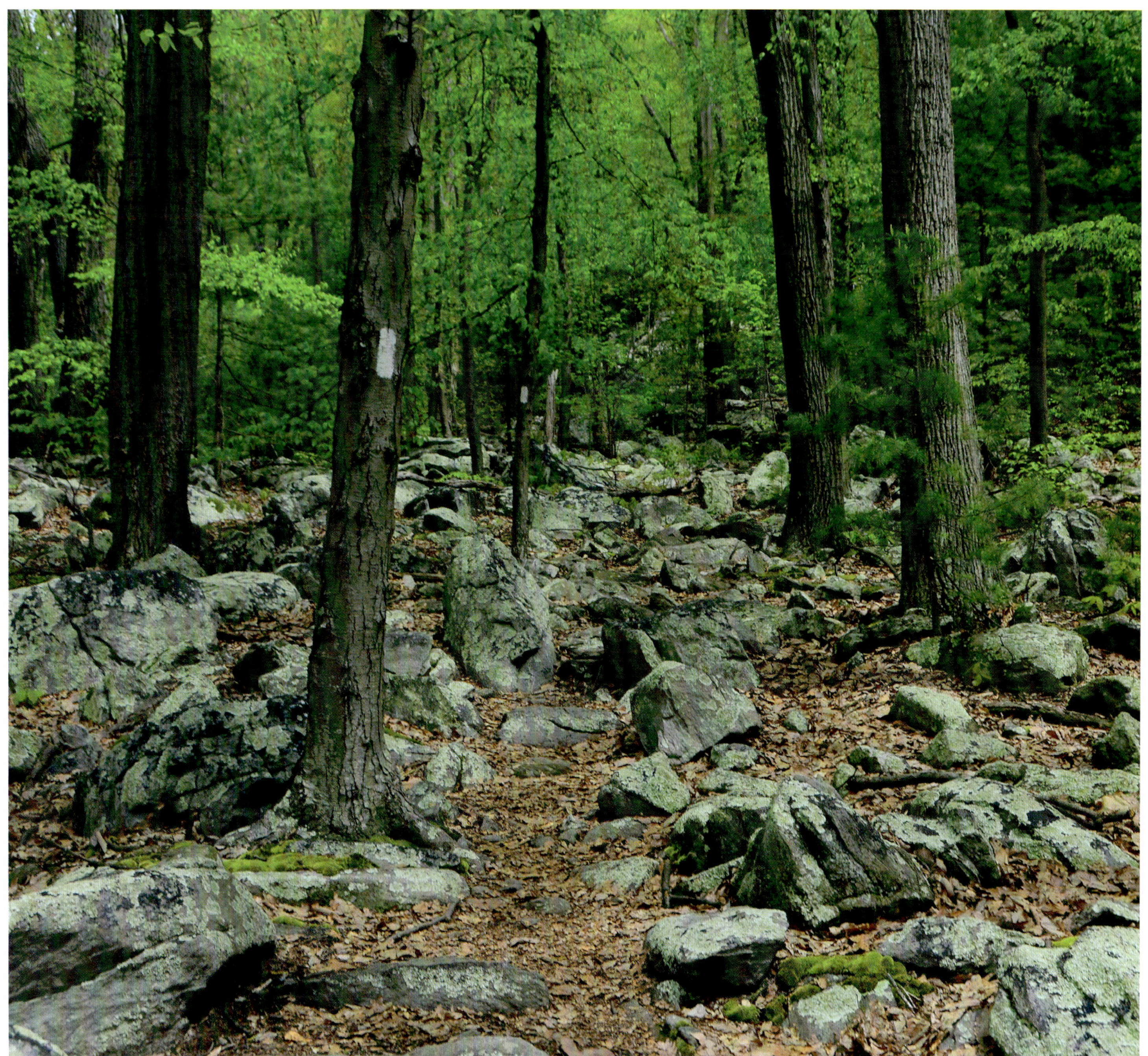

Northern Maryland, moss-covered rocks

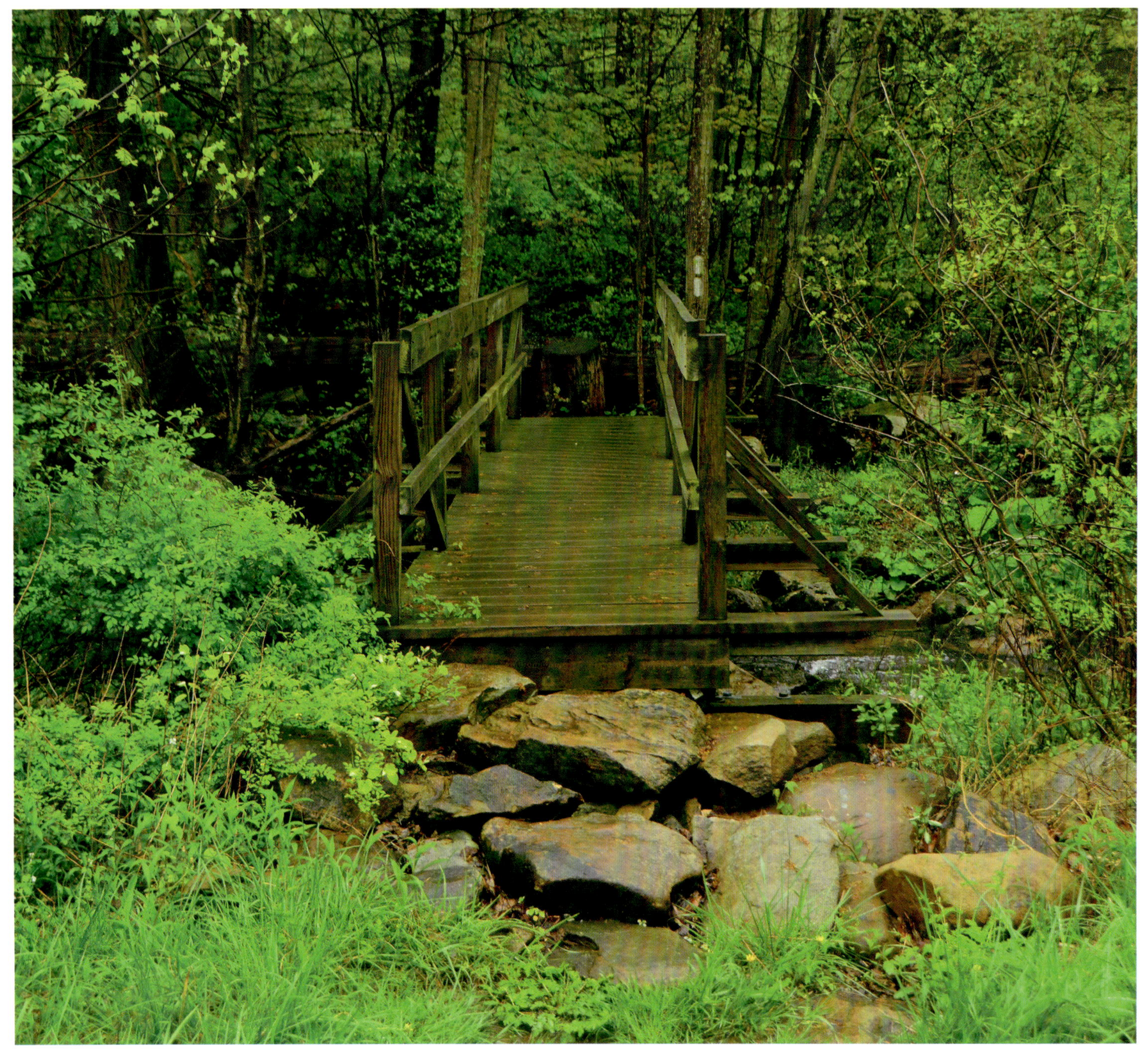

Stream bridge crossing on the Appalachian Trail in Pennsylvania

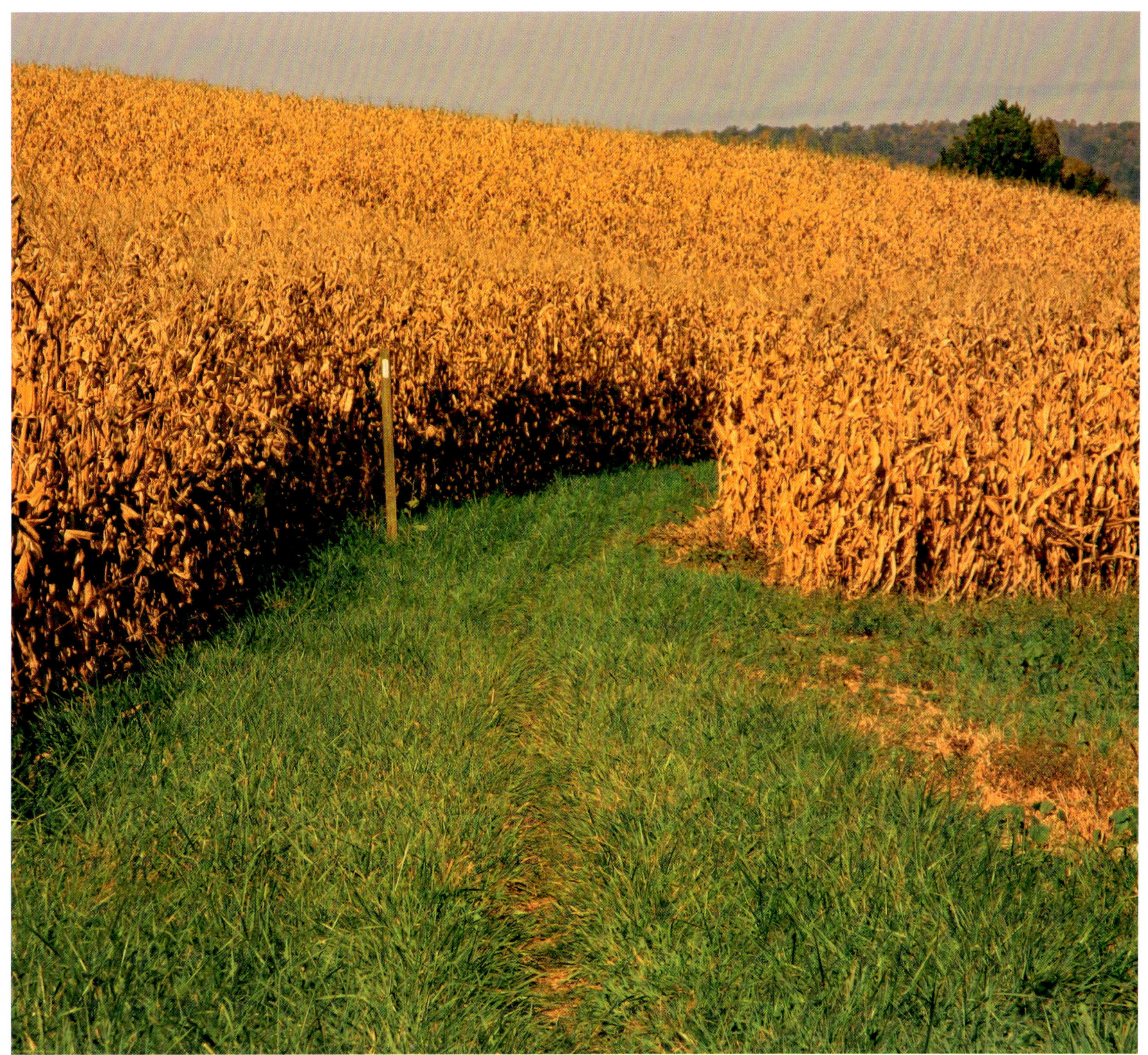

The Appalachian Trail in Pennsylvania cuts through a cornfield.

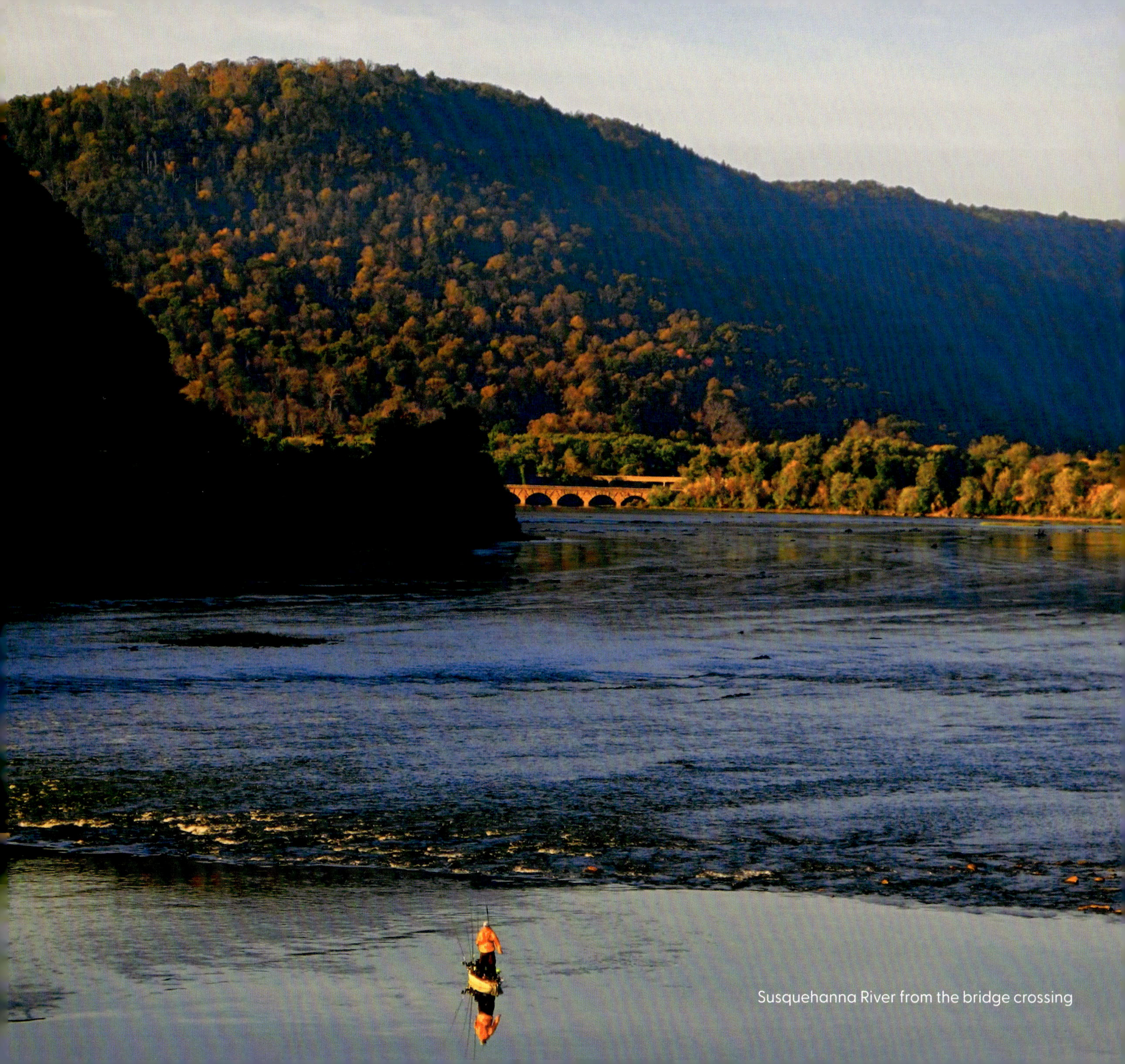
Susquehanna River from the bridge crossing

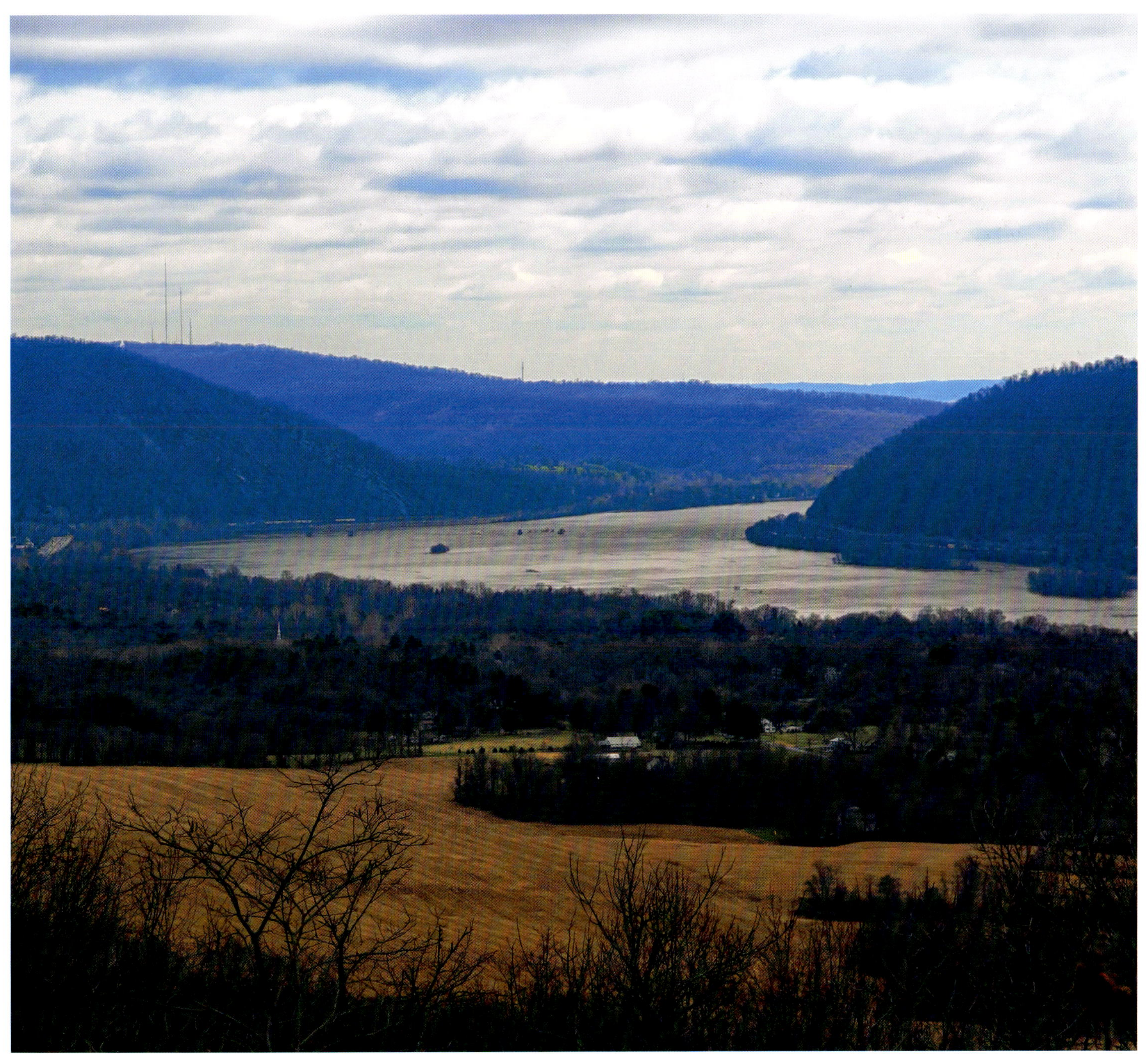

Section 8 of the Appalachian Trail in Pennsylvania, looking at the Susquehanna River

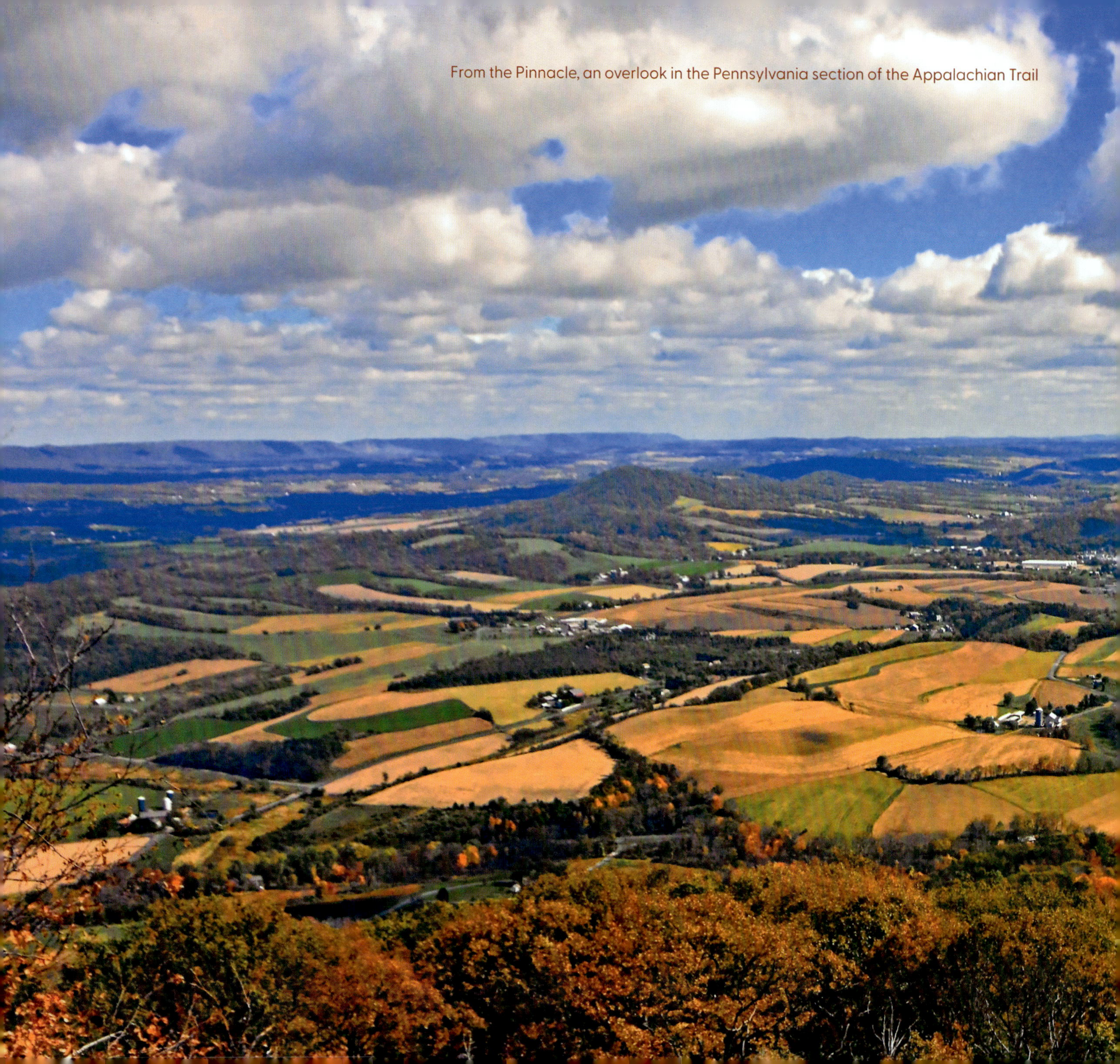

From the Pinnacle, an overlook in the Pennsylvania section of the Appalachian Trail

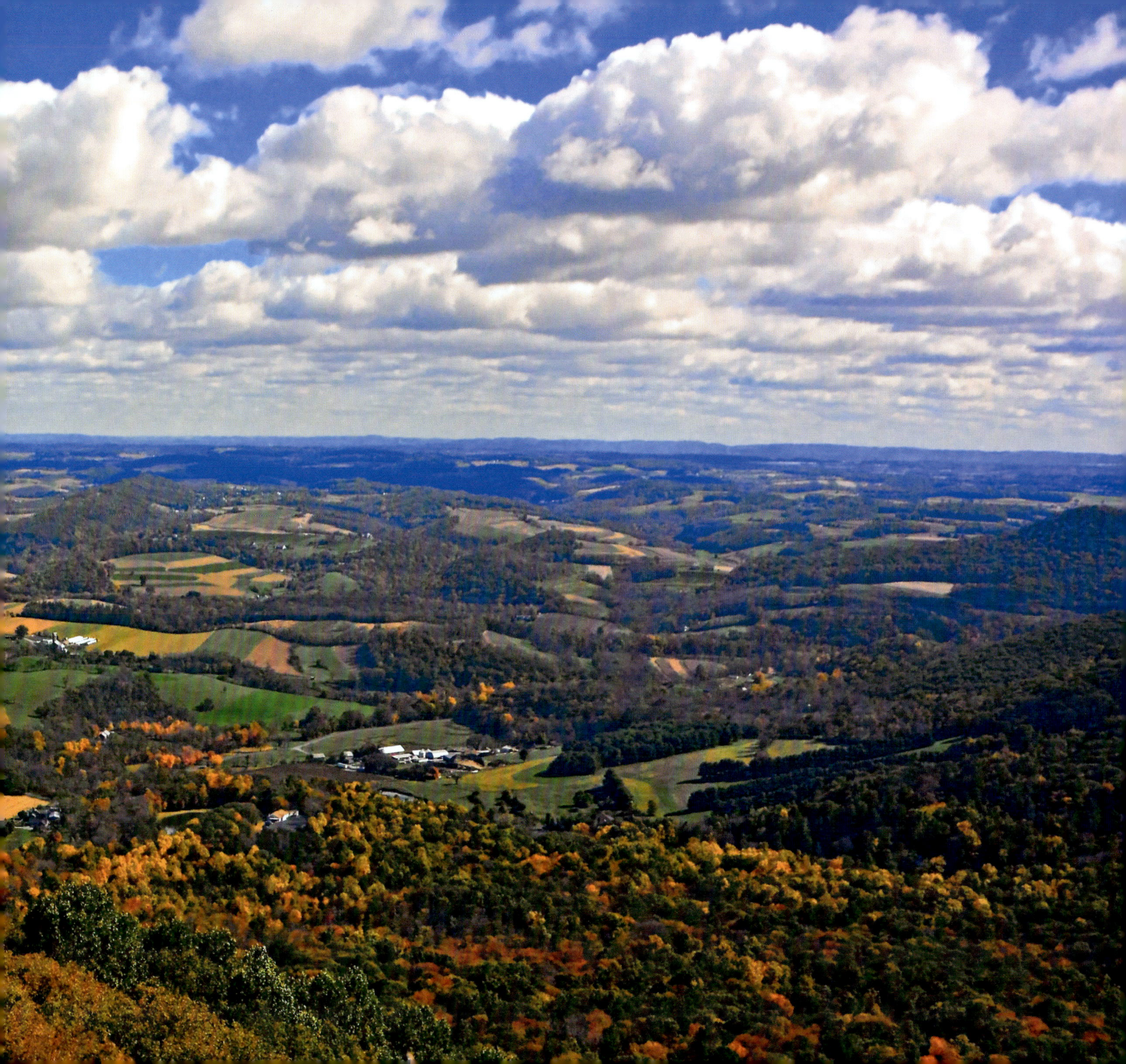

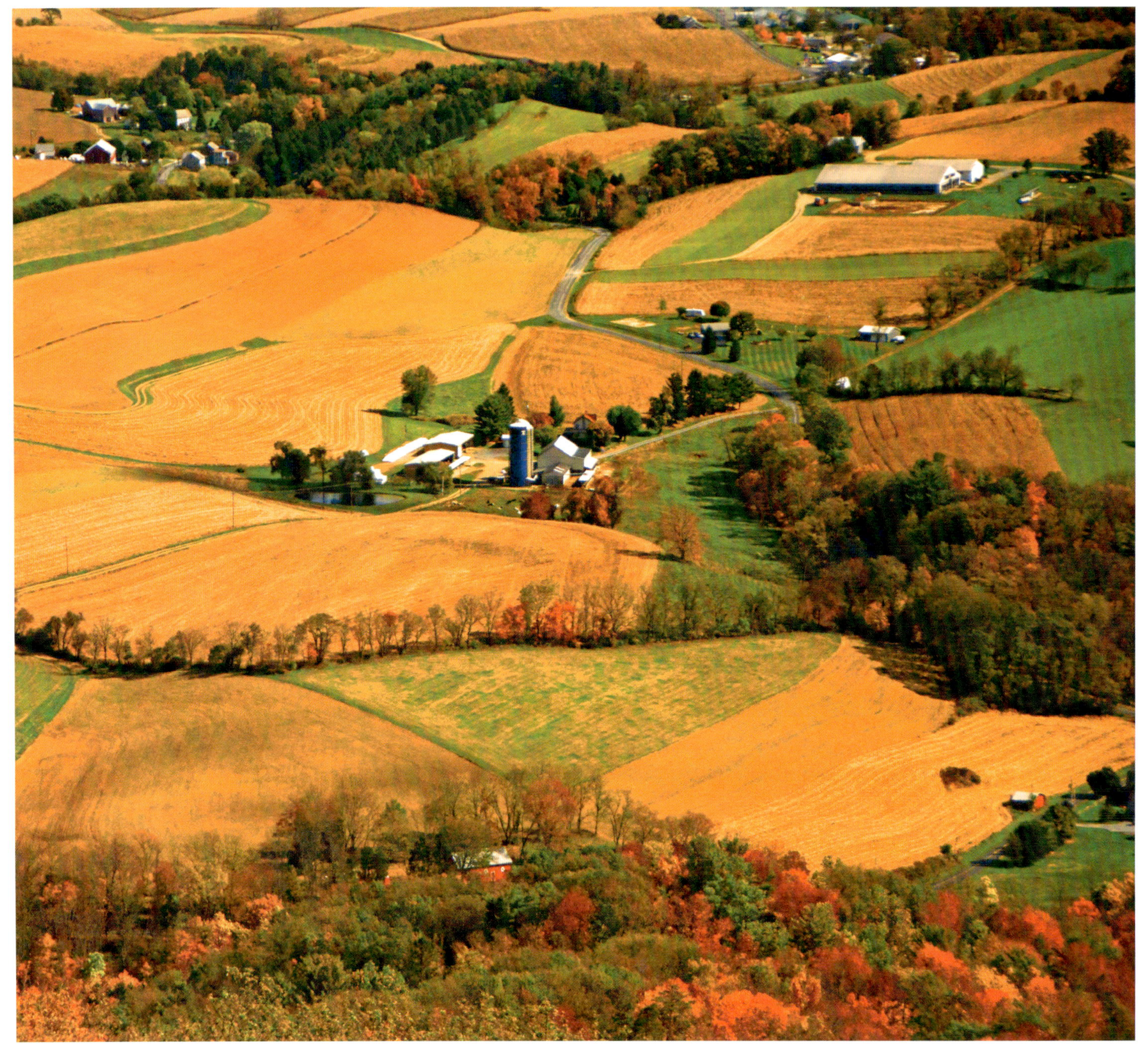

Pennsylvania farmland viewed from the Appalachian Trail

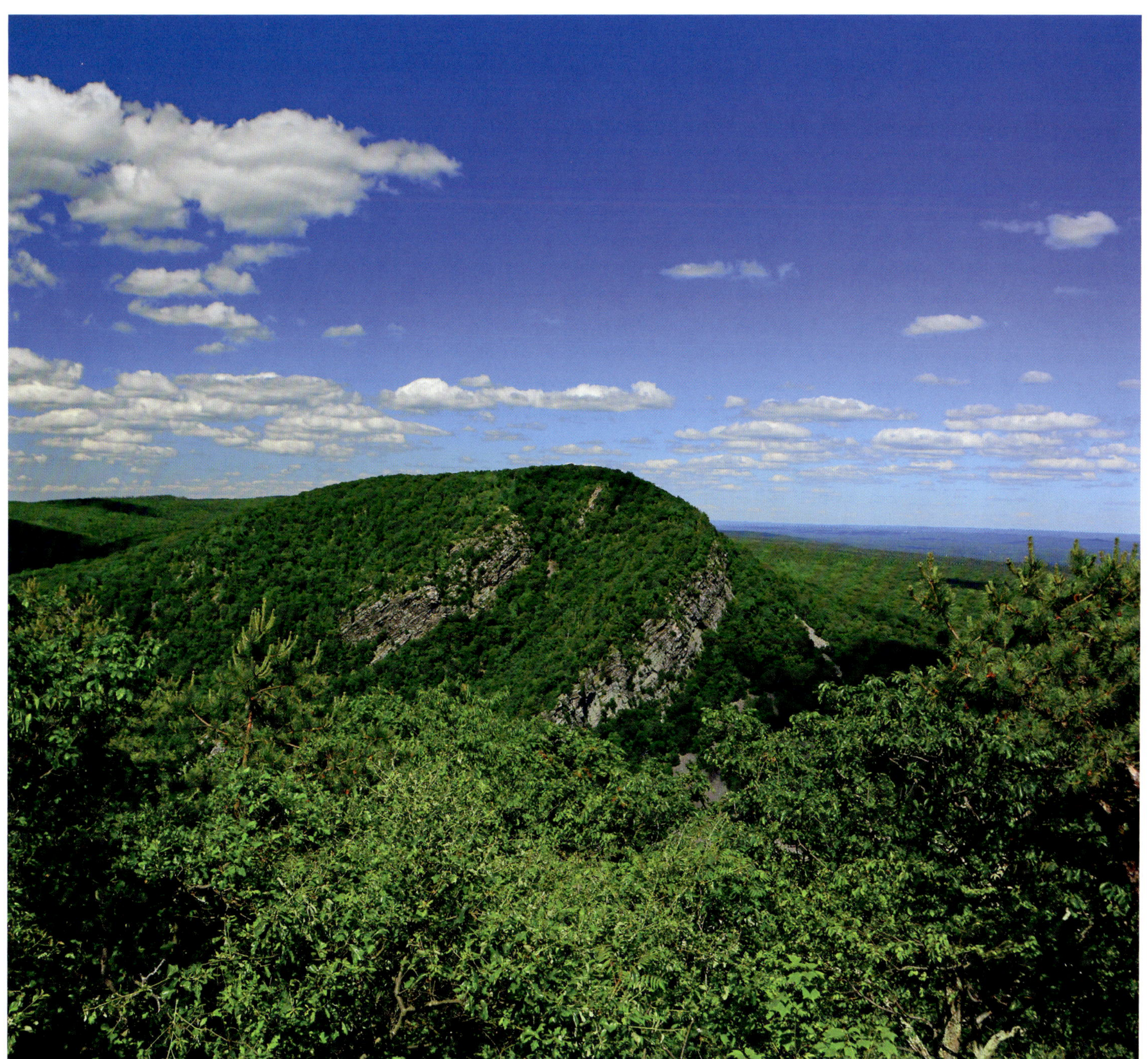

Mount Tammany from Mount Minsi

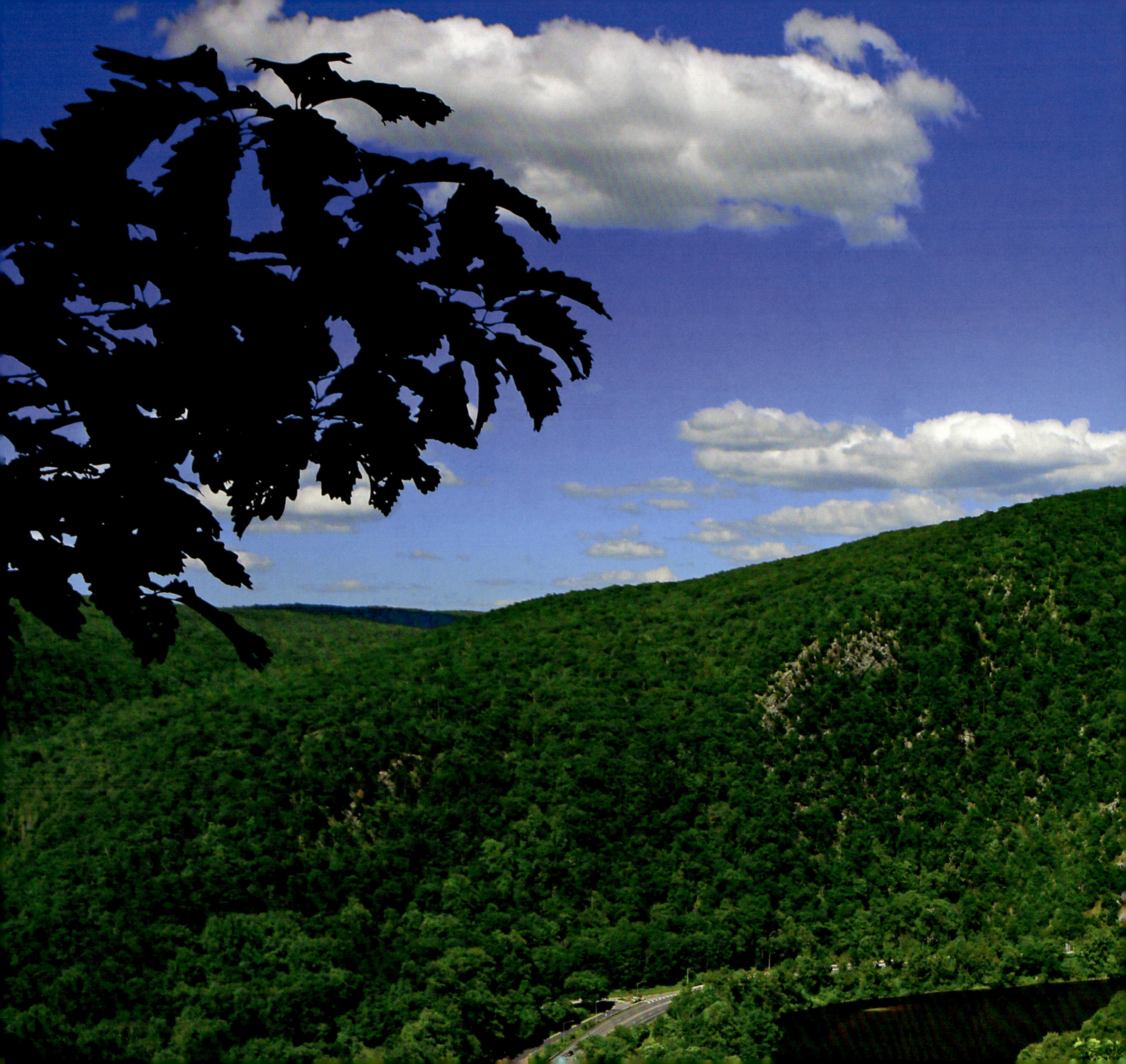

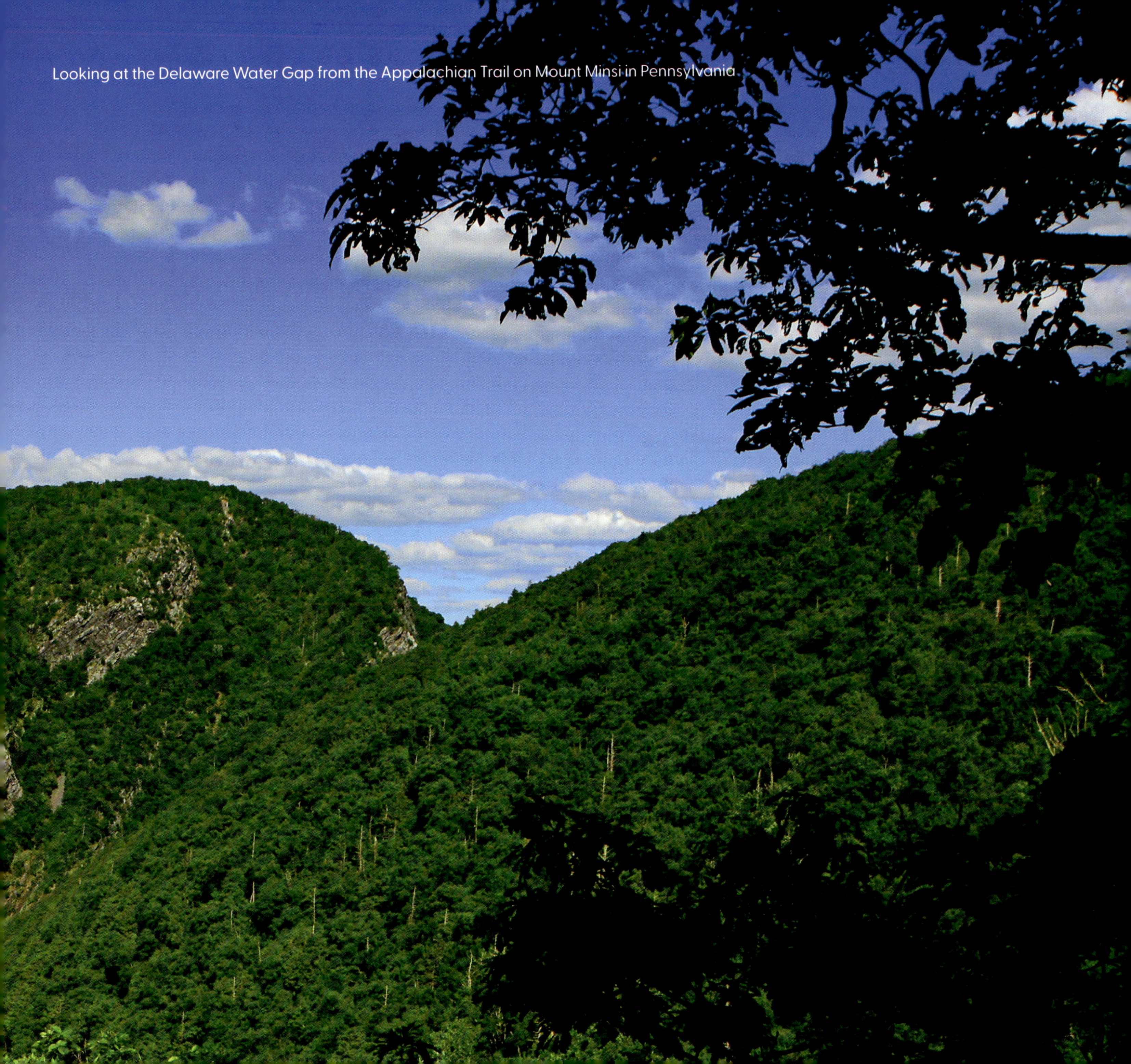

Looking at the Delaware Water Gap from the Appalachian Trail on Mount Minsi in Pennsylvania

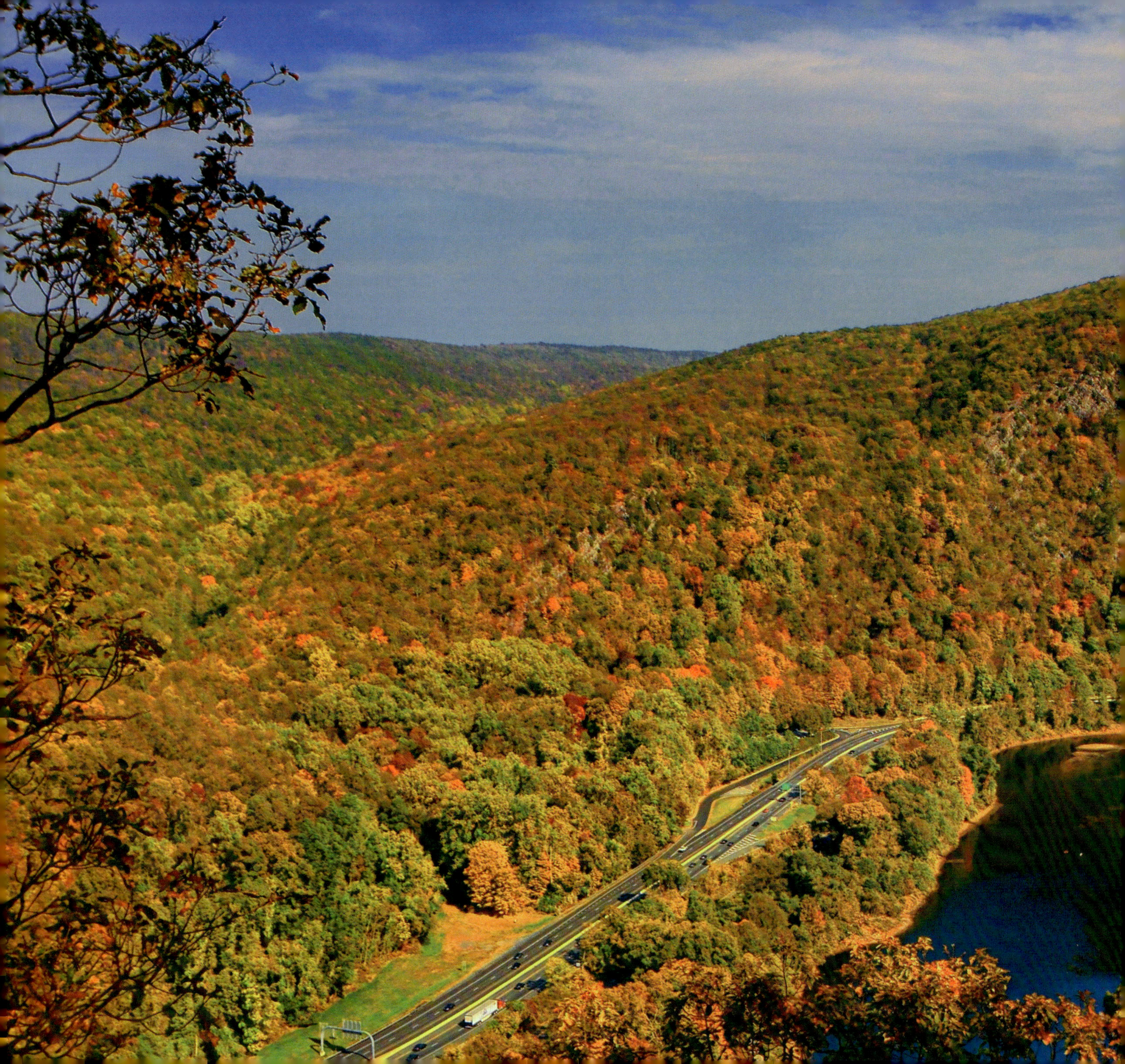

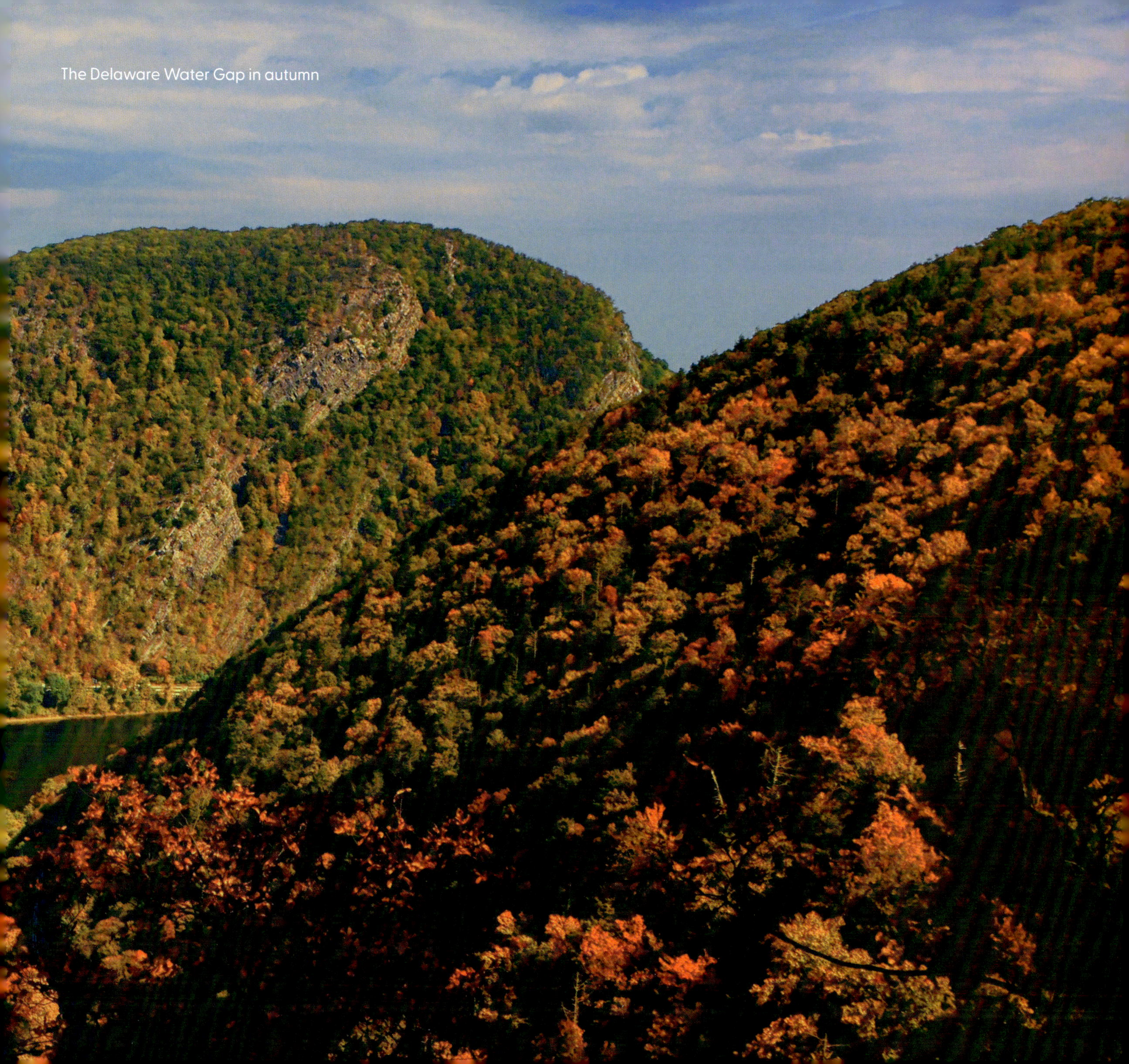

The Delaware Water Gap in autumn

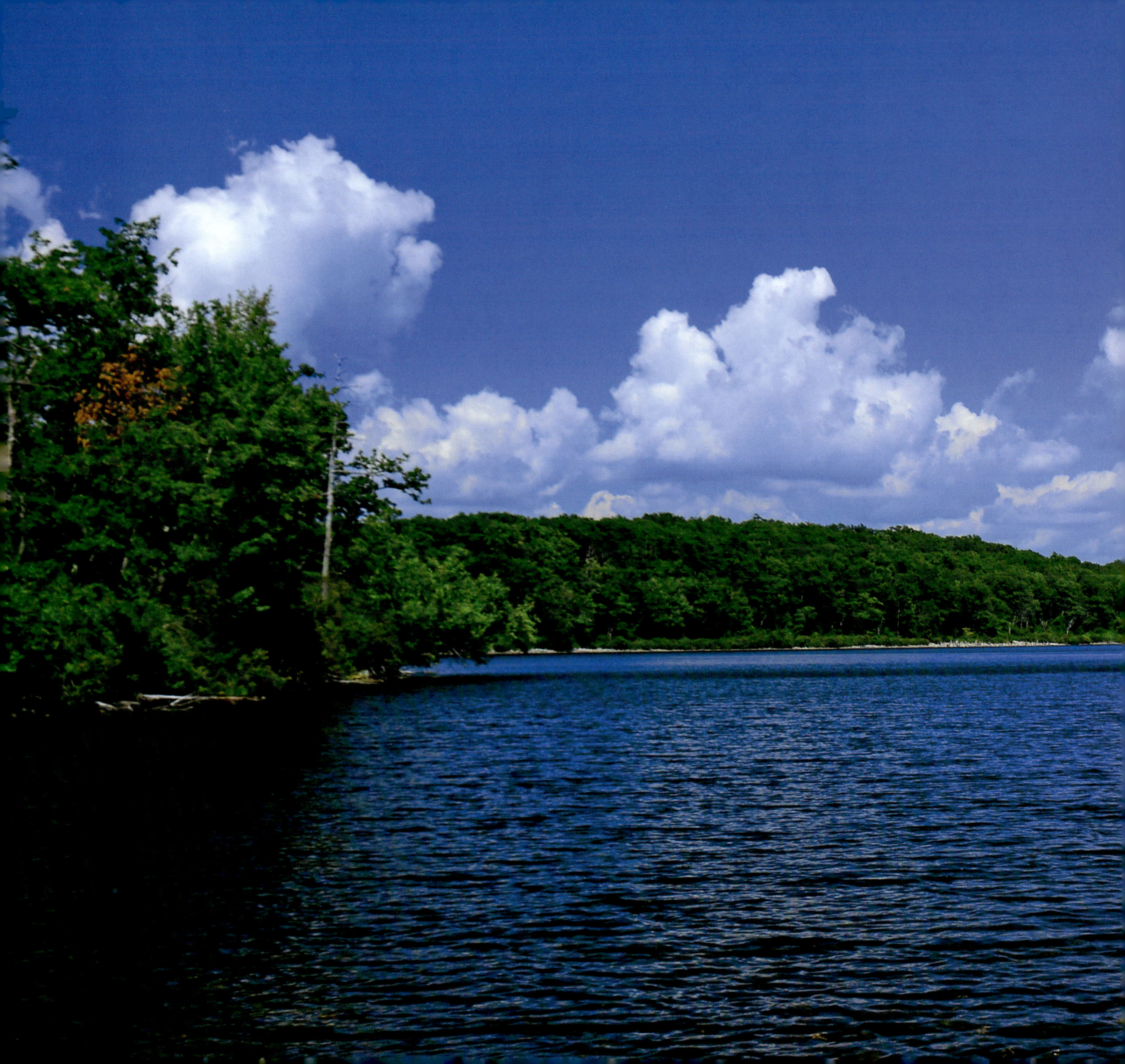

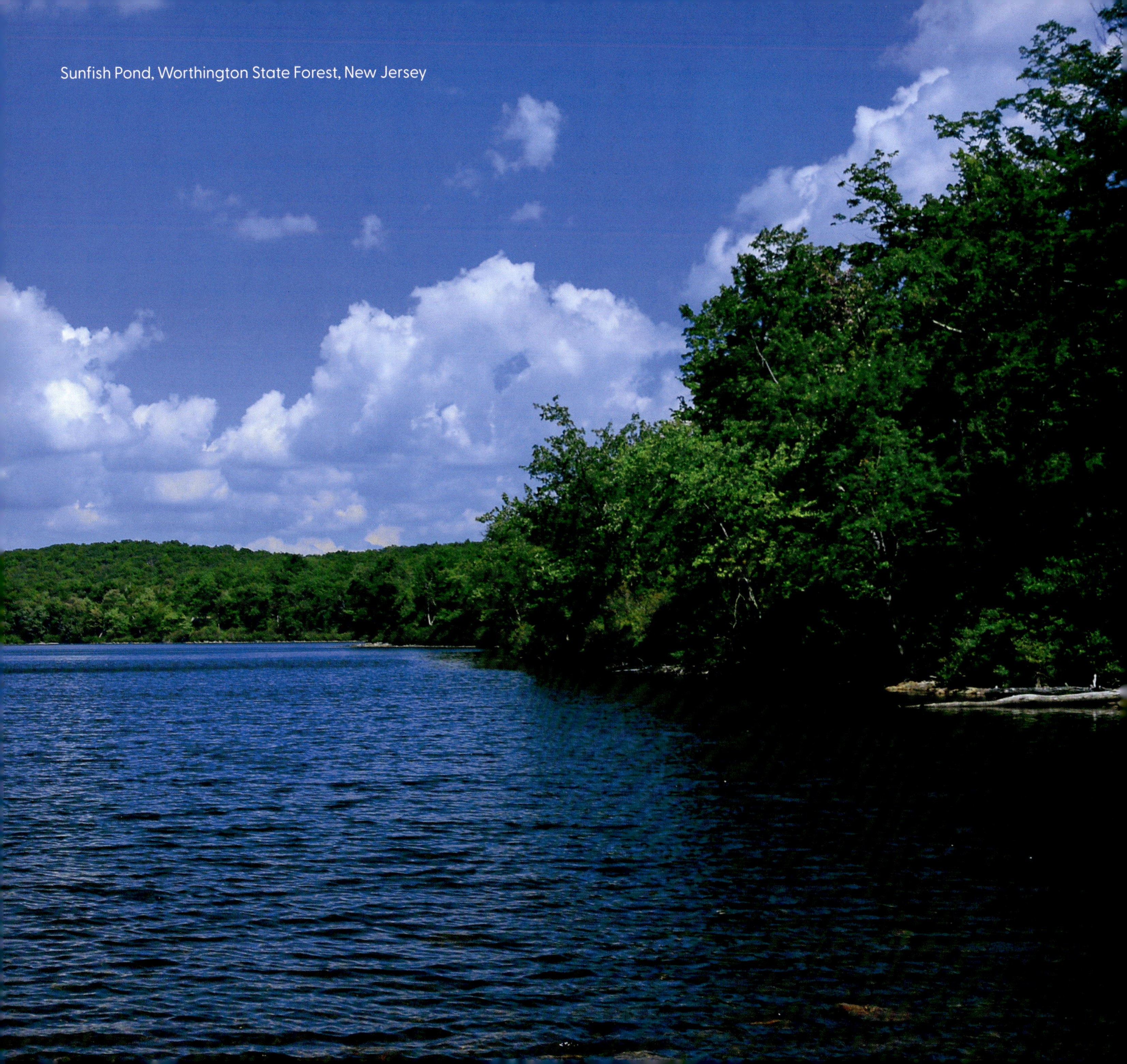

Sunfish Pond, Worthington State Forest, New Jersey

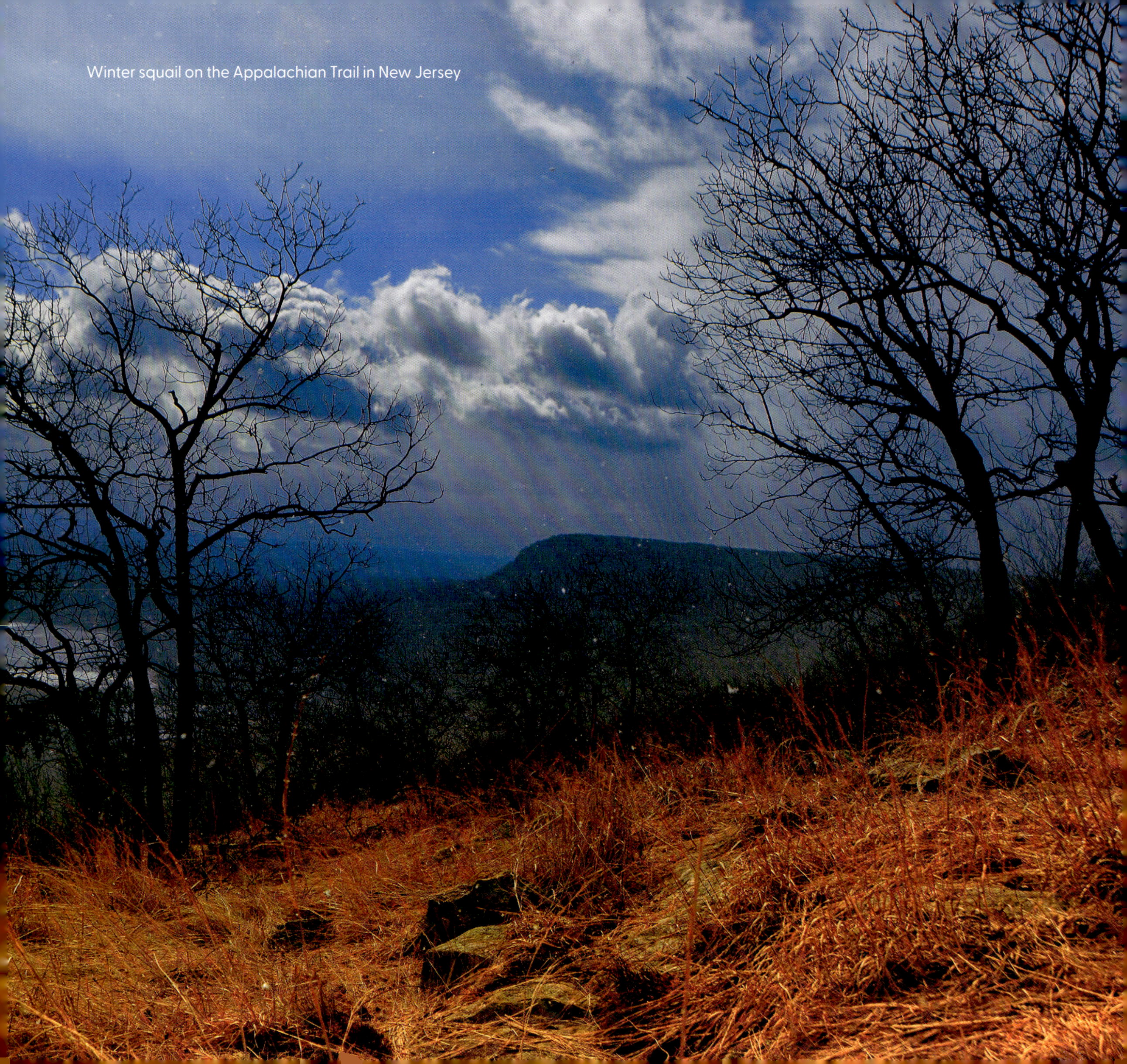

Winter squail on the Appalachian Trail in New Jersey

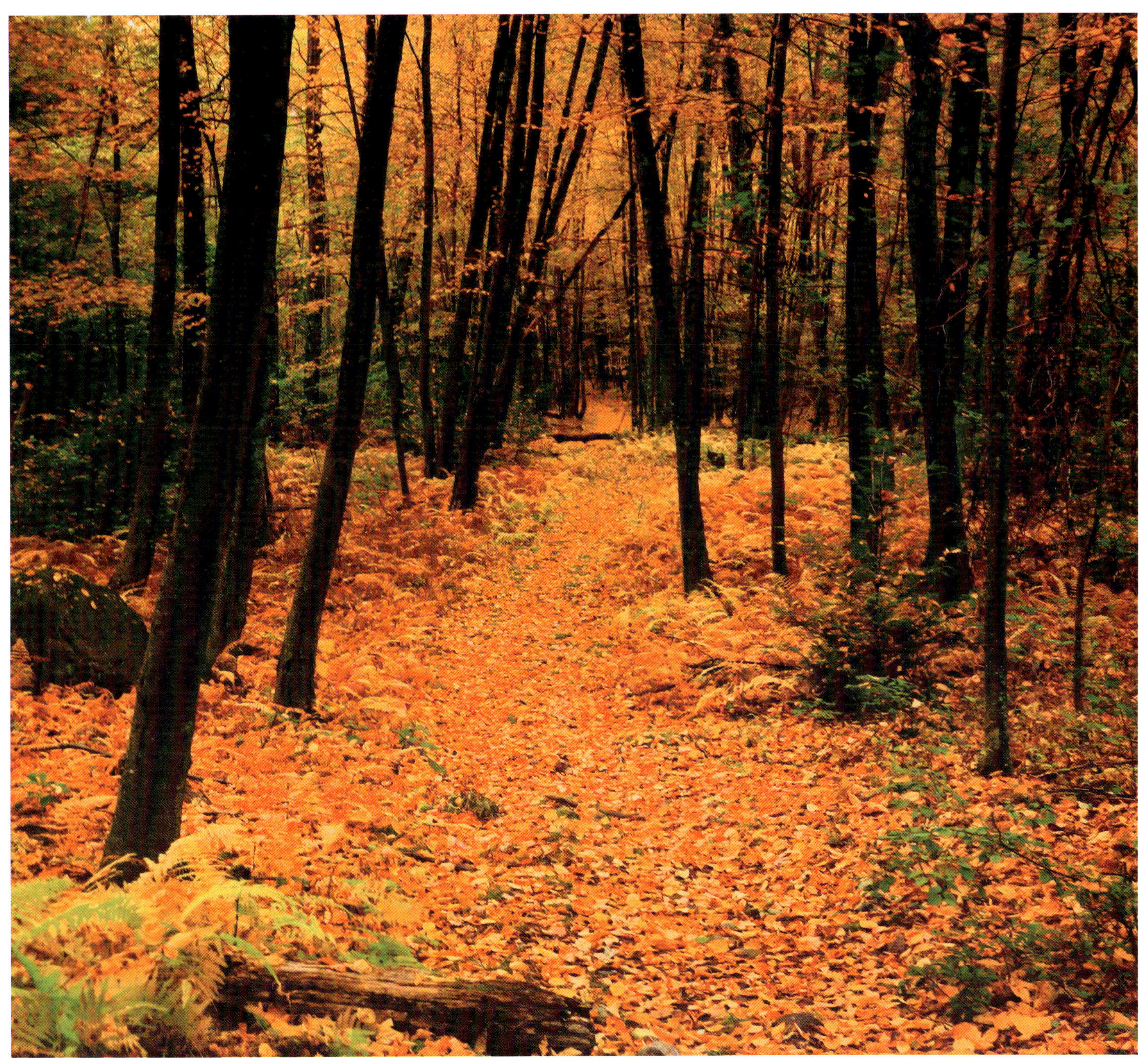

Autumn colors in the Delaware Water Gap National Recreation Area in New Jersey

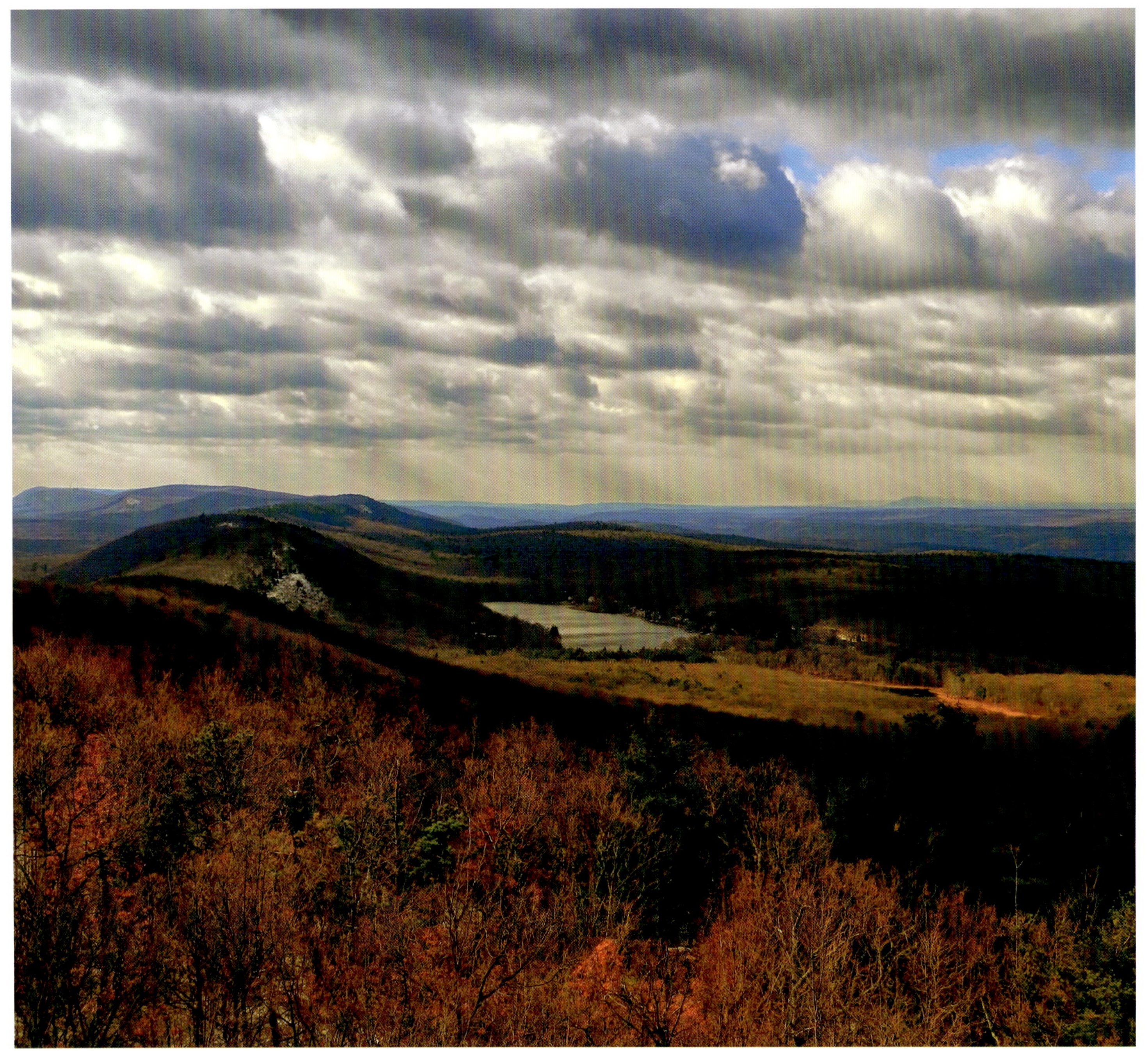

The Appalachian Trail from New Jersey's Culver Fire Tower

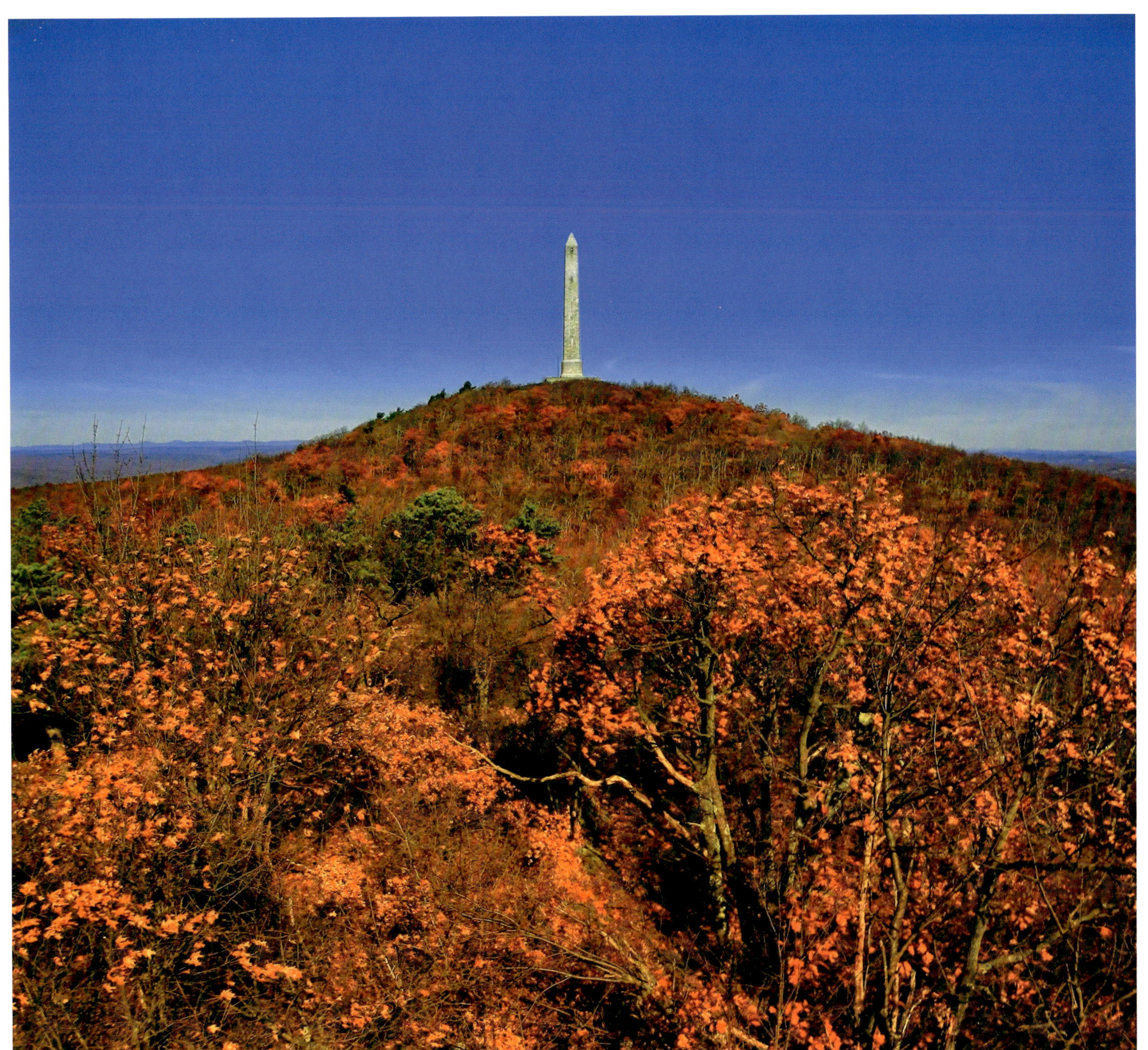

High Point, New Jersey, and peak colors

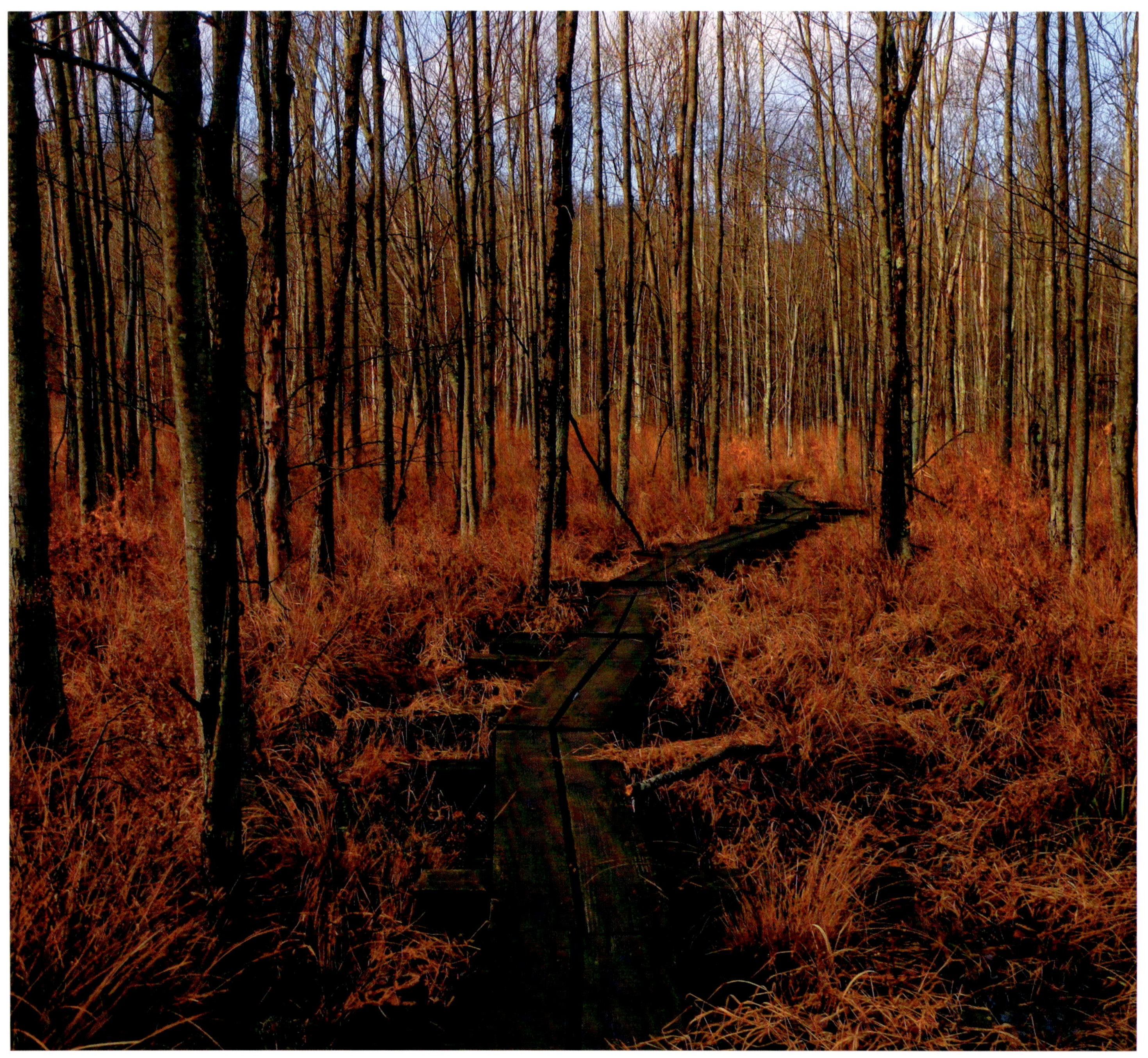

Pochuck Boardwalk, New Jersey

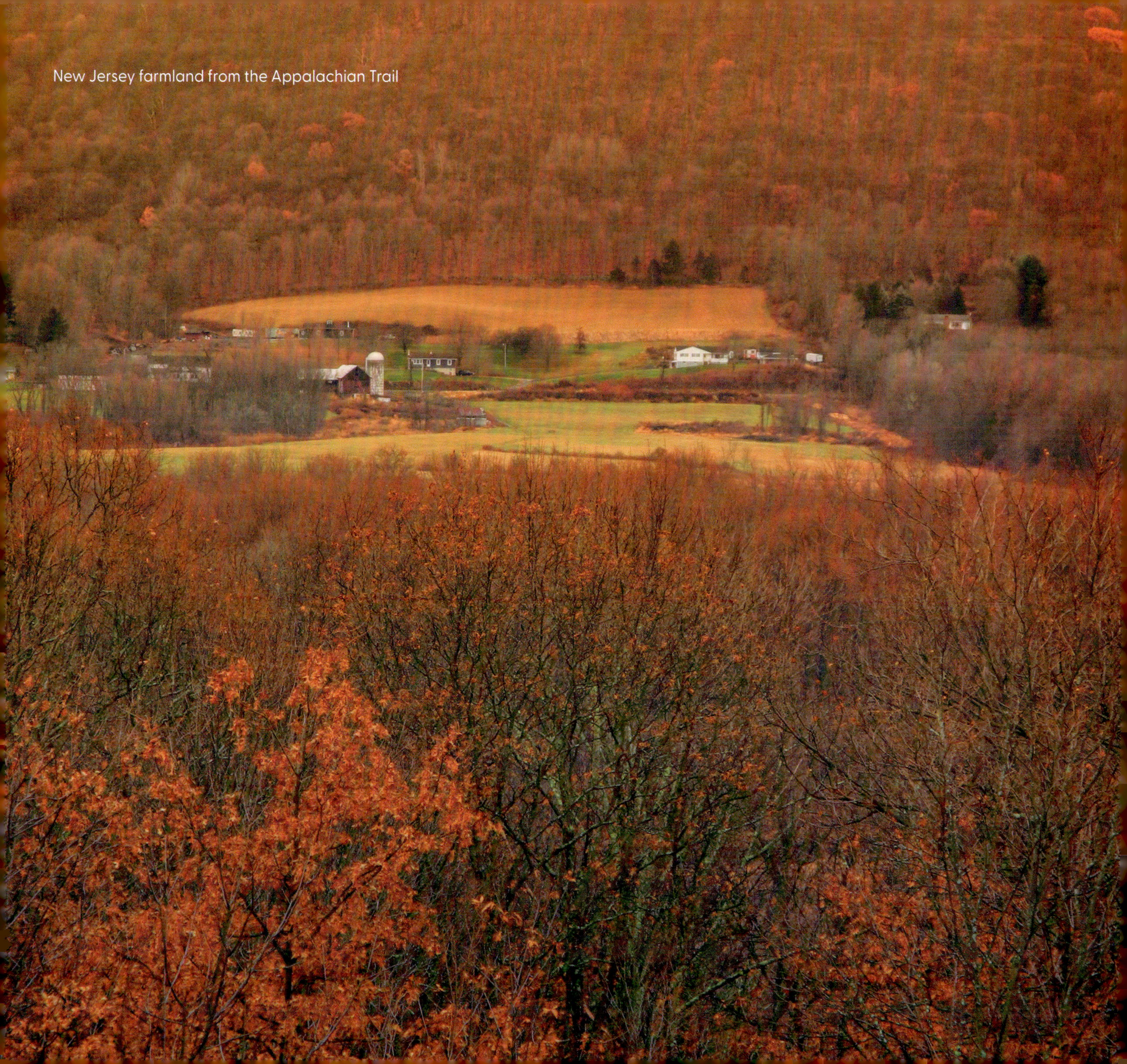

New Jersey farmland from the Appalachian Trail

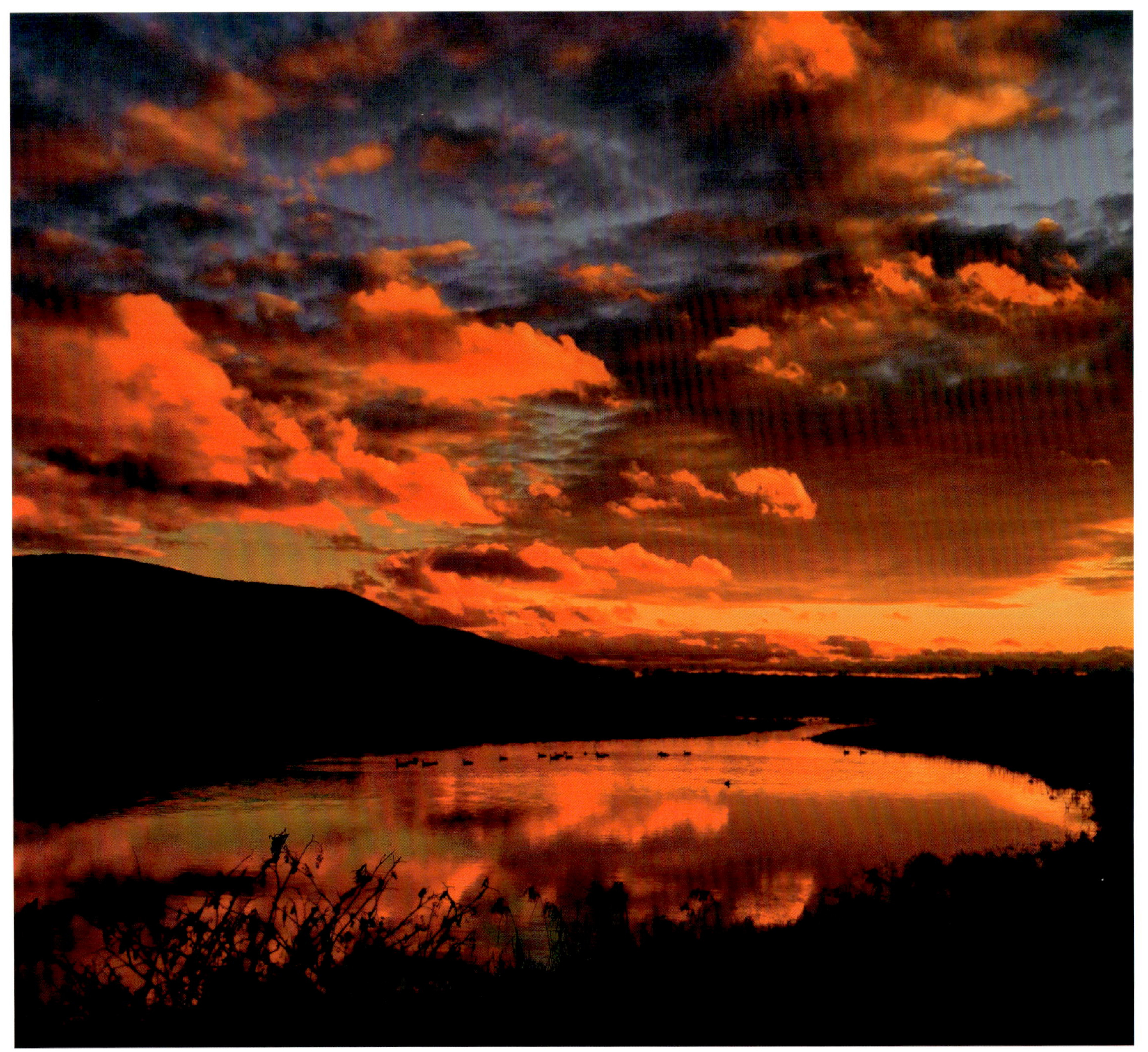

Sunset at Wallkill River National Wildlife Refuge

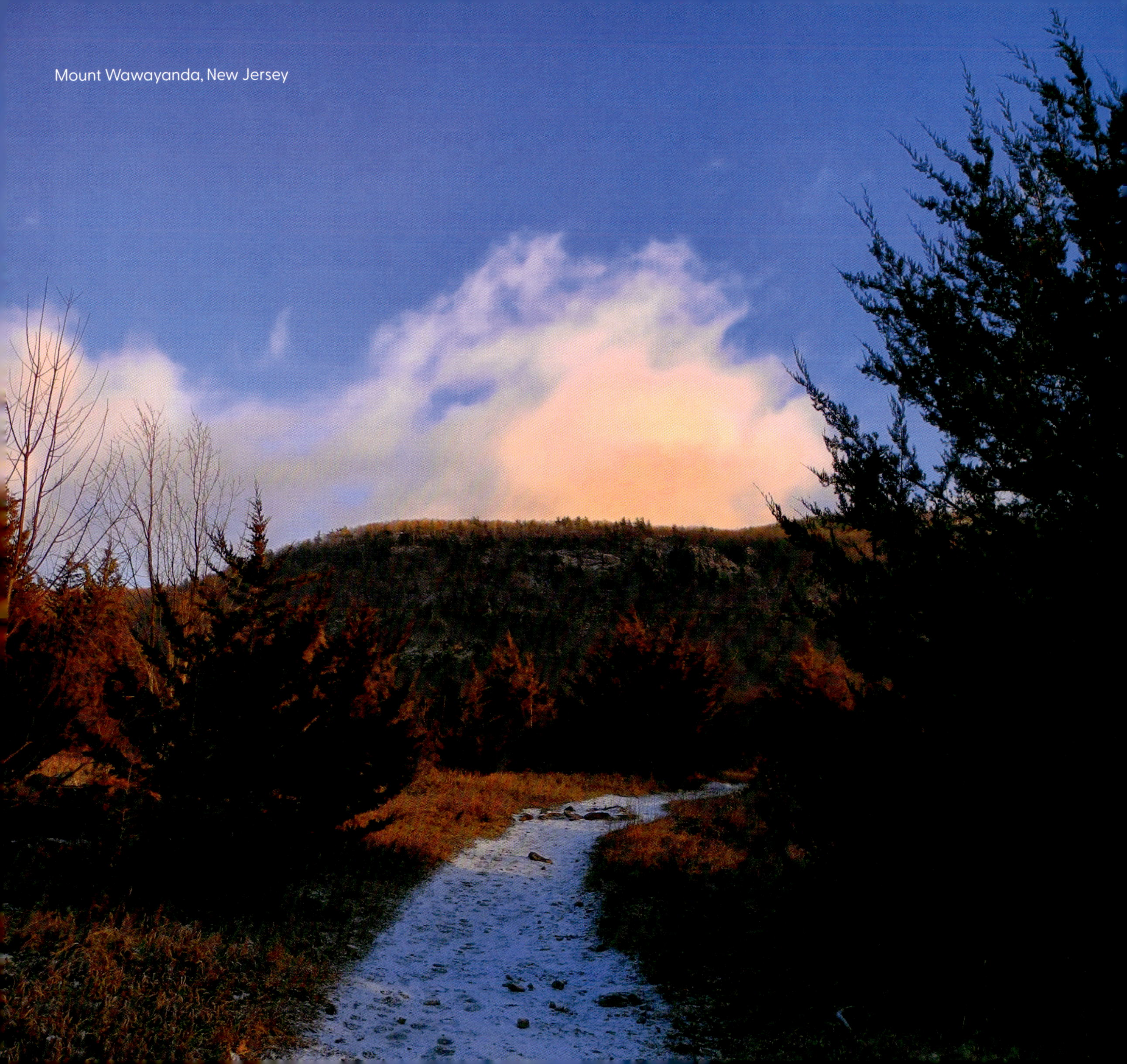

Mount Wawayanda, New Jersey

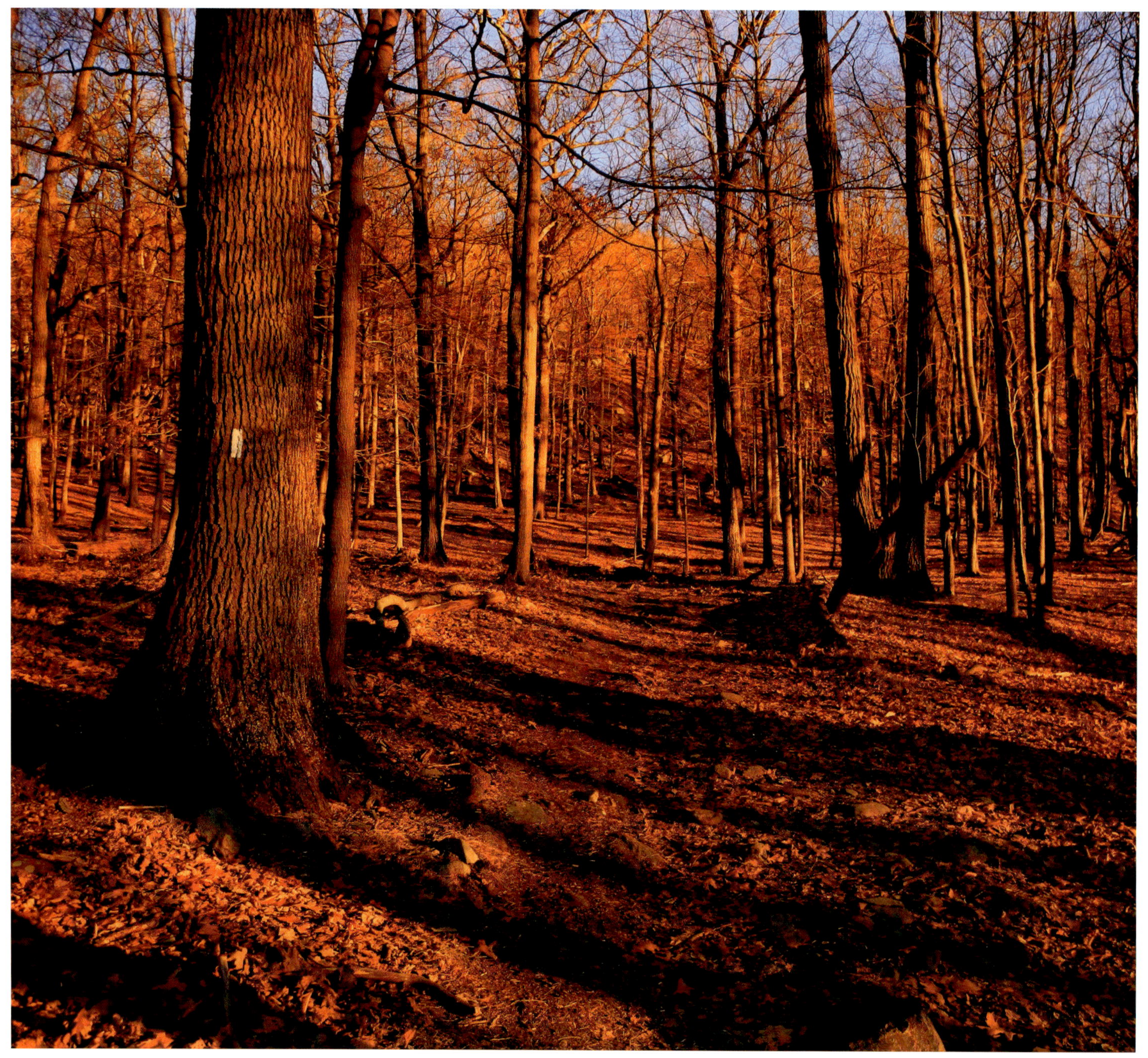

Harriman-Bear State Park, New York, at sunset on the Appalachian Trail

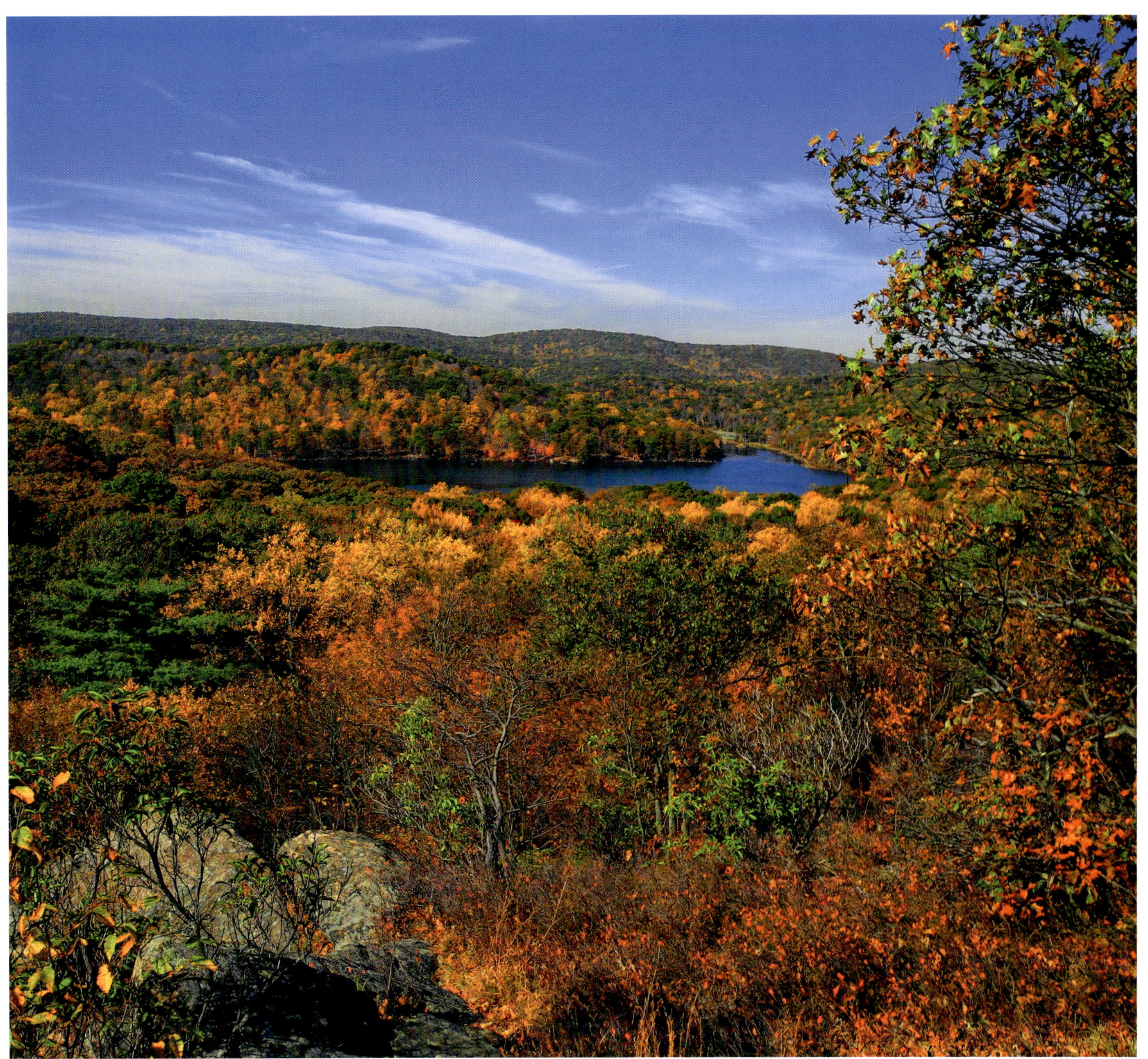

New York's Lake Tiorati from the Appalachian Trail

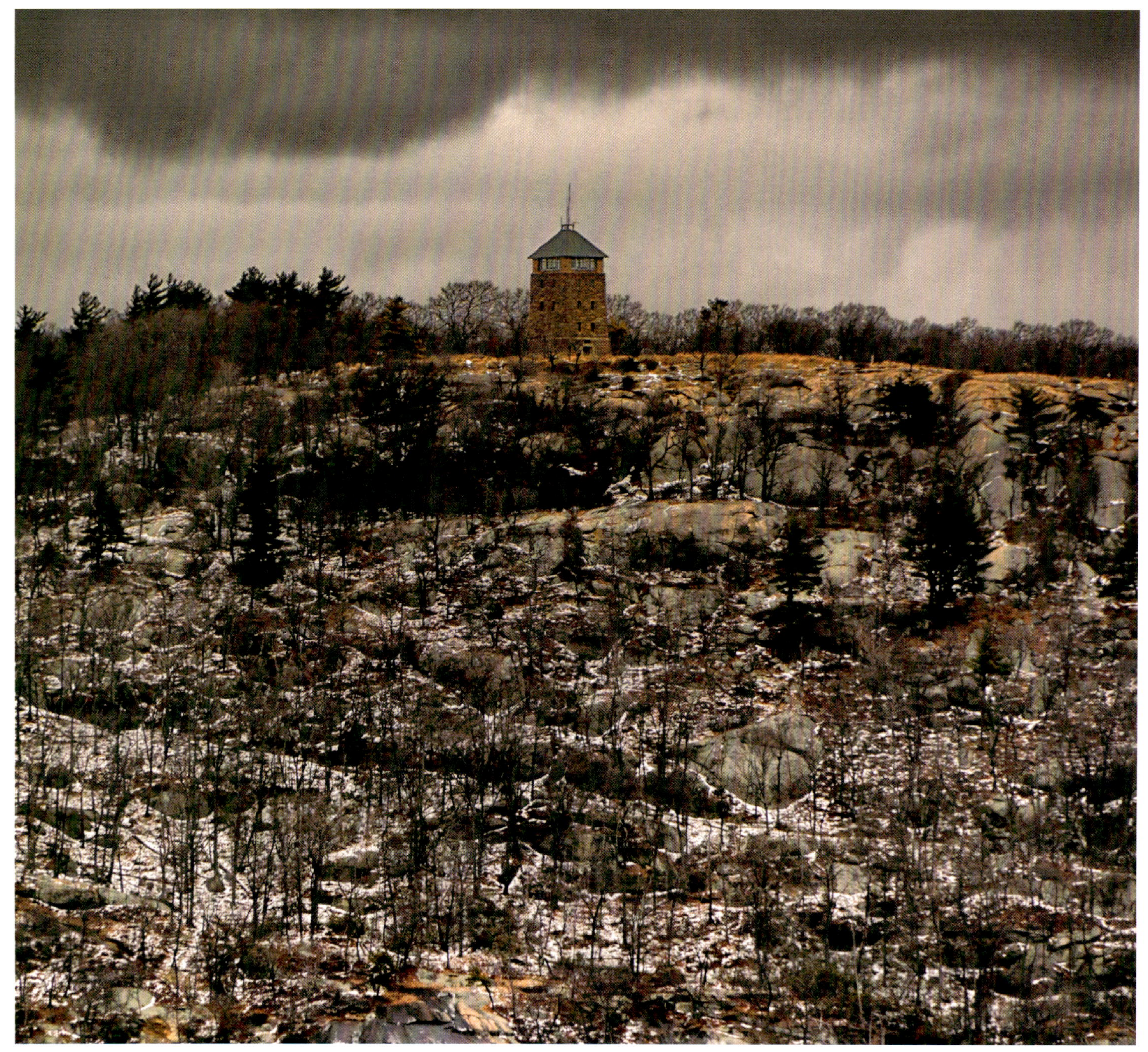

Bear Mountain's Perkins Tower

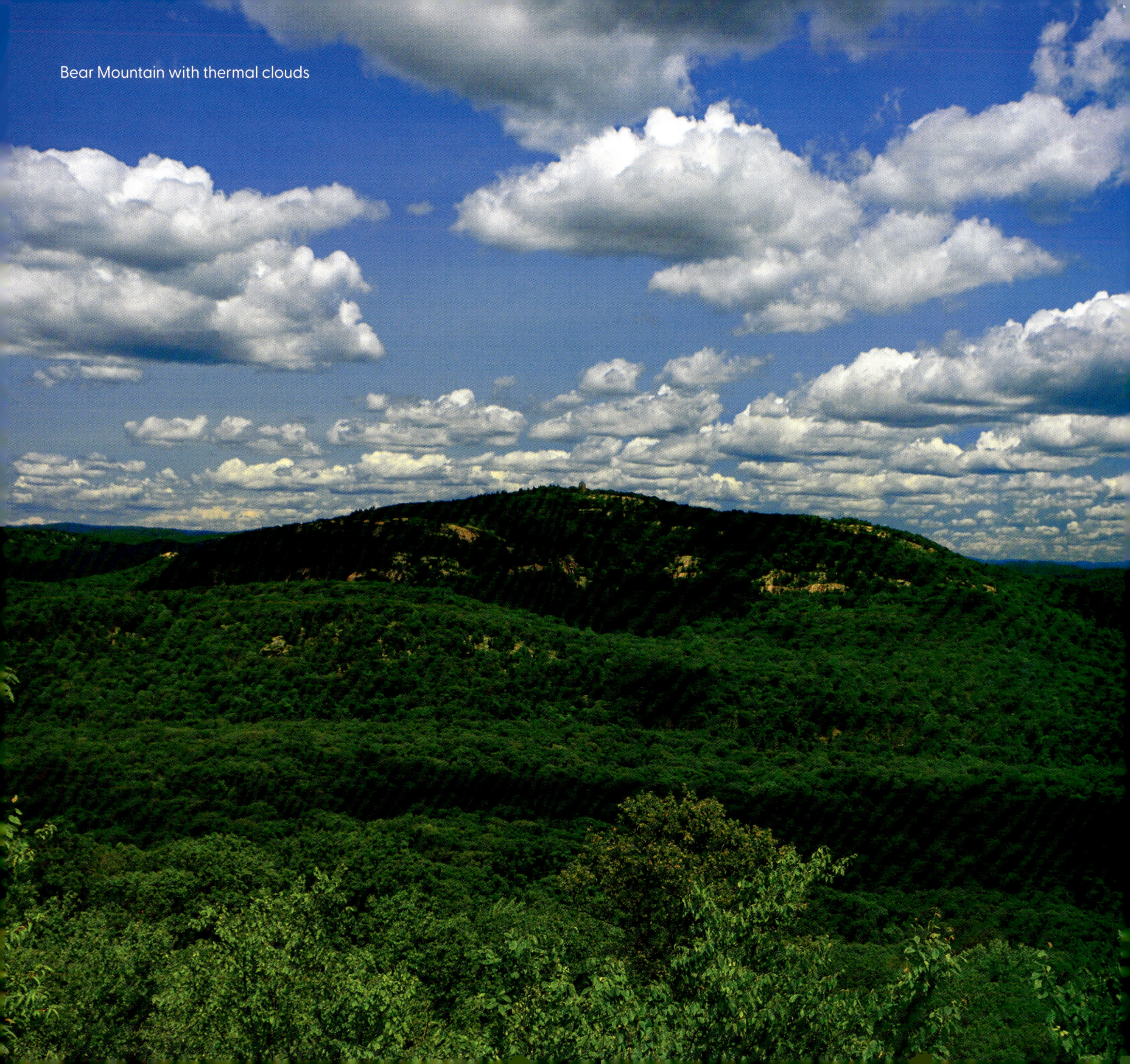

Bear Mountain with thermal clouds

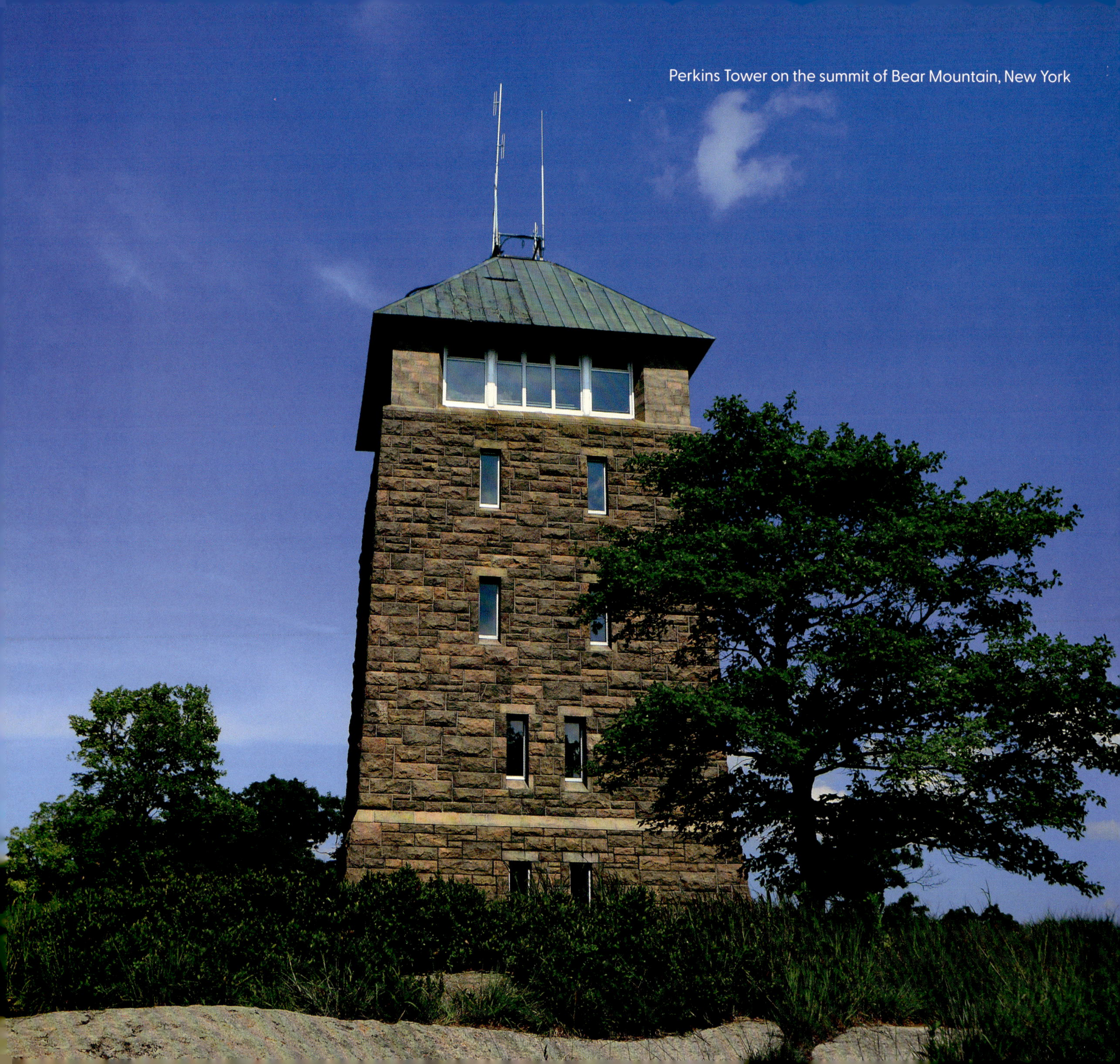
Perkins Tower on the summit of Bear Mountain, New York

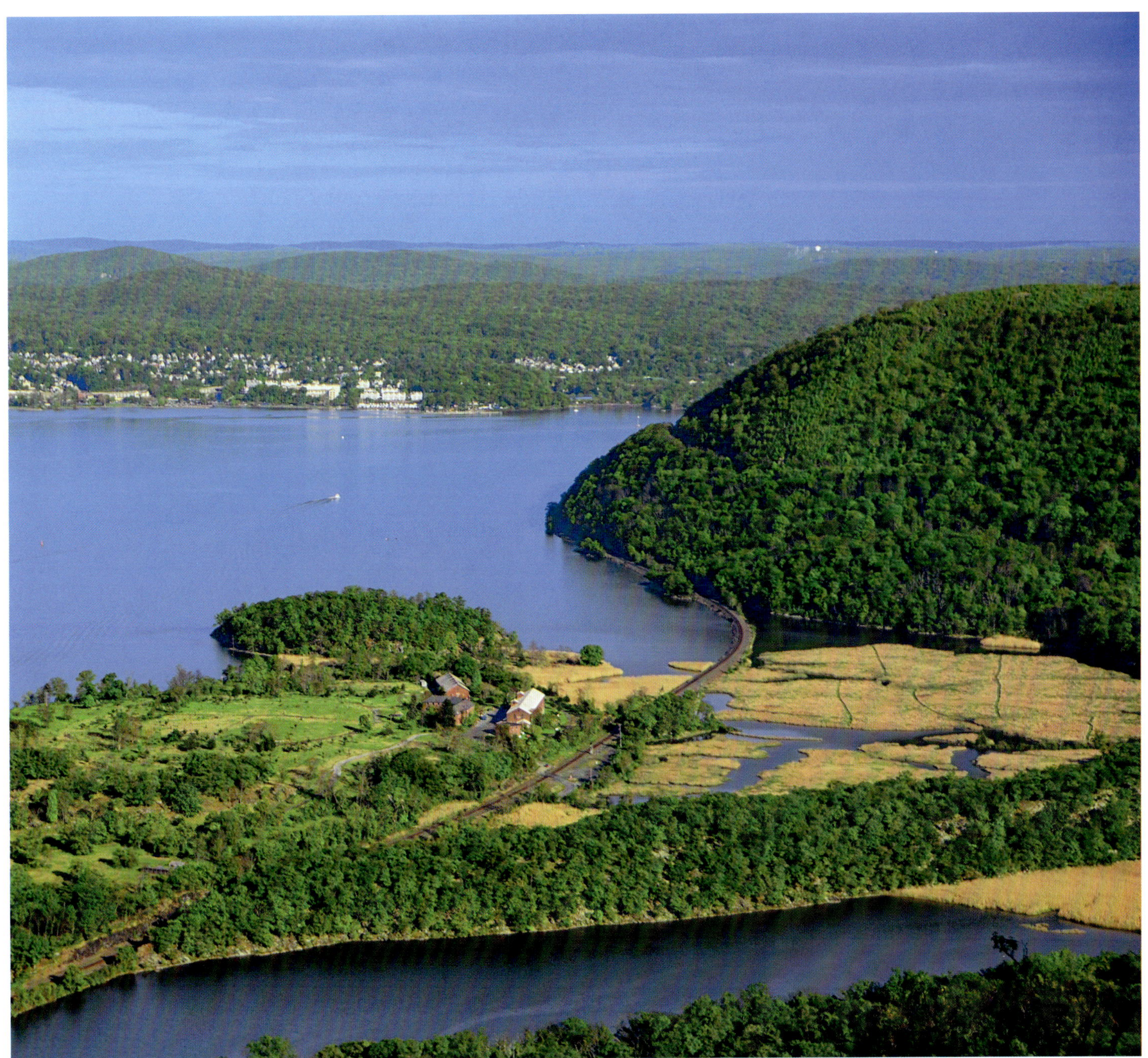

Hudson River from Bear Mountain, New York

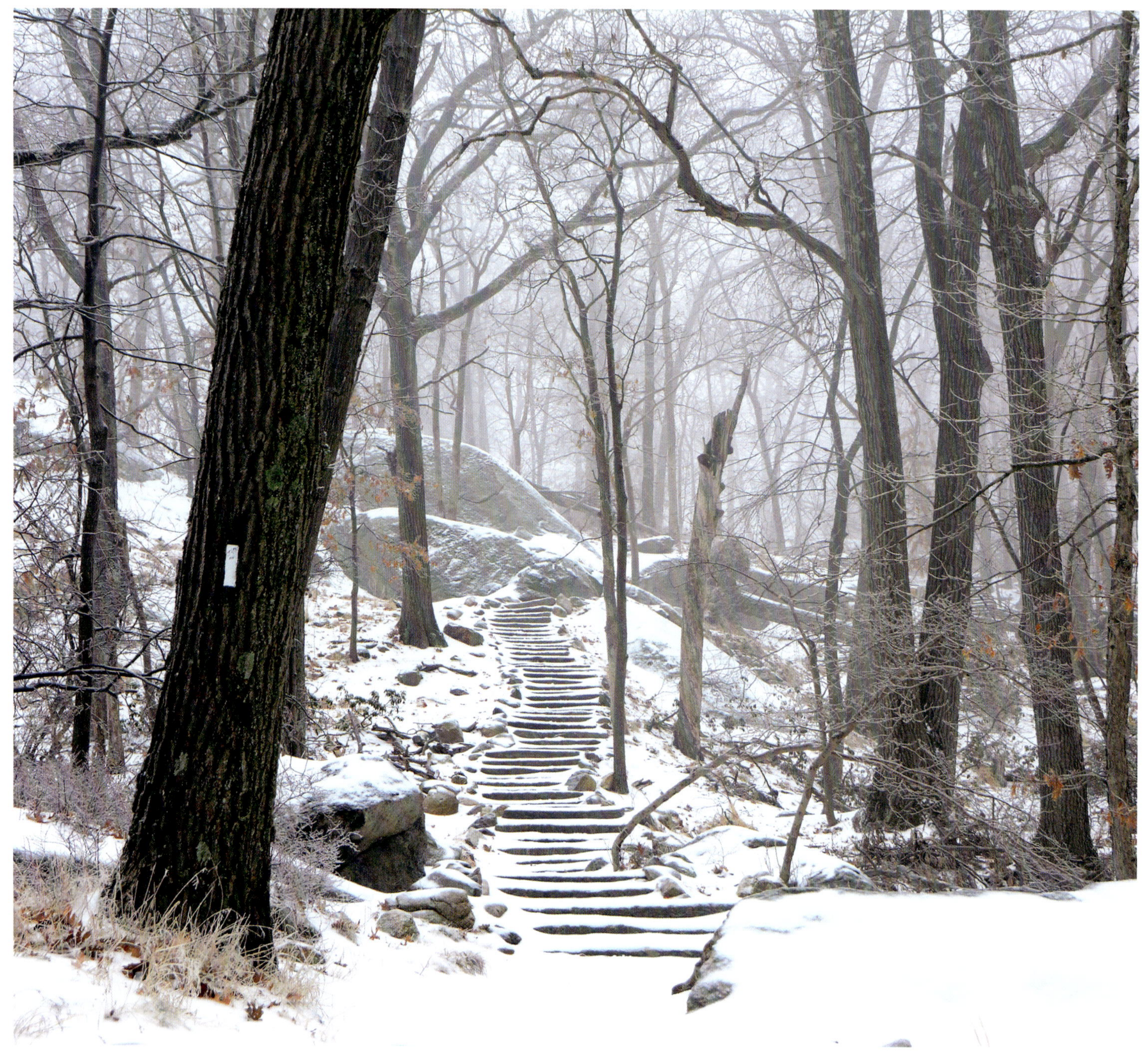
The Appalachian Trail on Bear Mountain, New York, in the winter

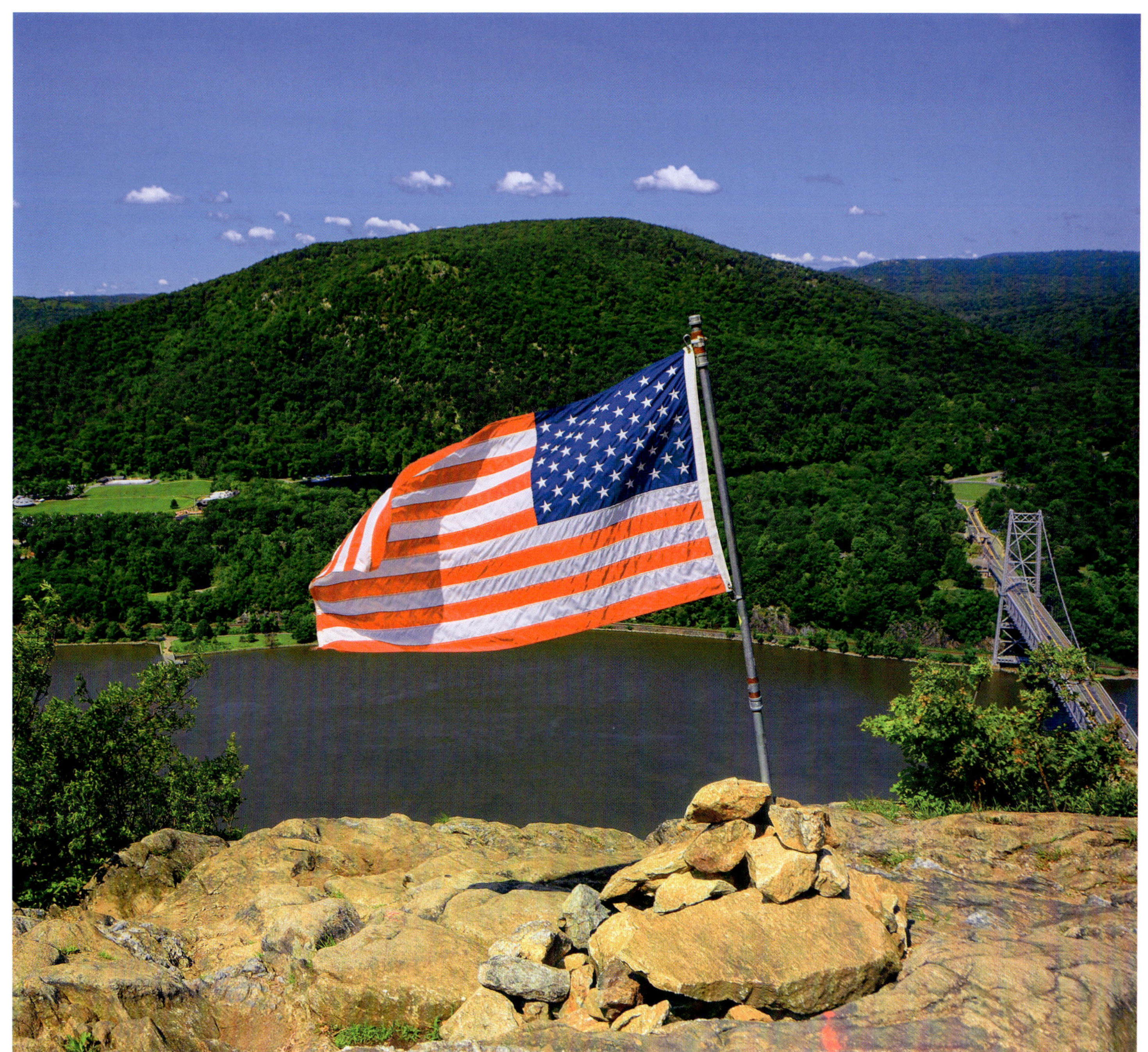

Anthony's Nose, summit view

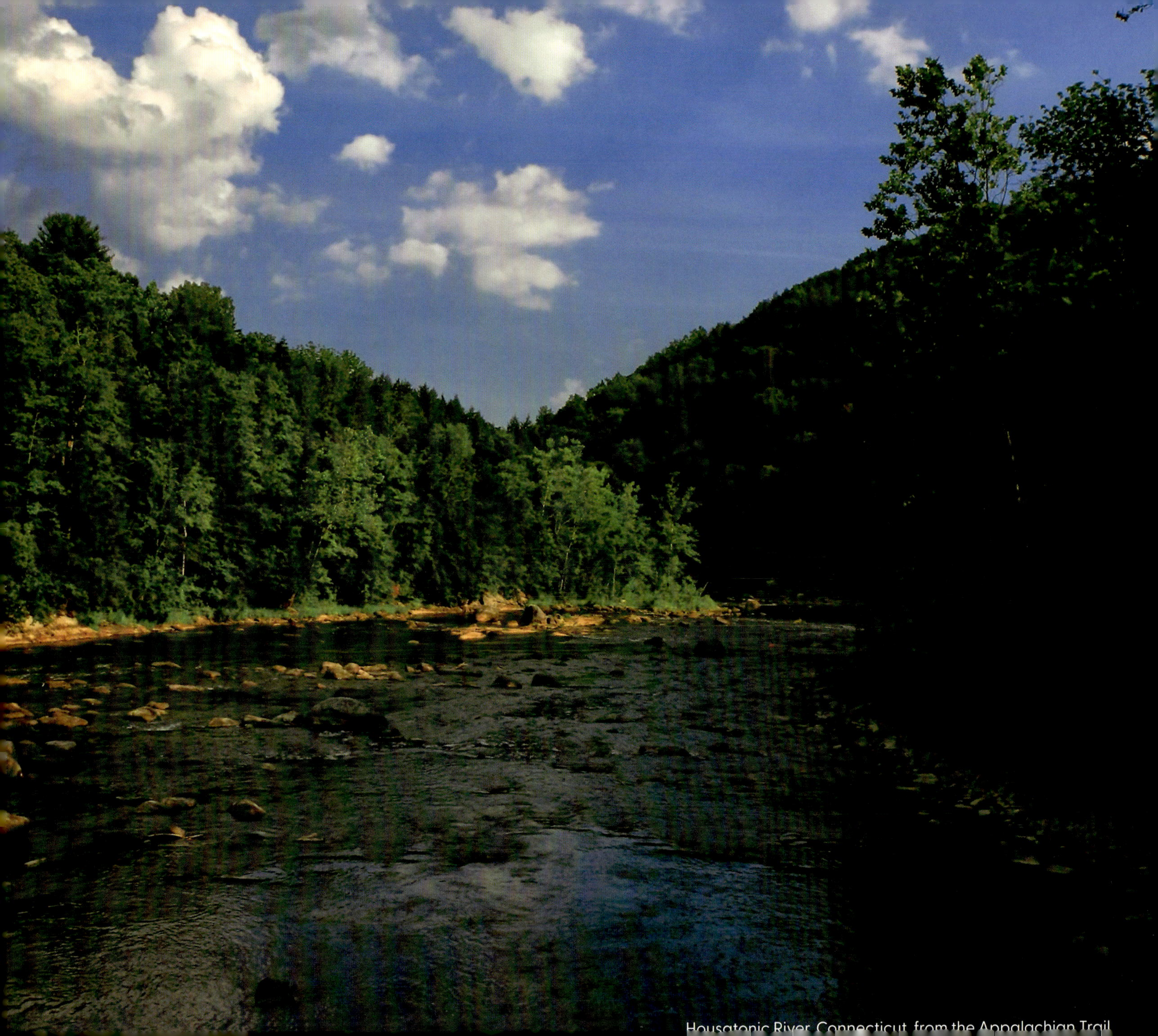

Housatonic River, Connecticut, from the Appalachian Trail

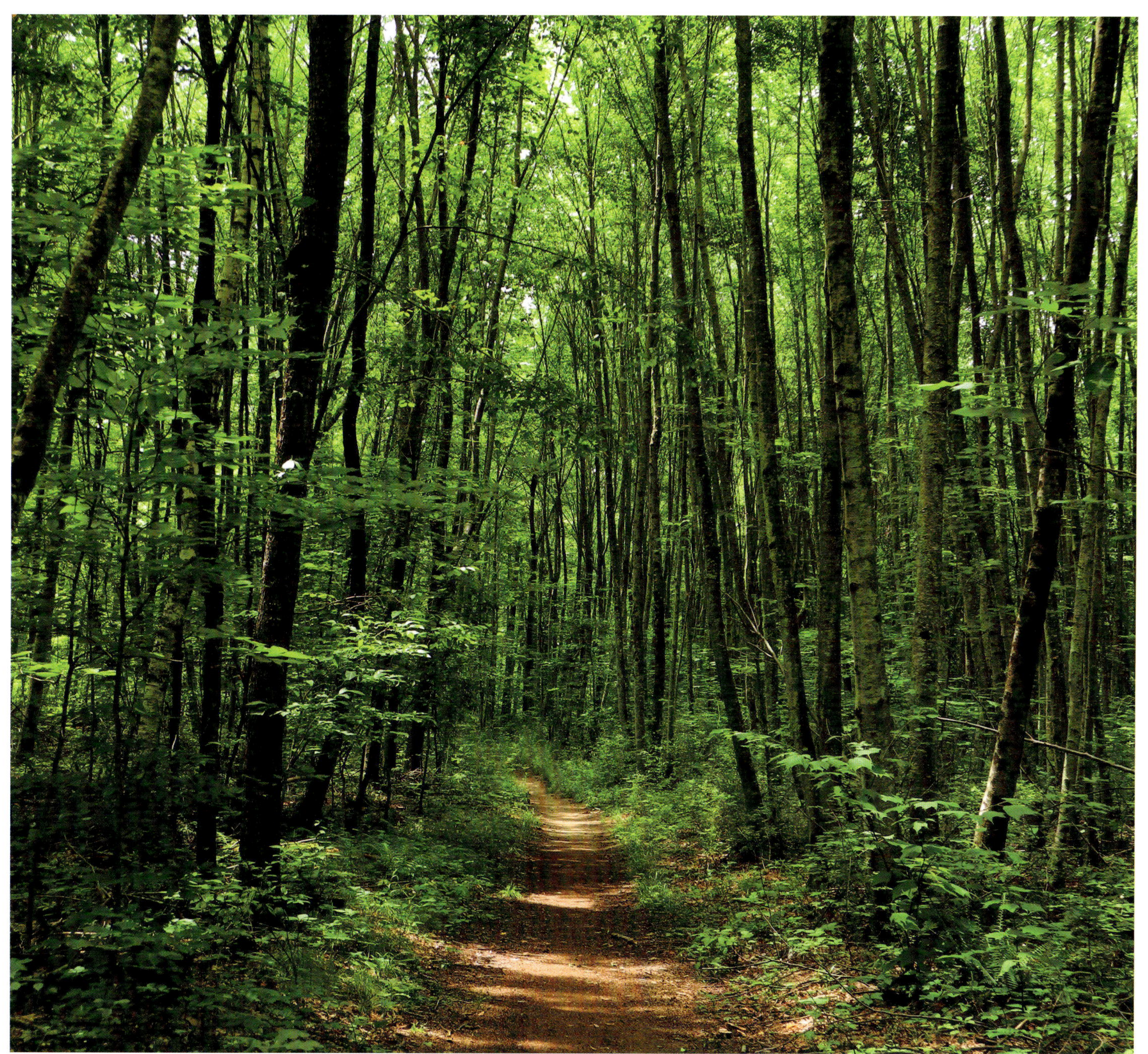

Aspen grove in Connecticut on the Appalachian Trail

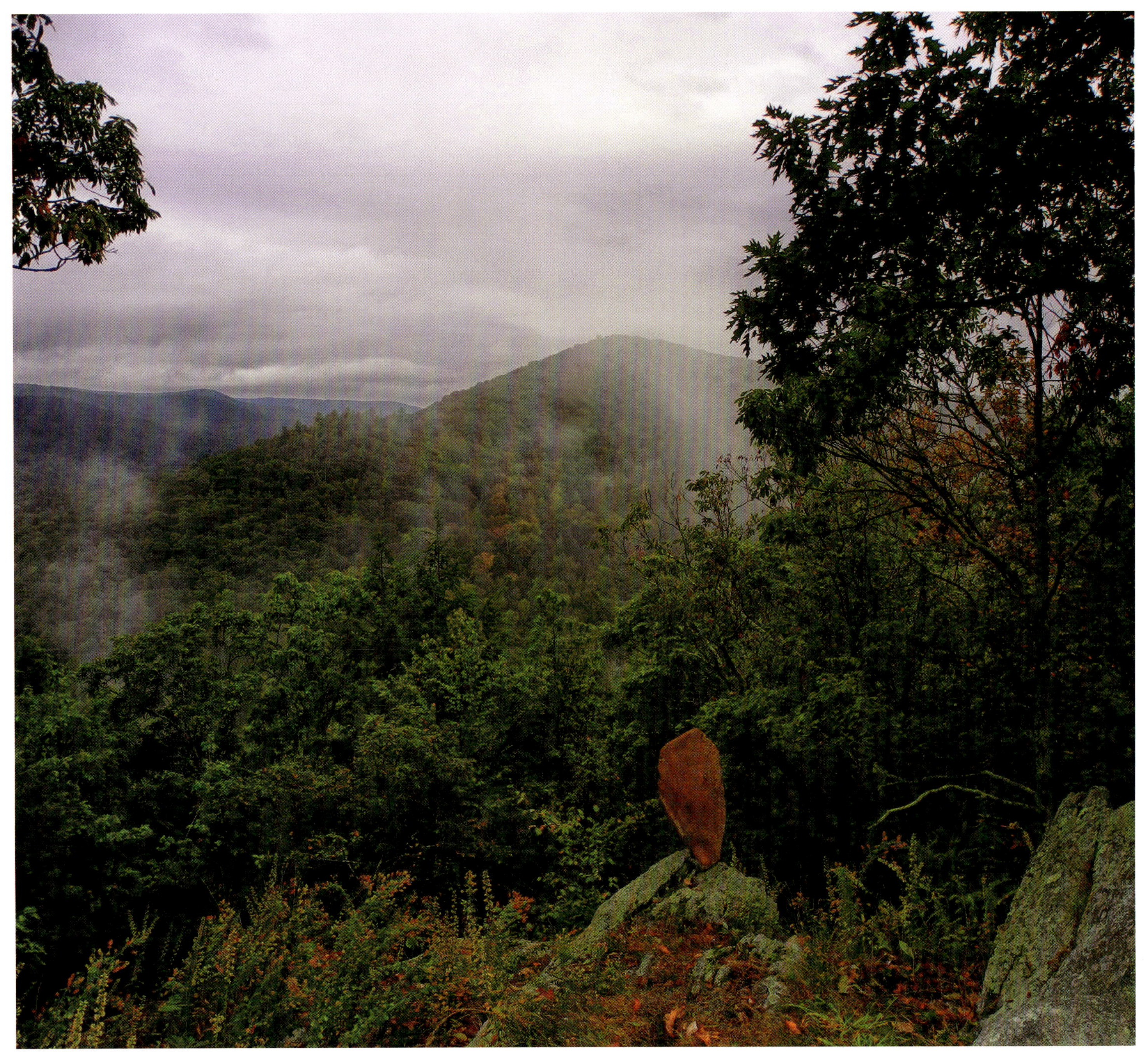

Misty morning in Connecticut on the Appalachian Trail

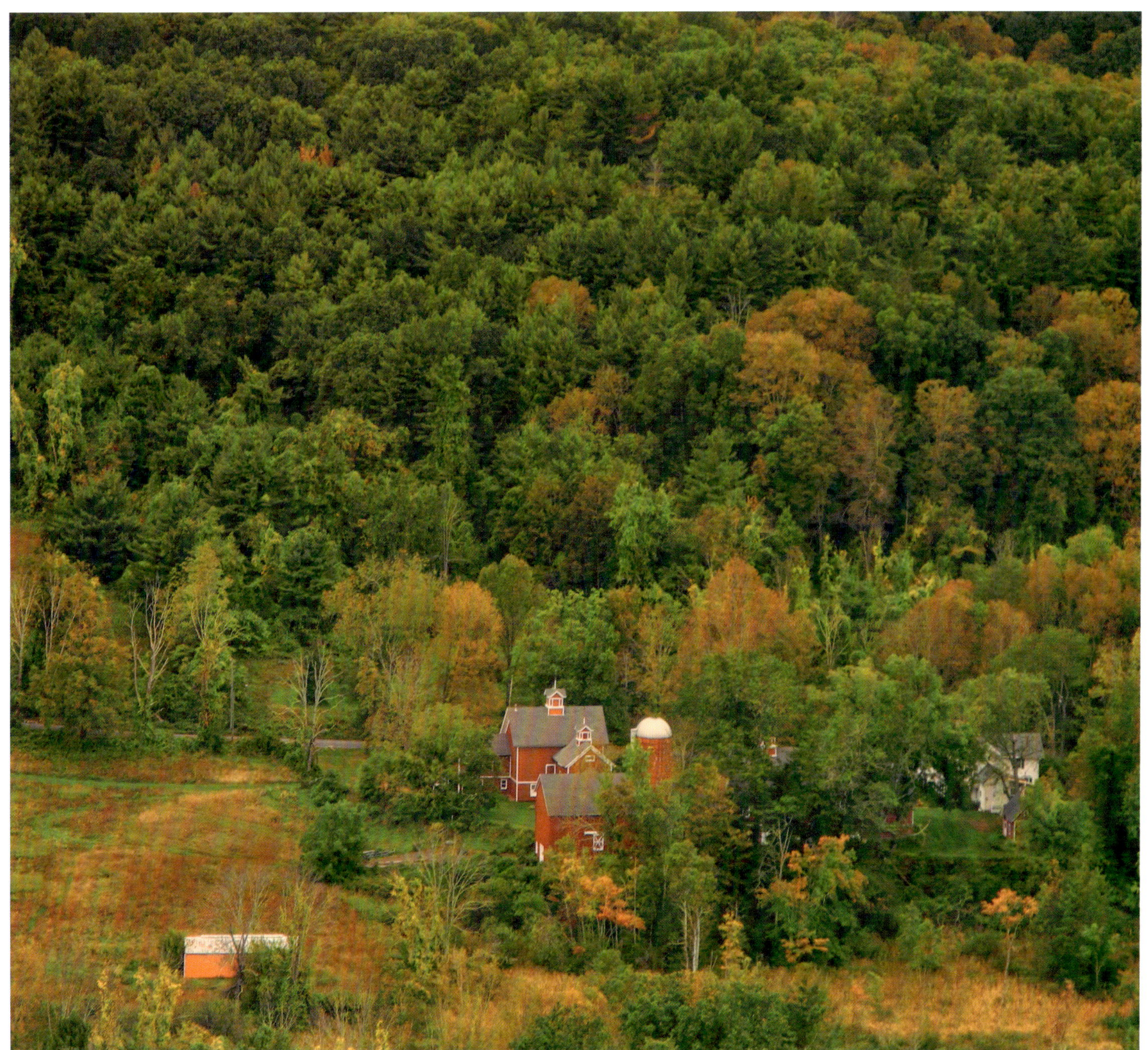

Connecticut farmland from the Appalachian Trail

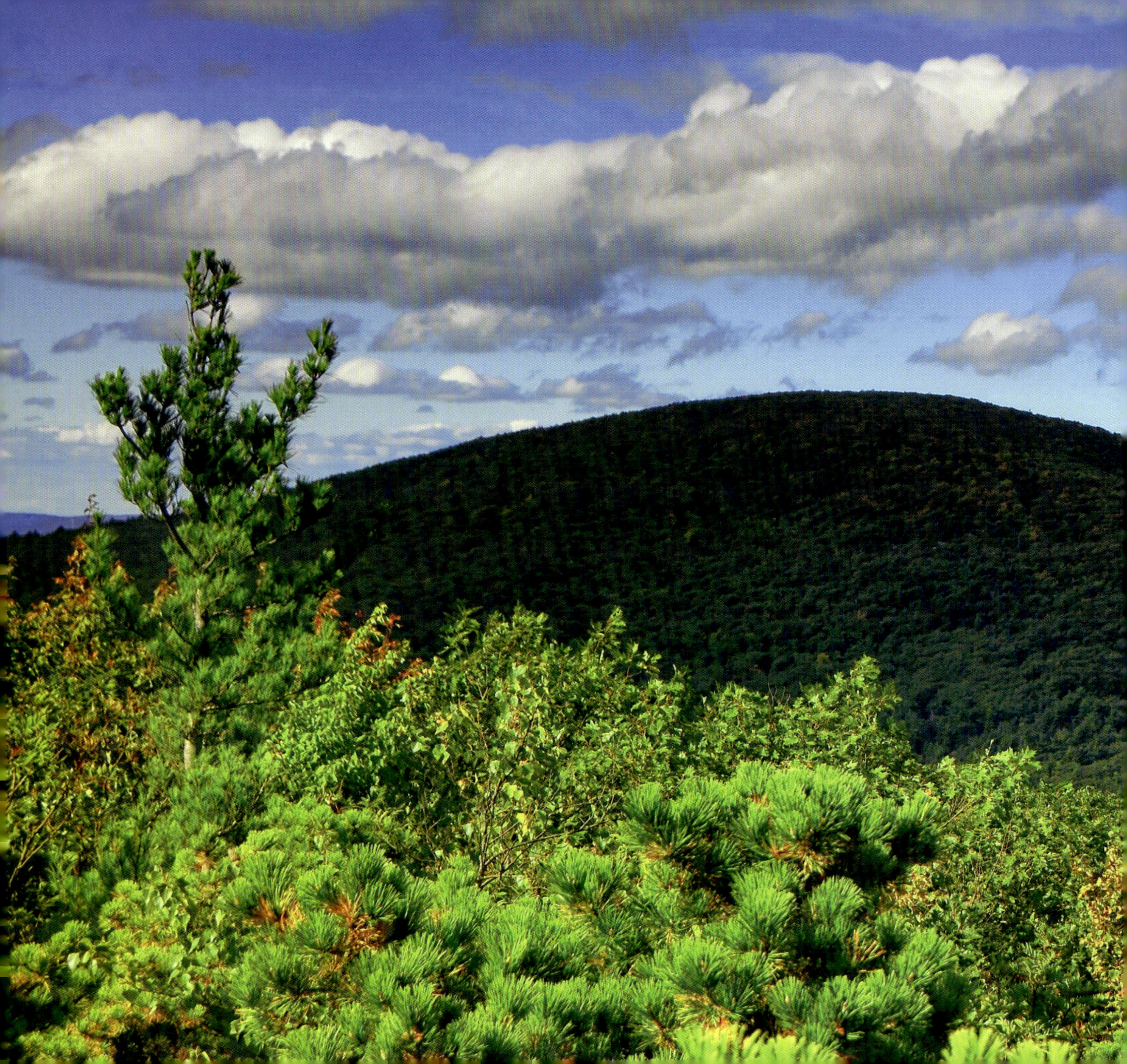

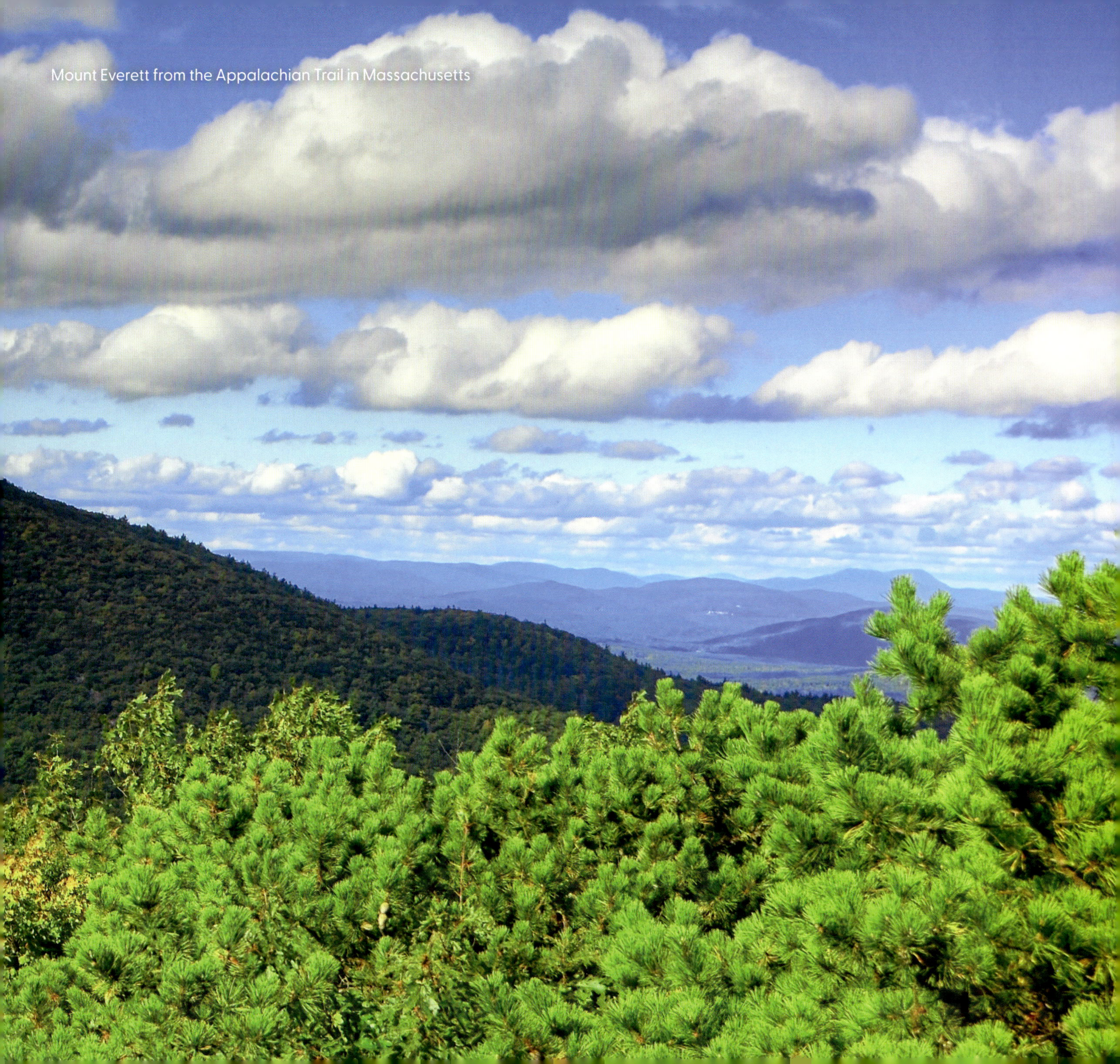

Mount Everett from the Appalachian Trail in Massachusetts

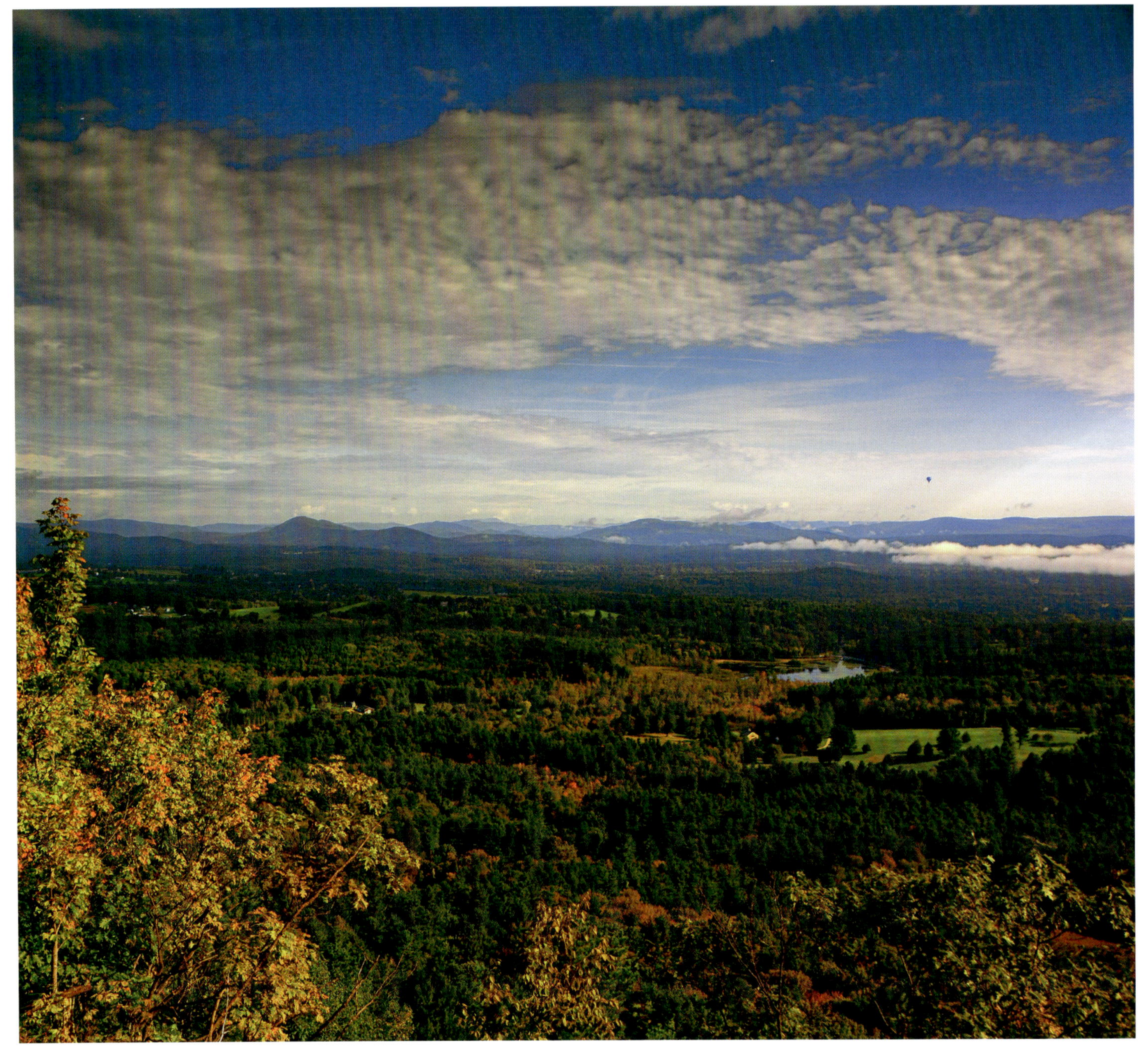

Massachusetts Berkshires

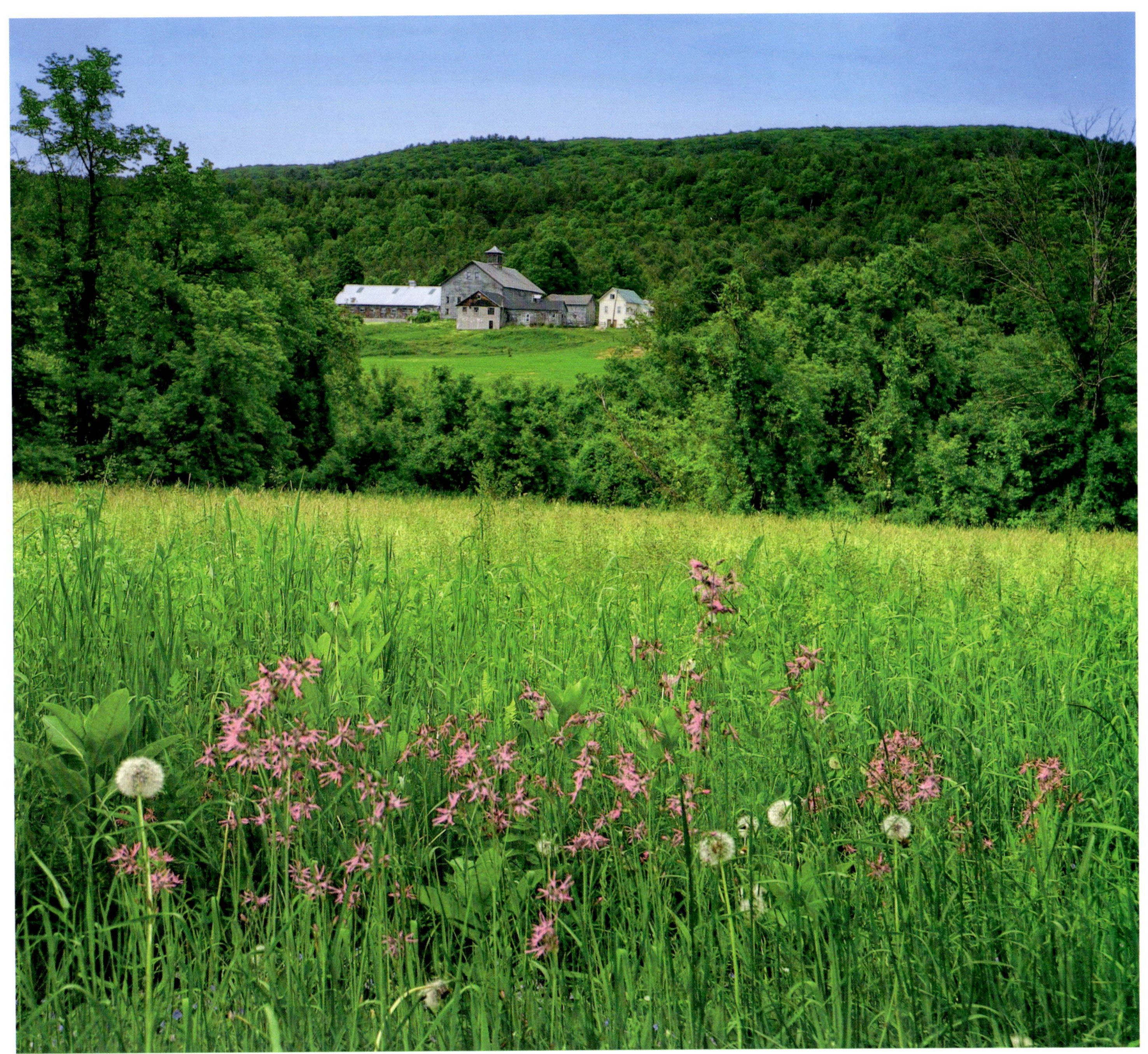

Farmland and spring wildflowers in Massachusetts from along the Appalachian Trail

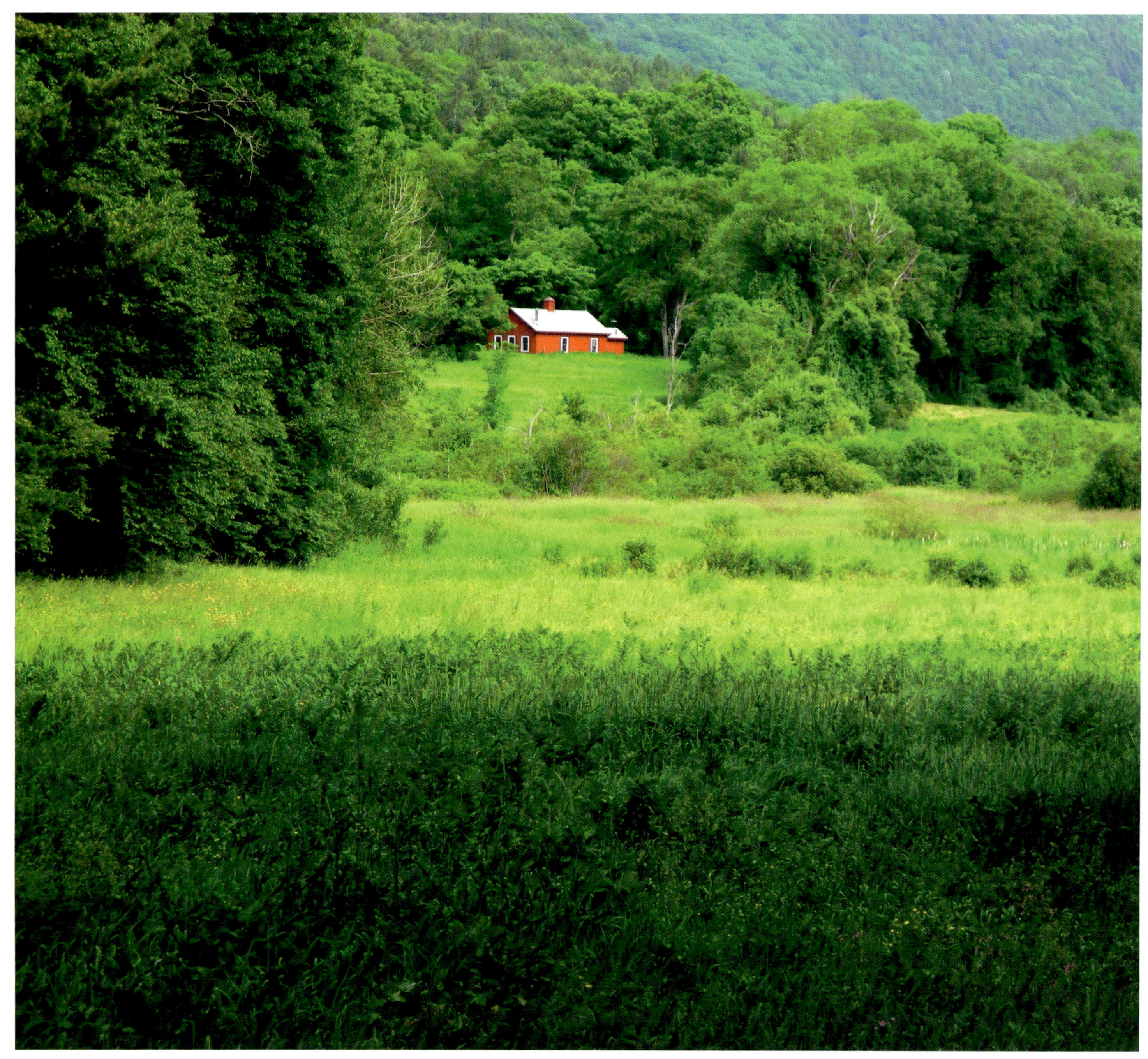

Red barn surrounded by Massachusetts spring green

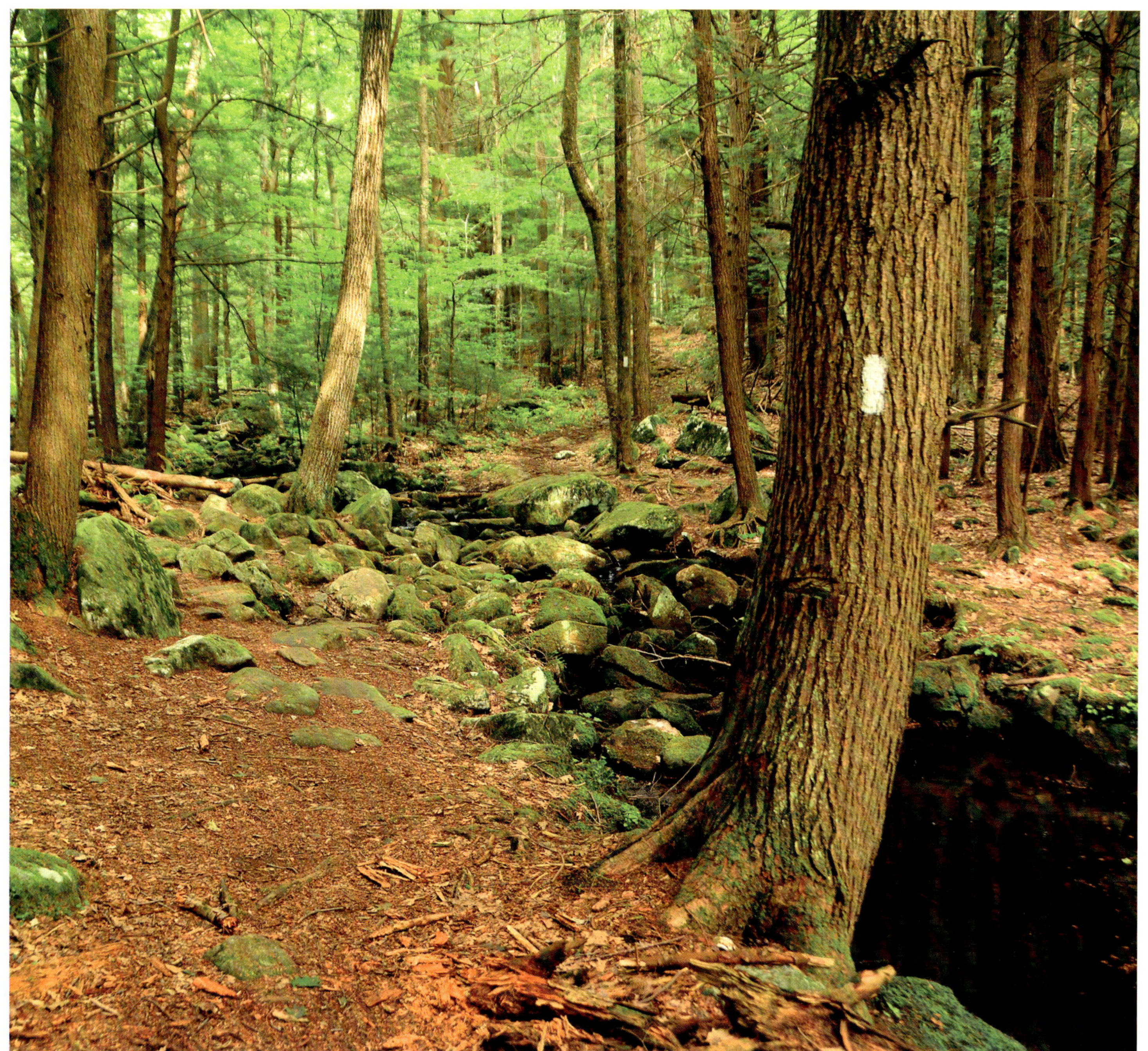

The Appalachian Trail in Massachusetts, green tunnel

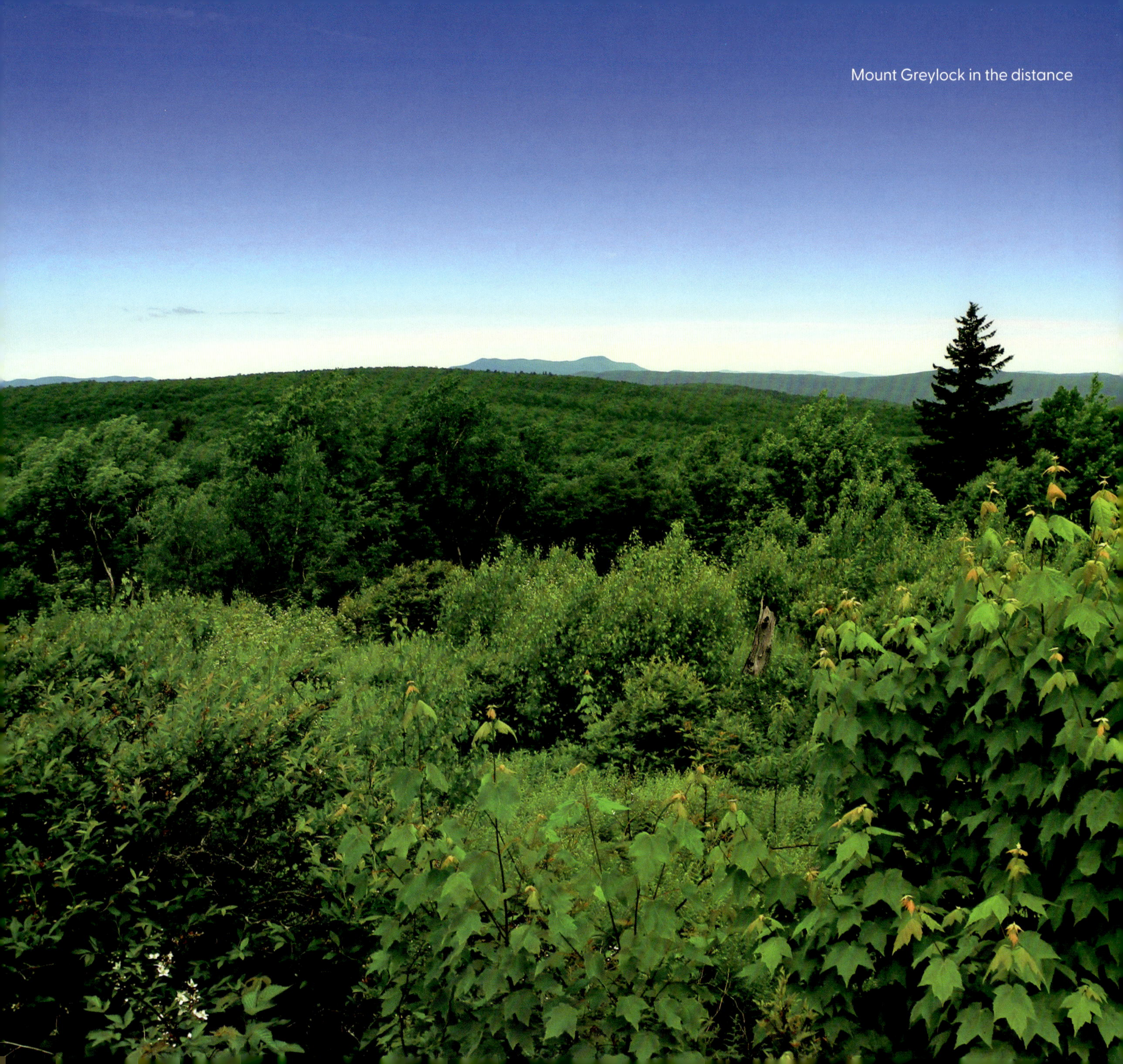

Mount Greylock in the distance

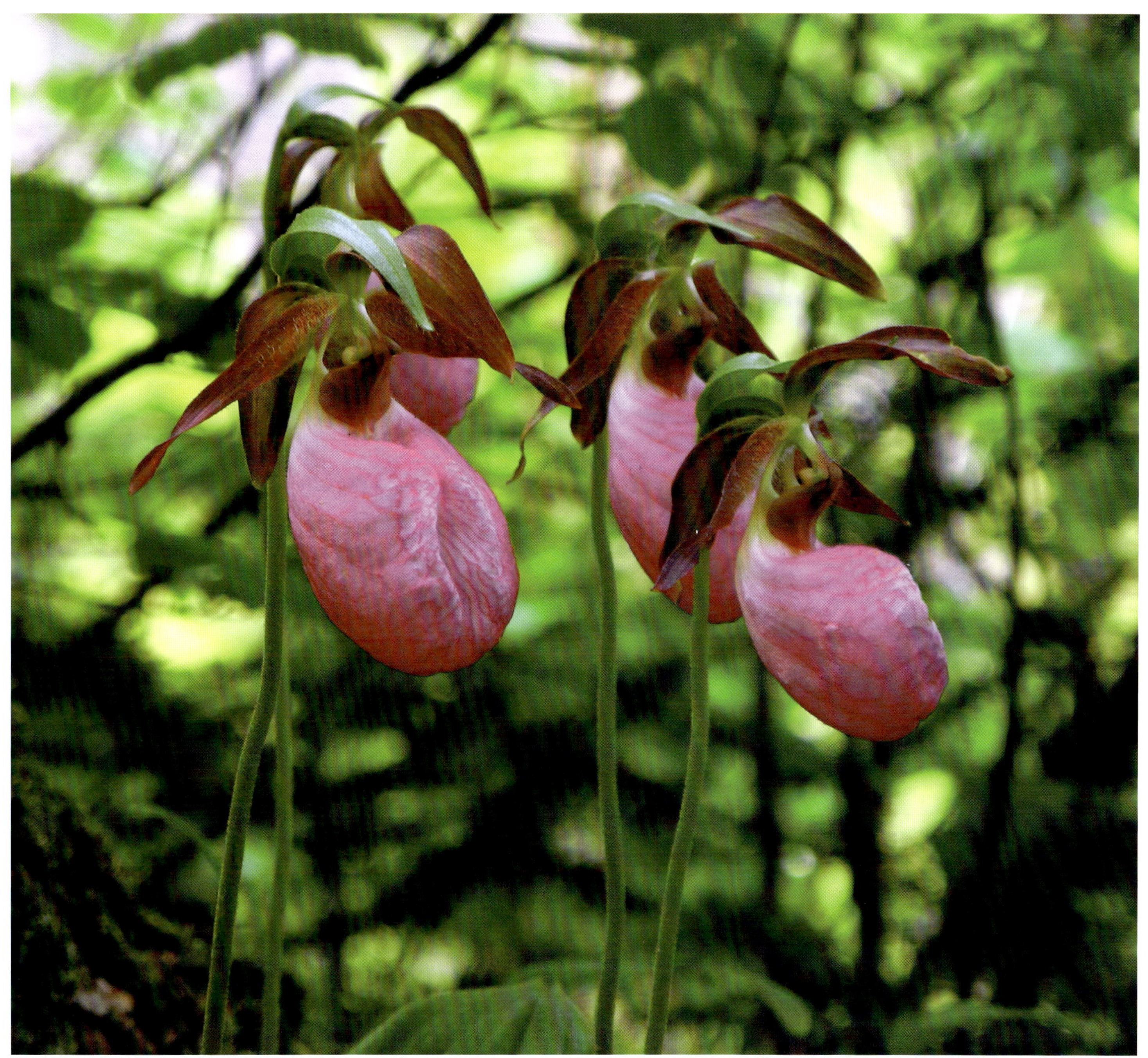

Pink lady slippers in Massachusetts

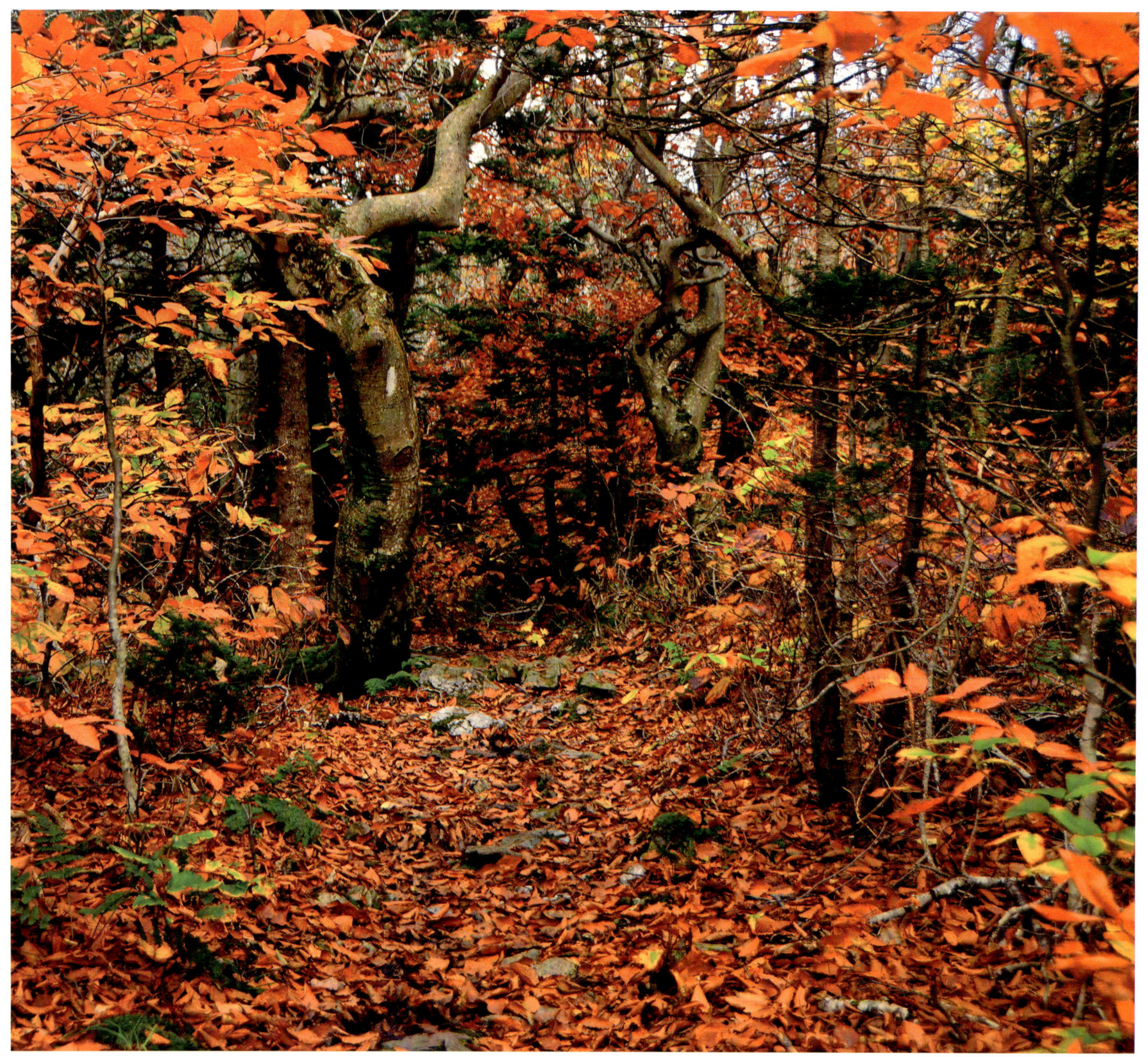

The Appalachian Trail in Massachusetts in autumn

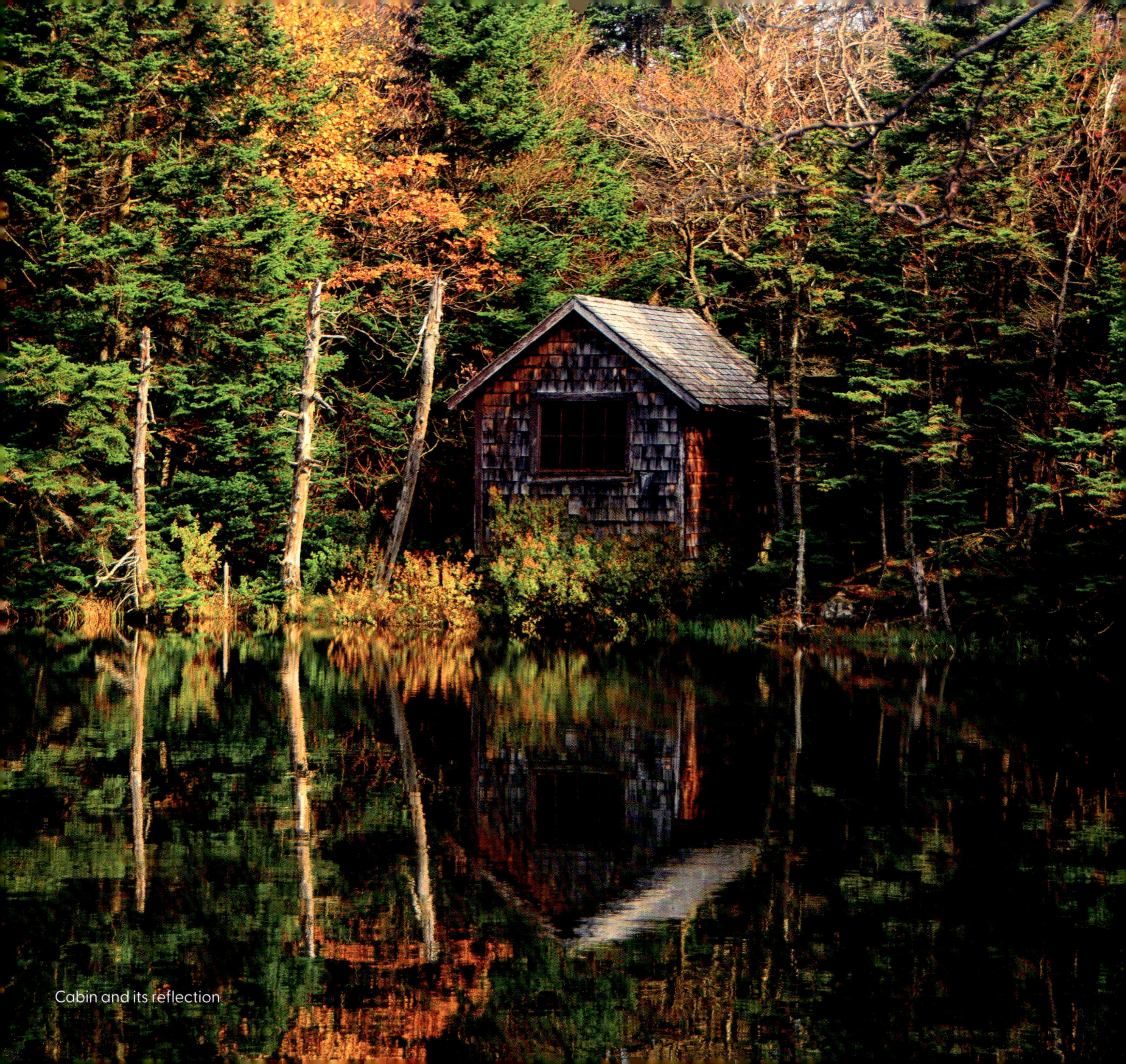
Cabin and its reflection

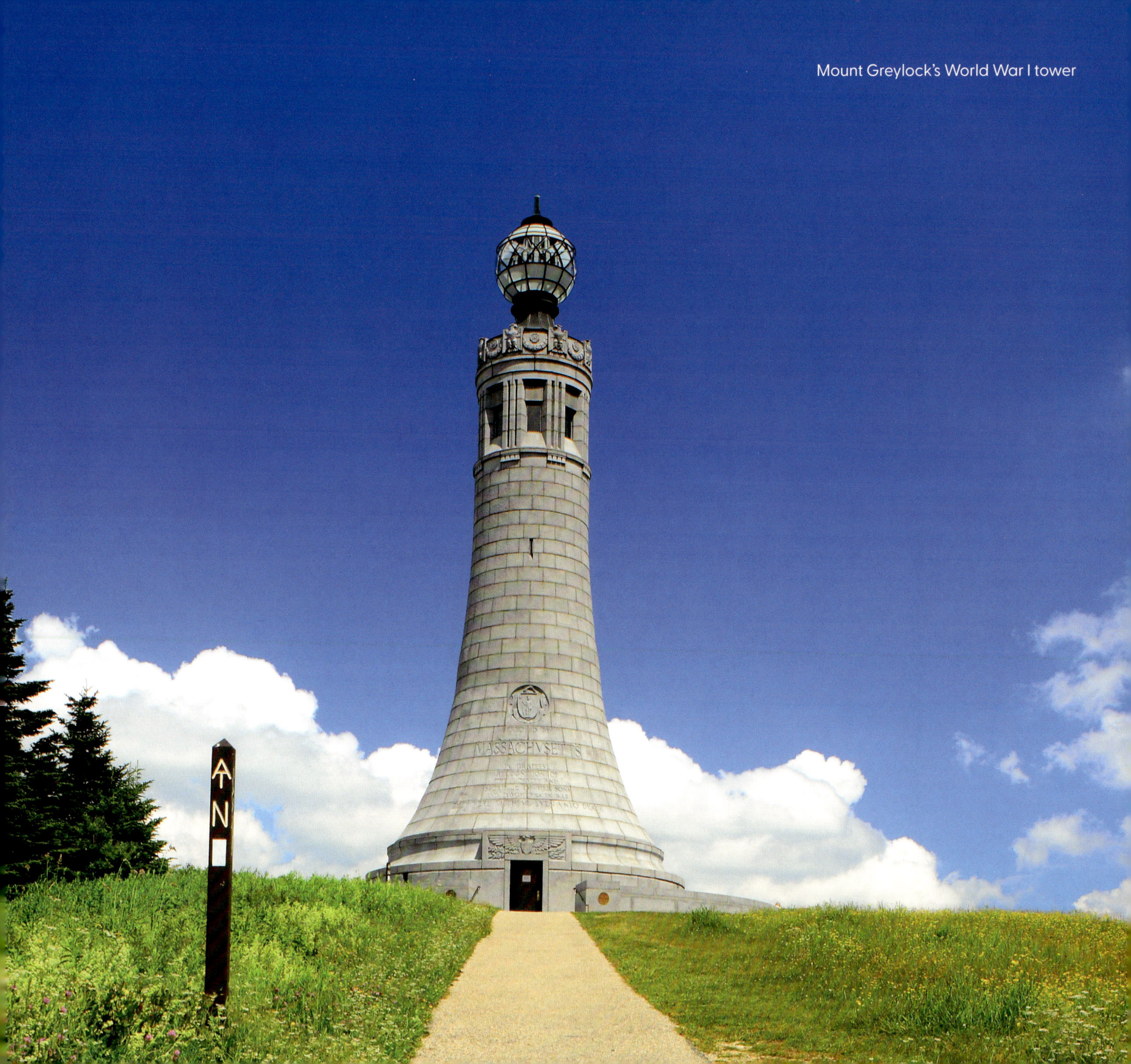

Mount Greylock's World War I tower

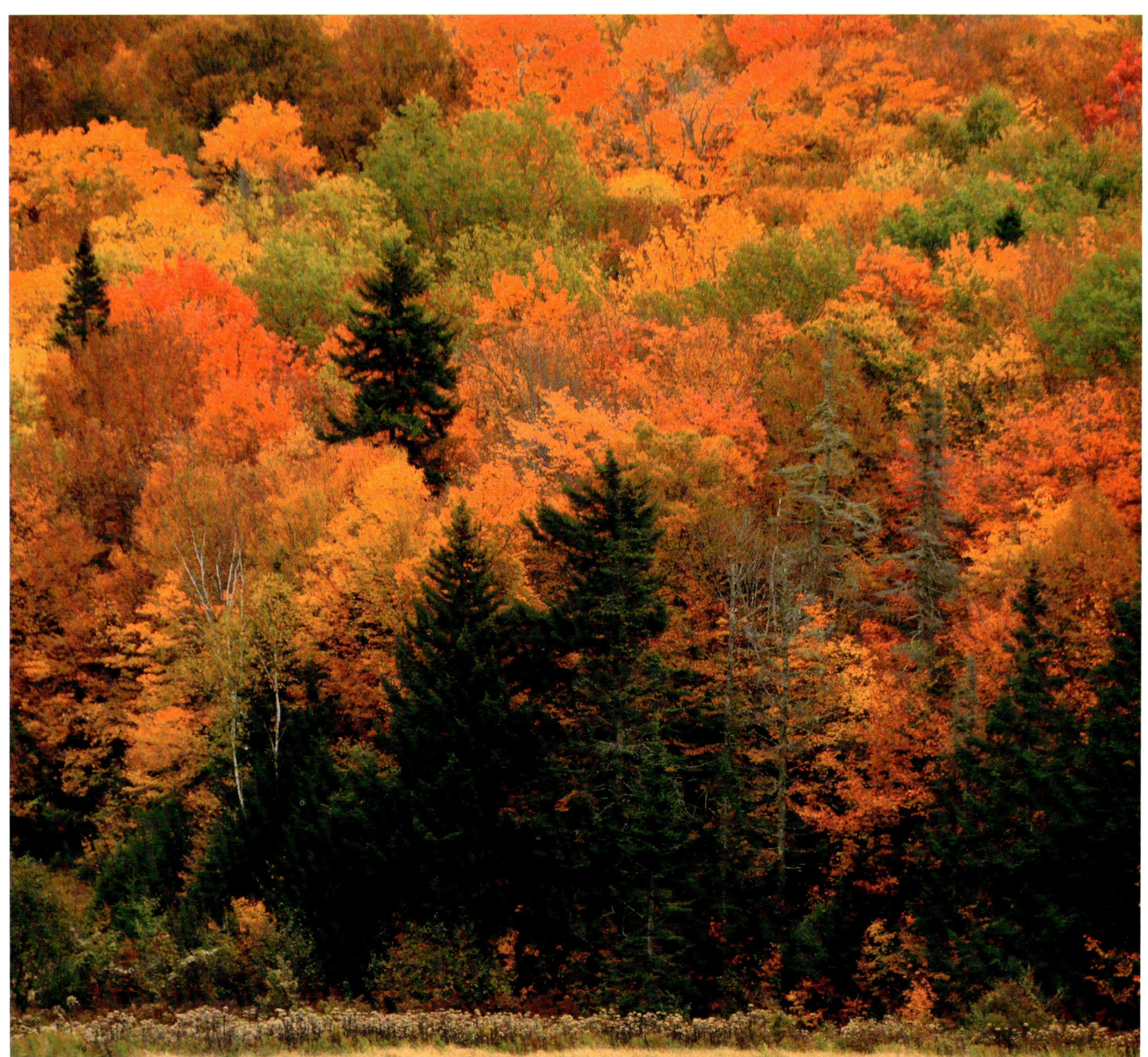

Autumn colors on the Appalachian Trail in Vermont

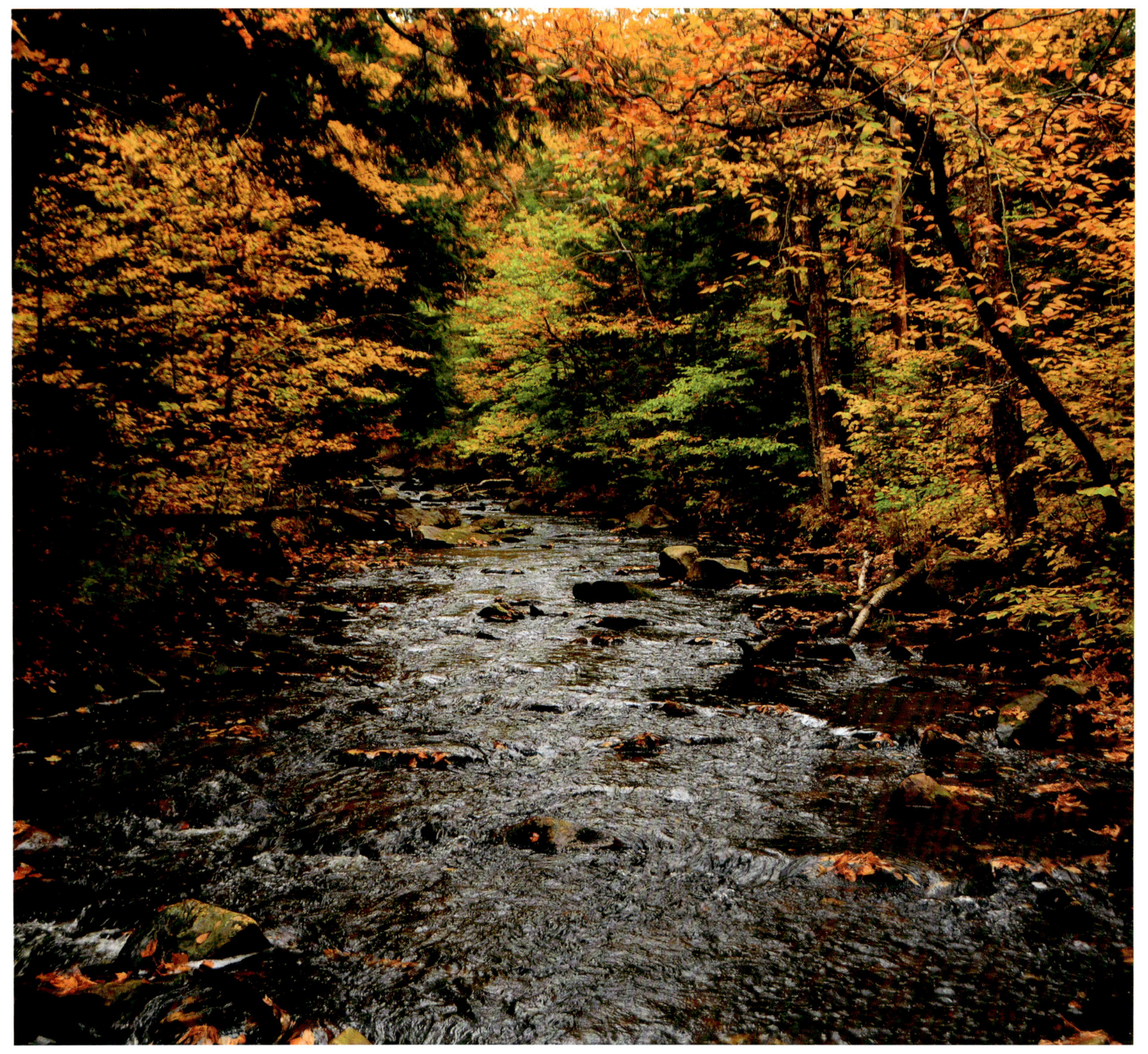

Creek on the Appalachian Trail in Vermont

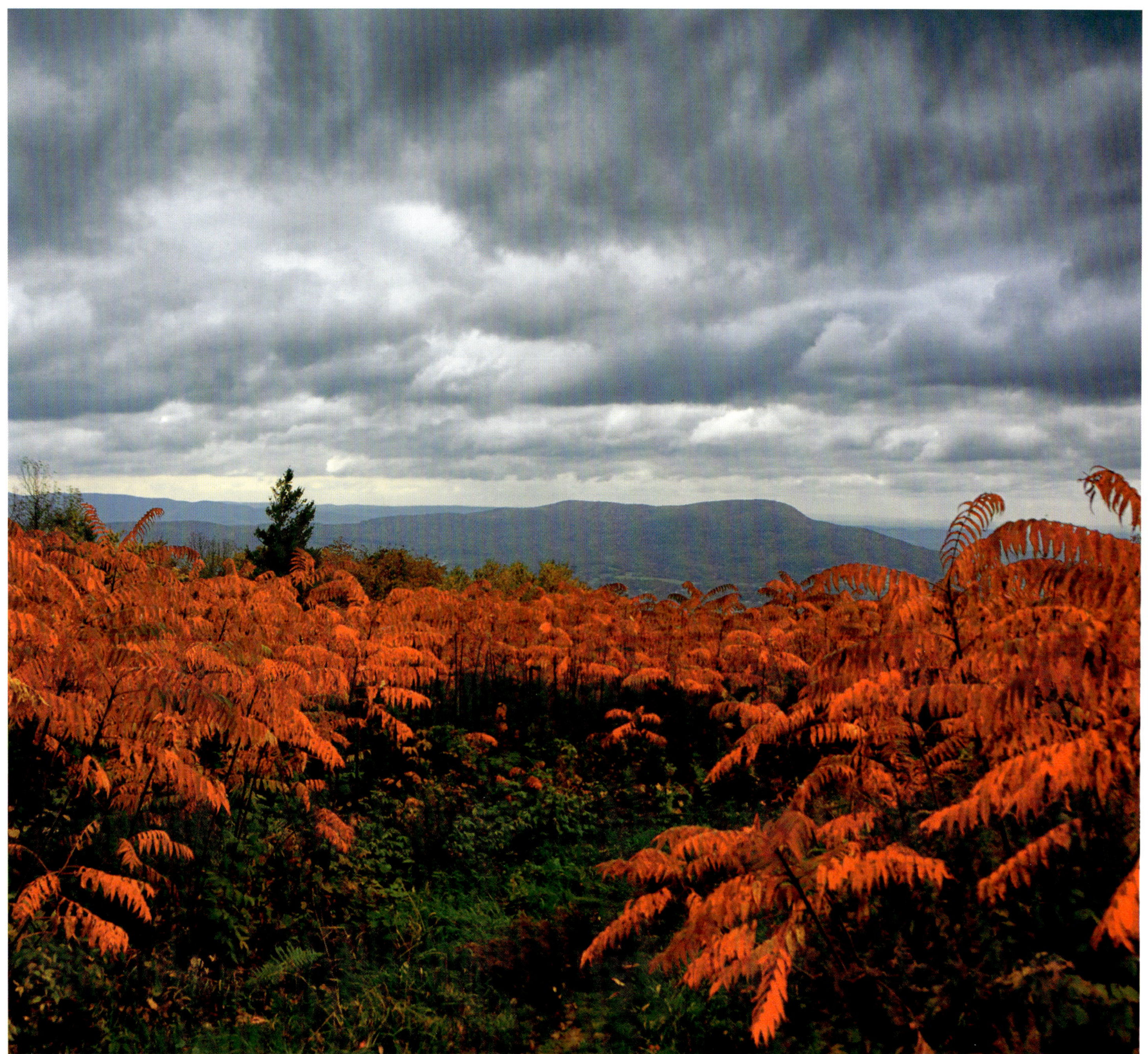
The Appalachian Trail in Vermont

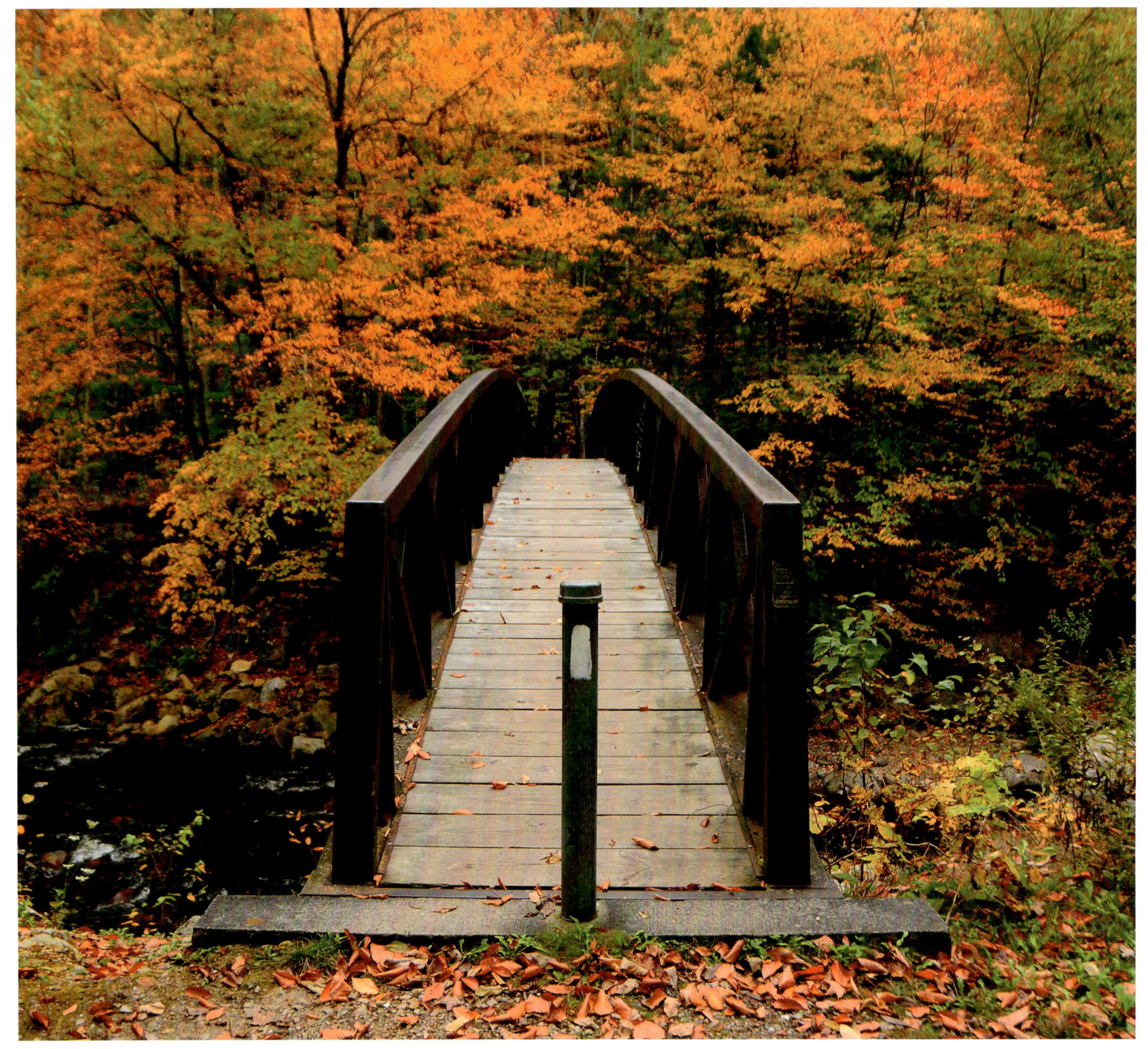

Glastenbury Creek Bridge

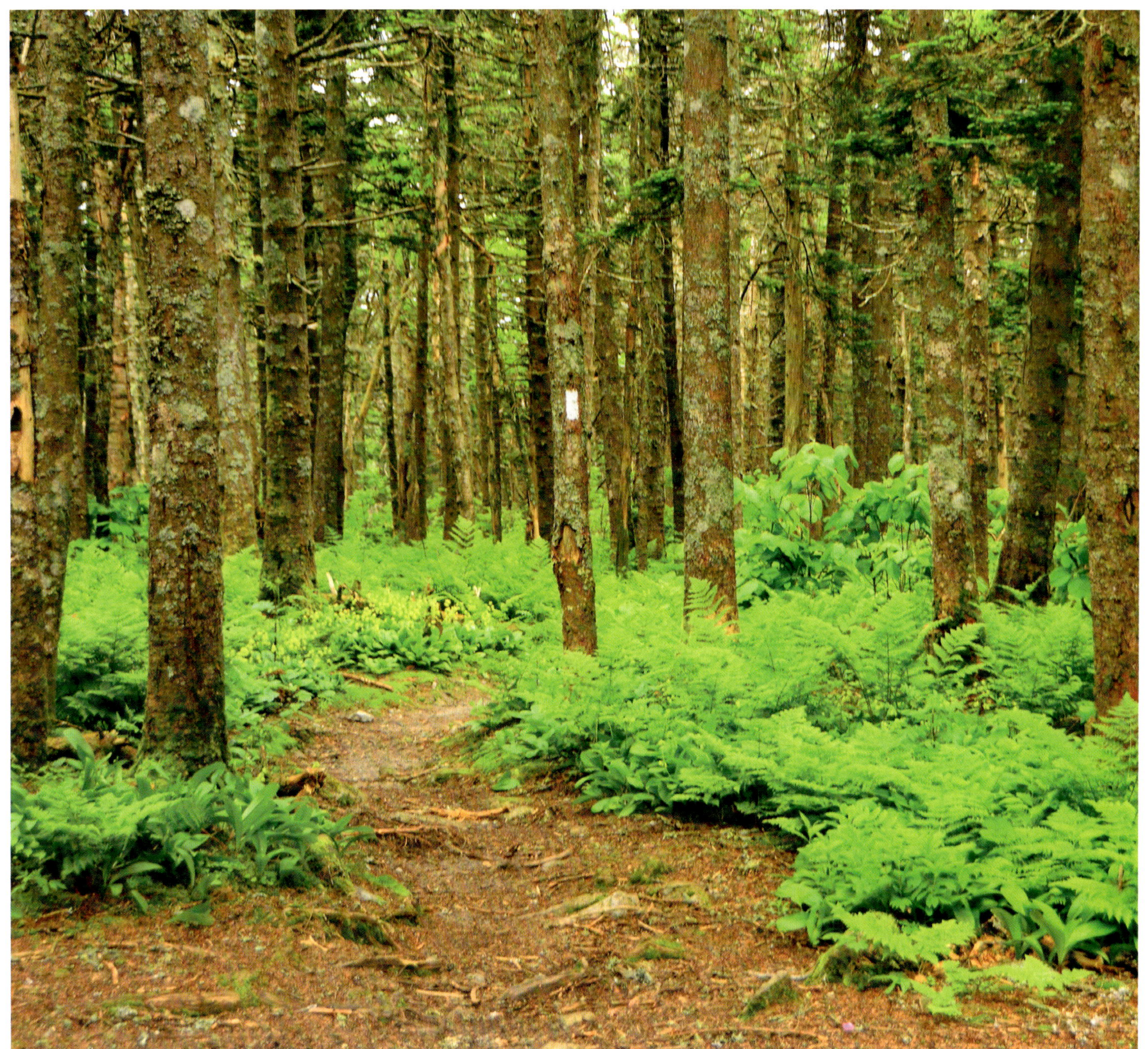

The upper elevations of Glastenbury Wilderness

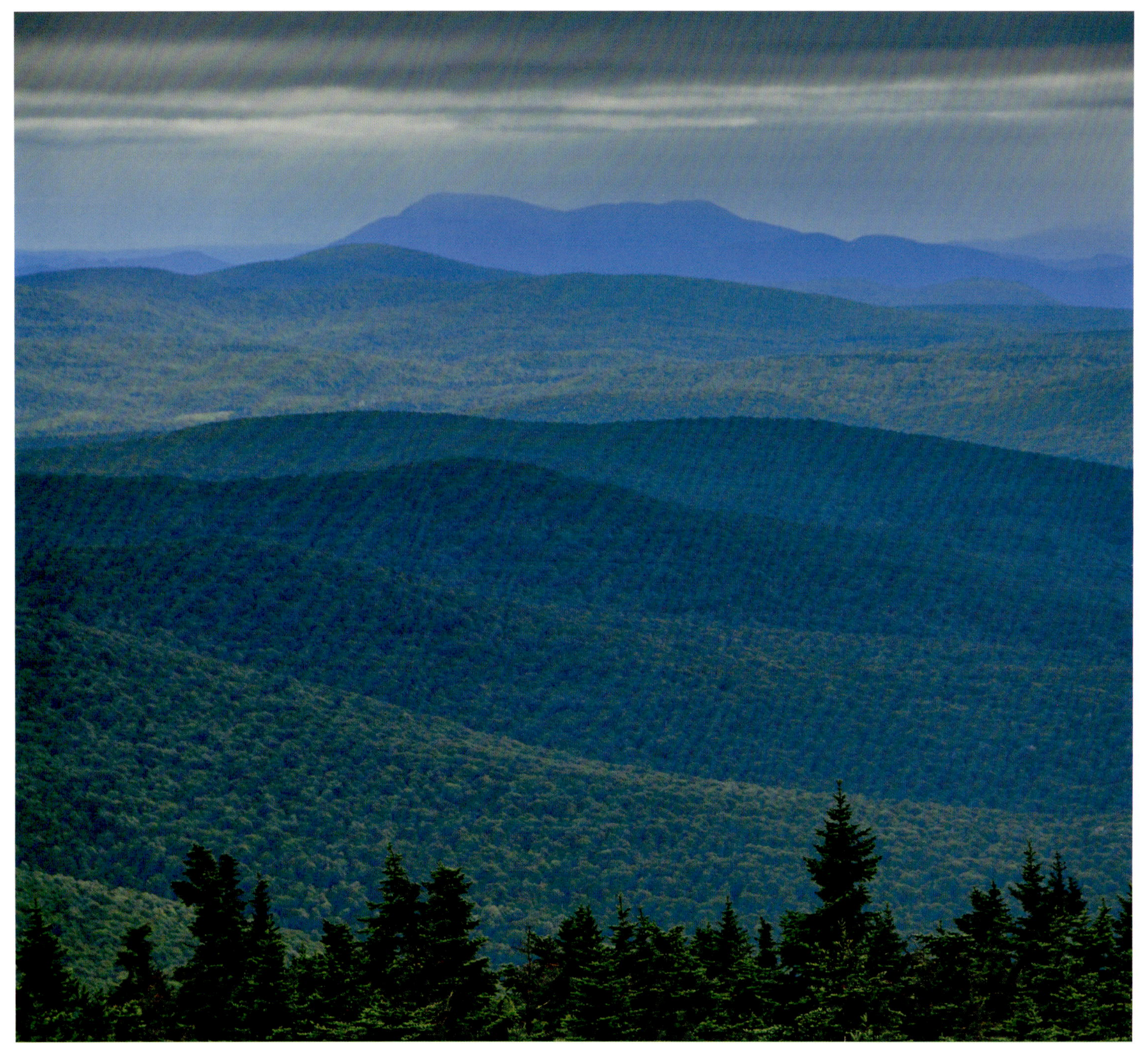

Mount Greylock and Southern Green Mountains from Glastenbury Mountain's summit

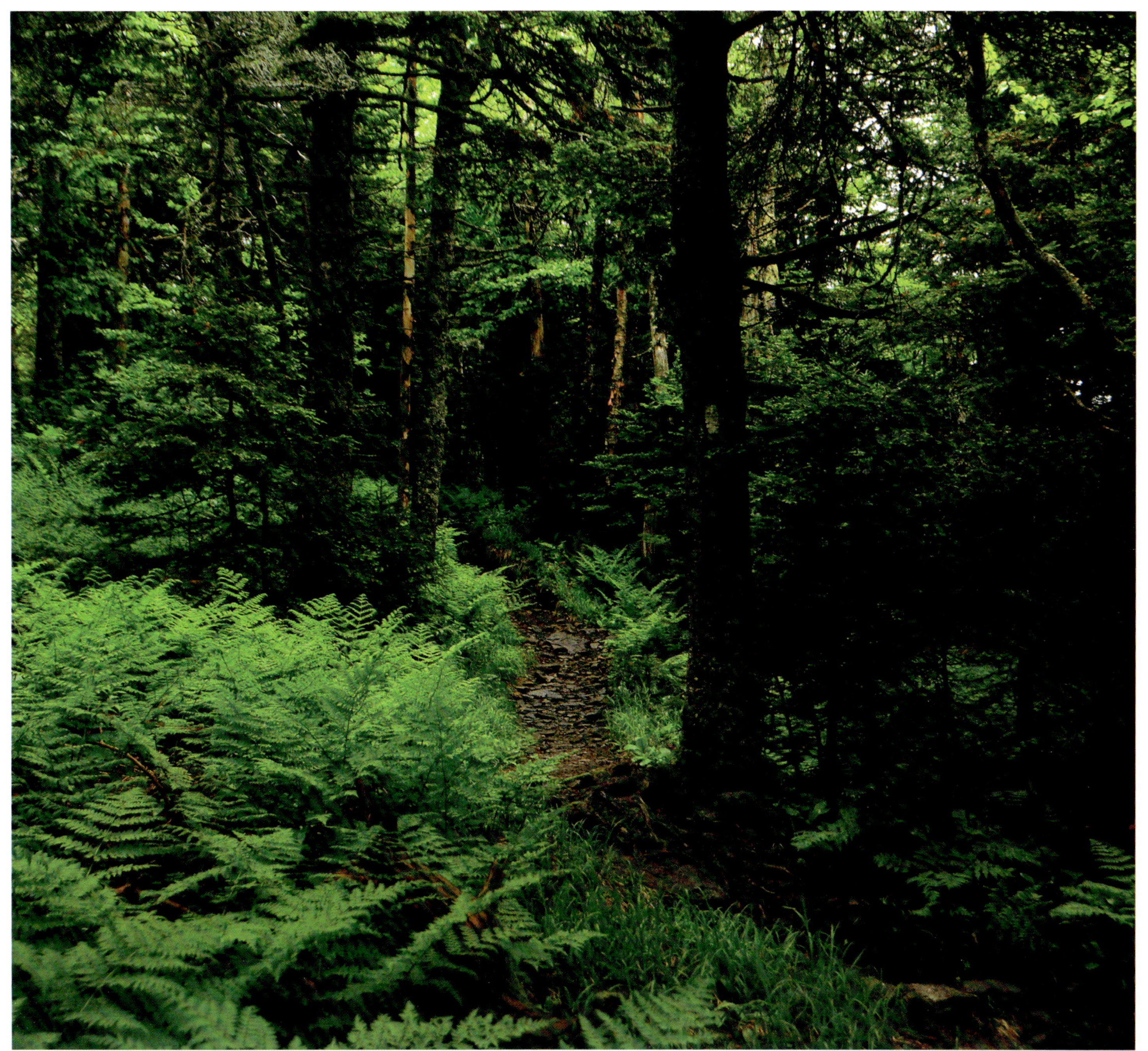

Stratton Mountain, Vermont, ferns and spring green

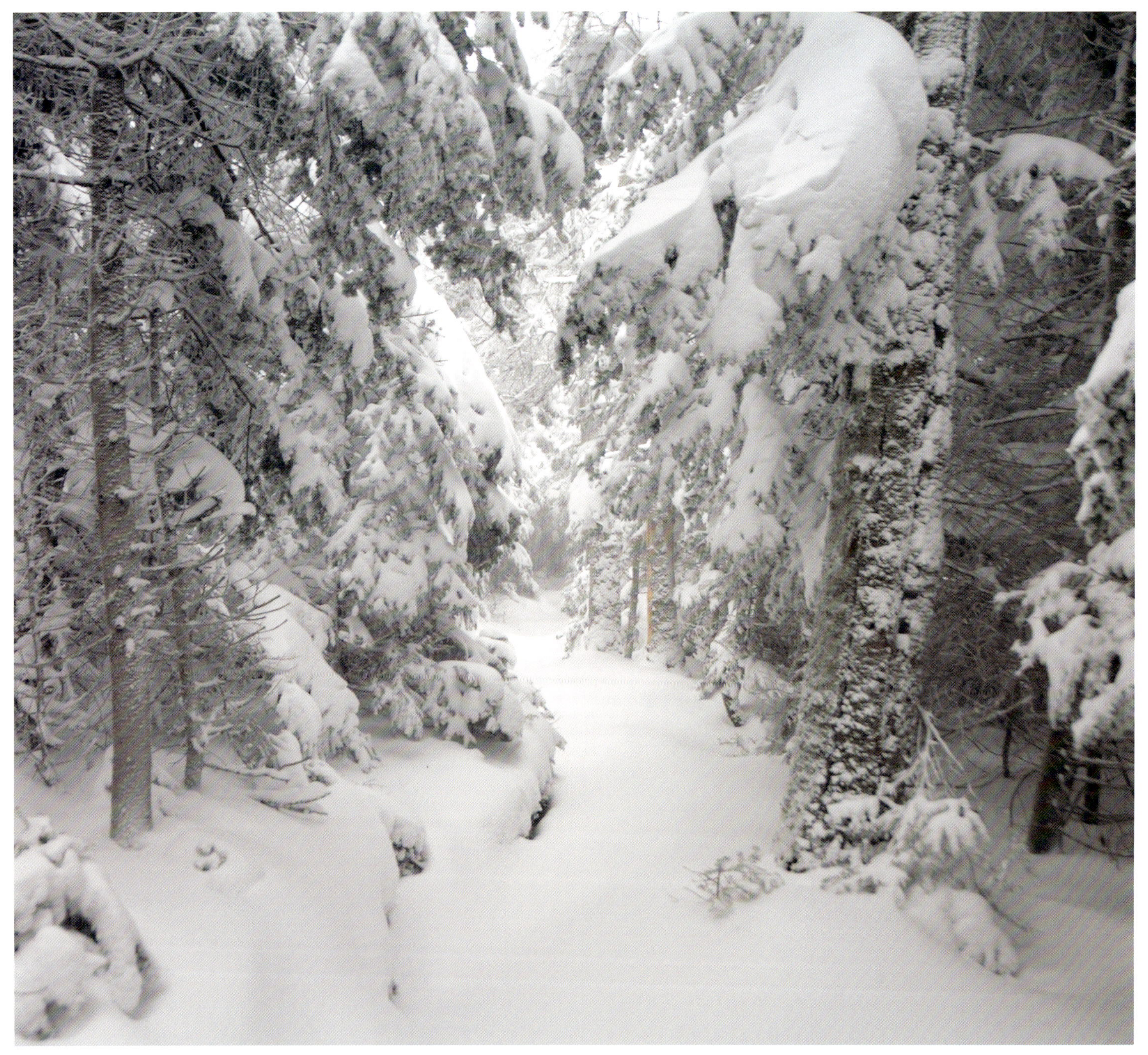

Stratton Mountain, blizzard-covered trees

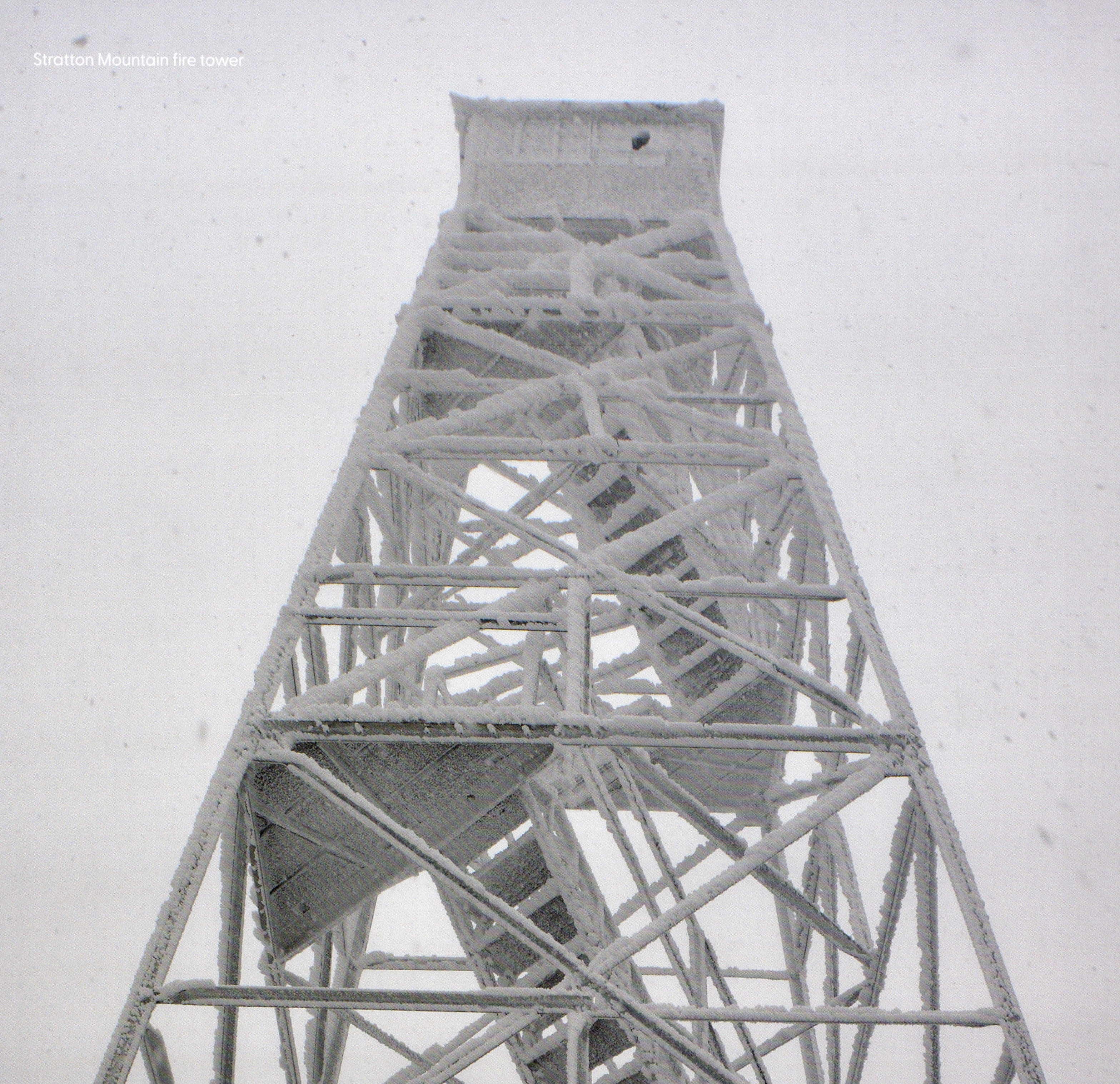

Stratton Mountain fire tower

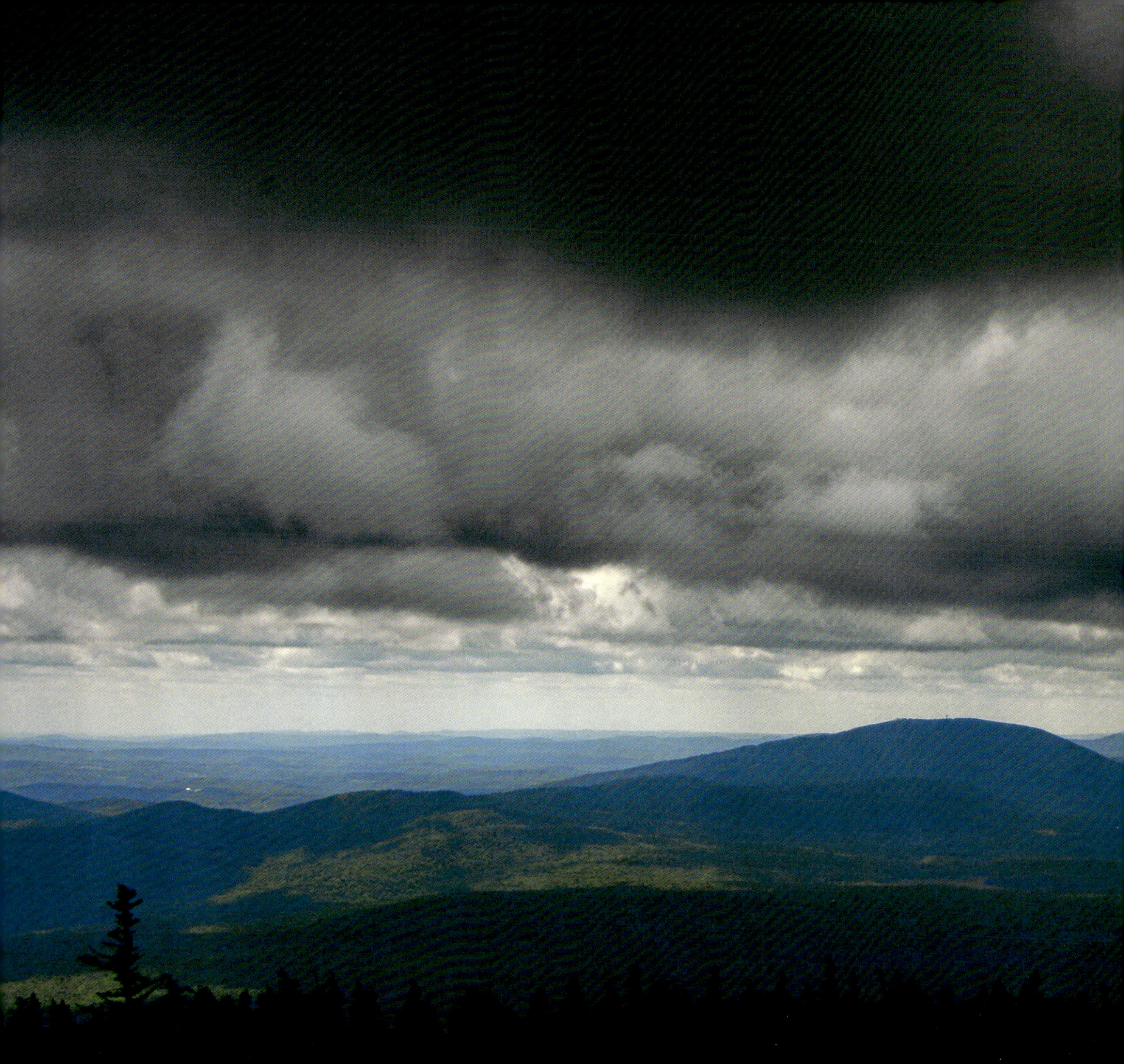

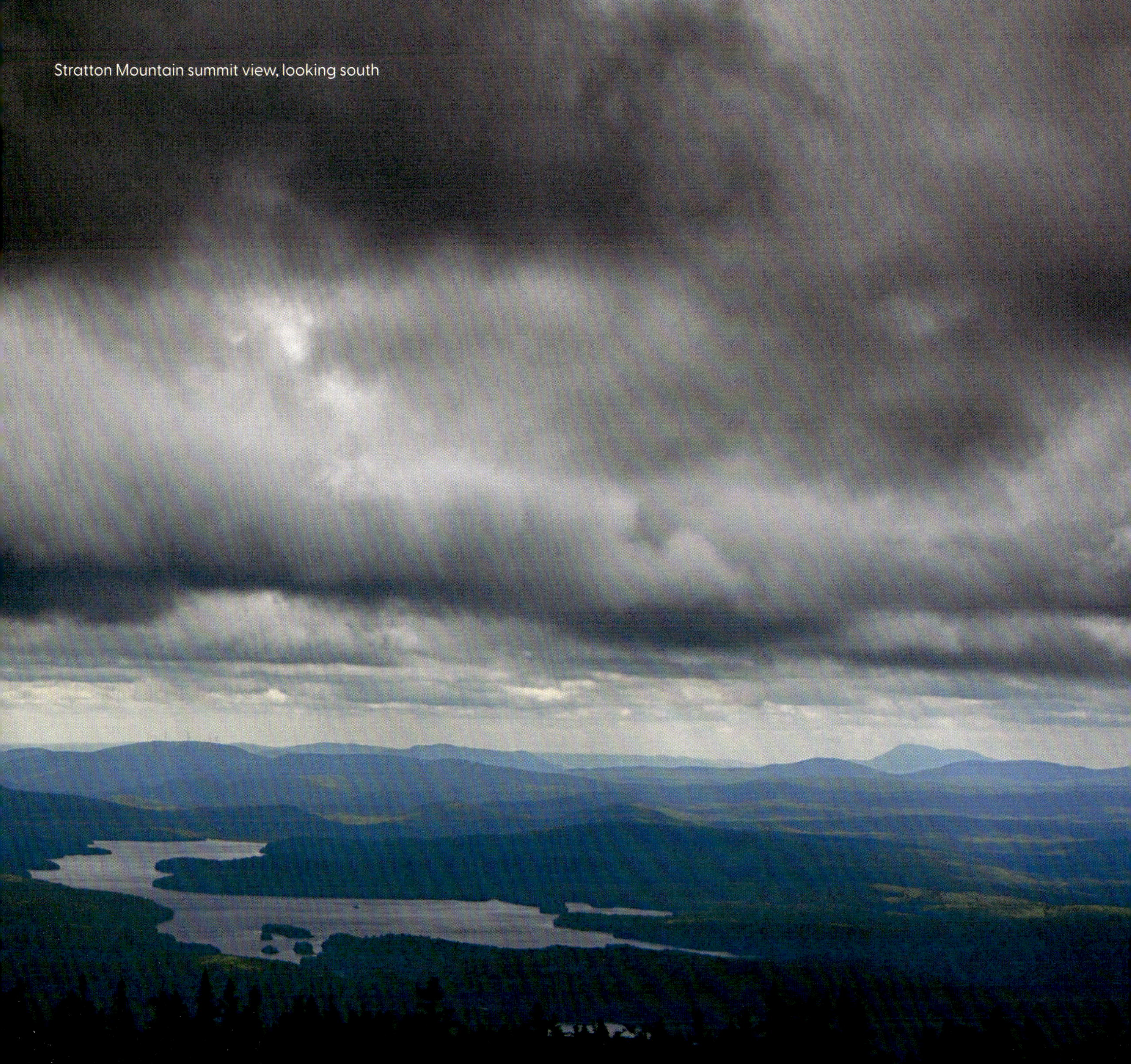
Stratton Mountain summit view, looking south

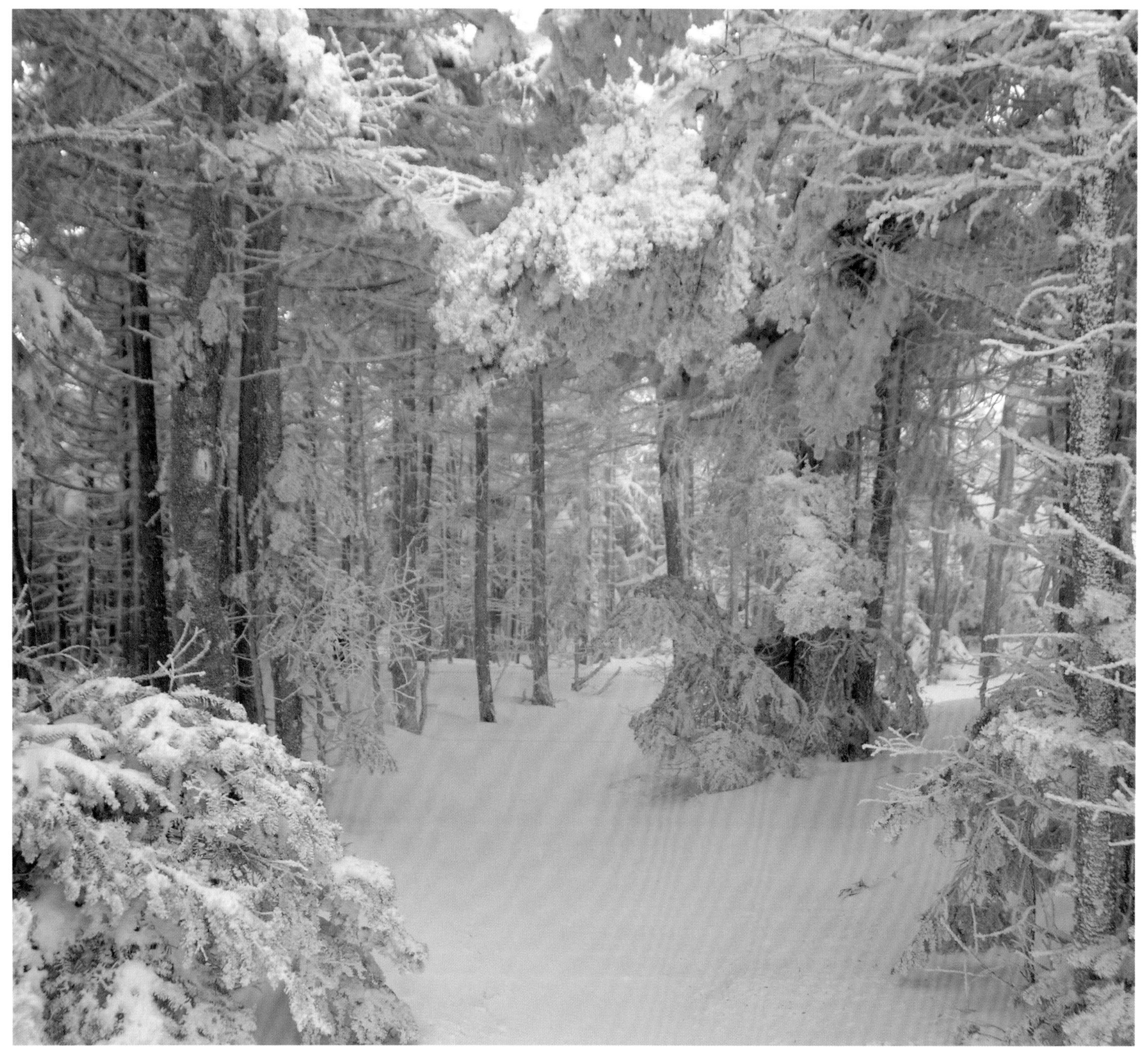

Hiking north of the summit of Stratton Mountain

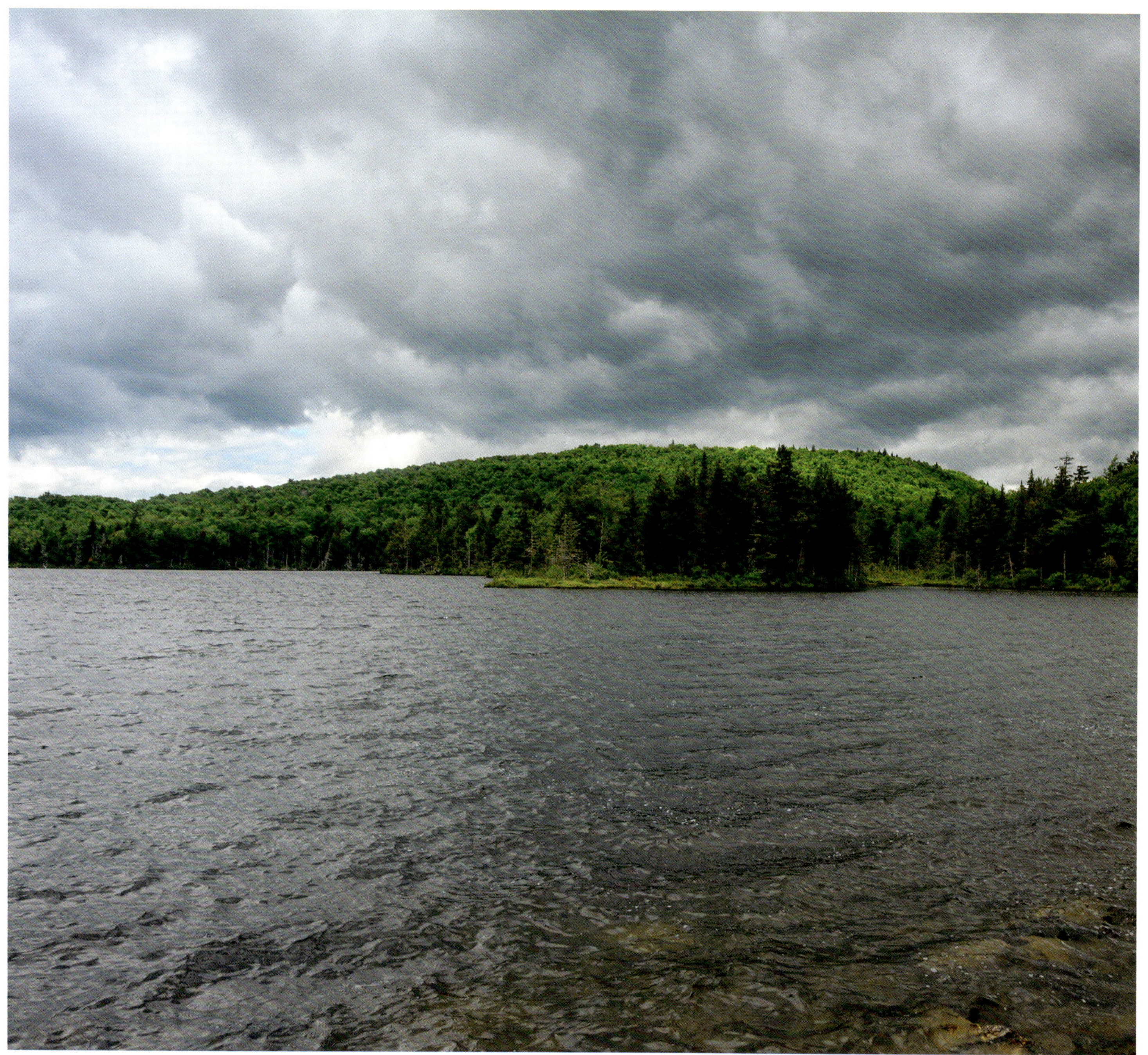

Stratton Pond, Vermont

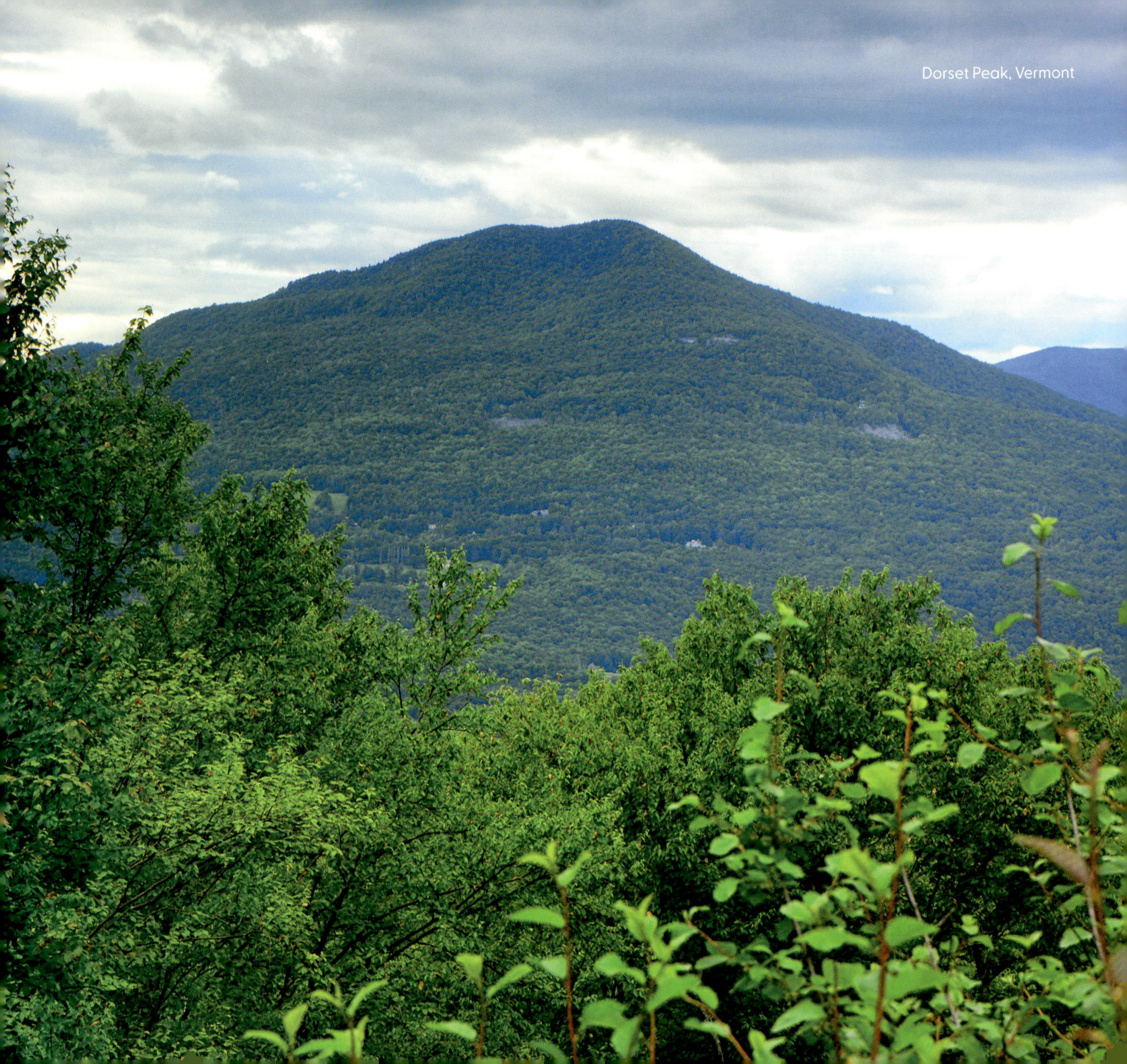
Dorset Peak, Vermont

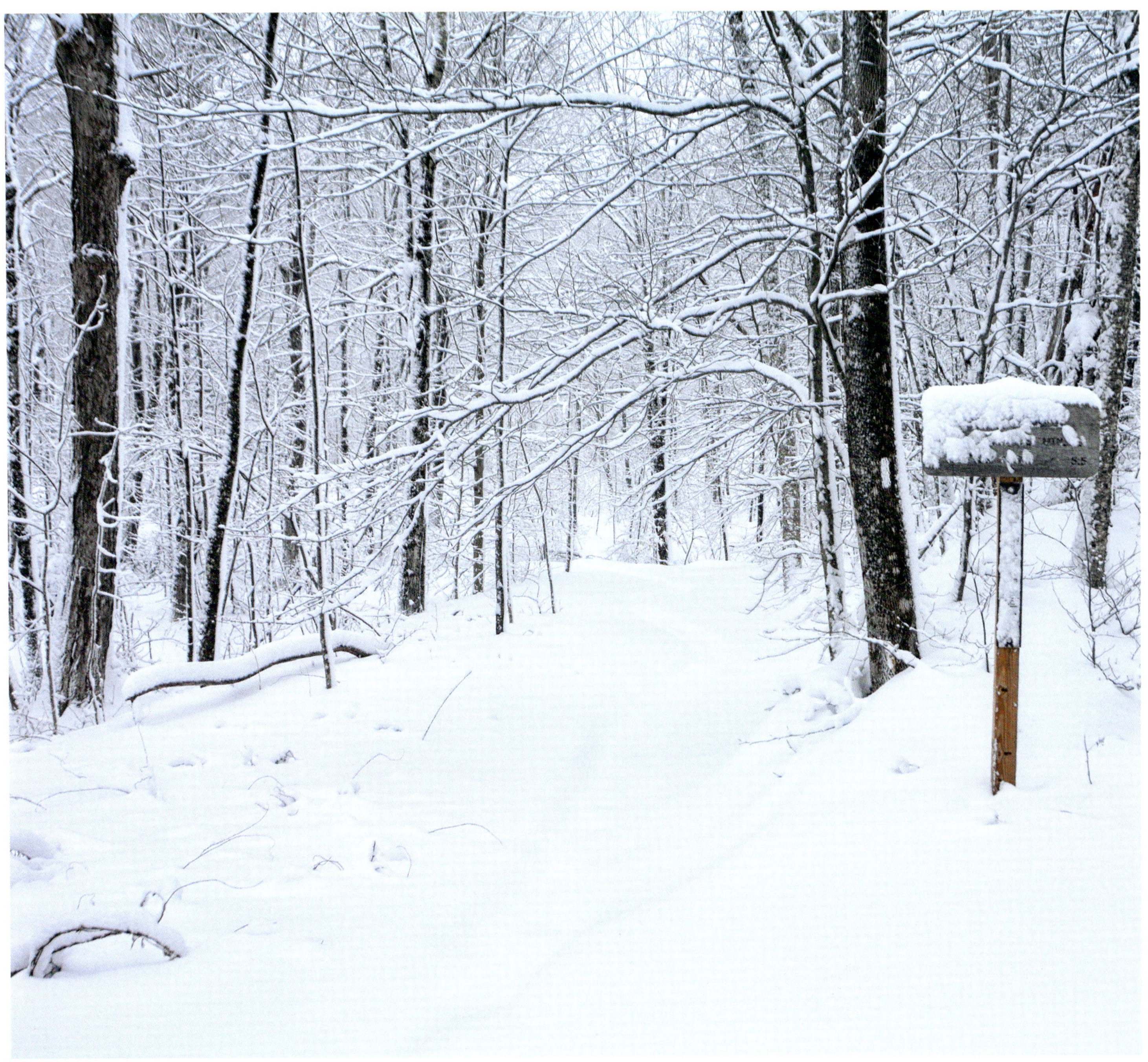

The Appalachian Trail on Bromley Mountain, Vermont

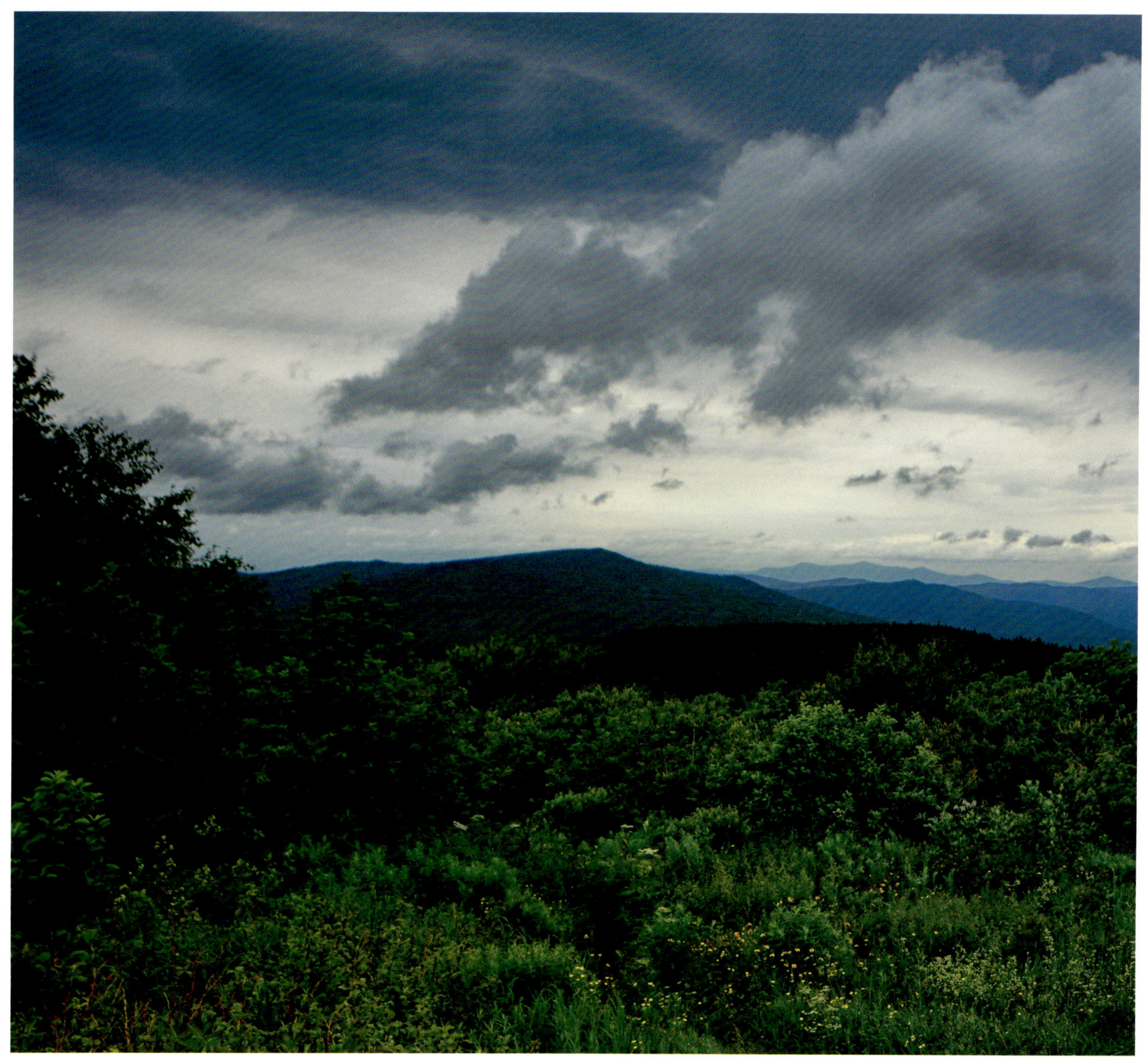

From the summit of Bromley Mountain, looking north

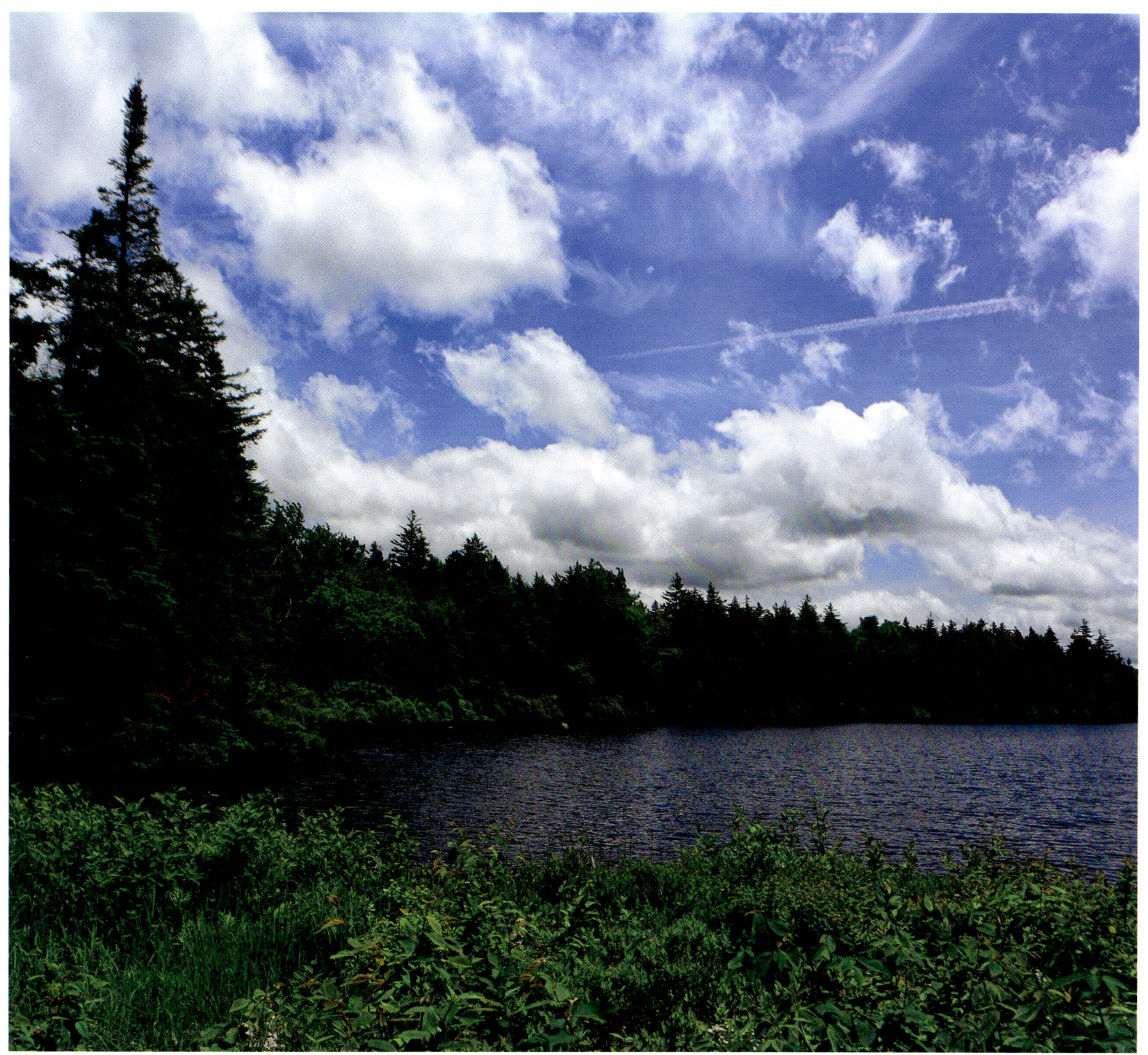

Griffith Lake, Vermont, on the Appalachian Trail

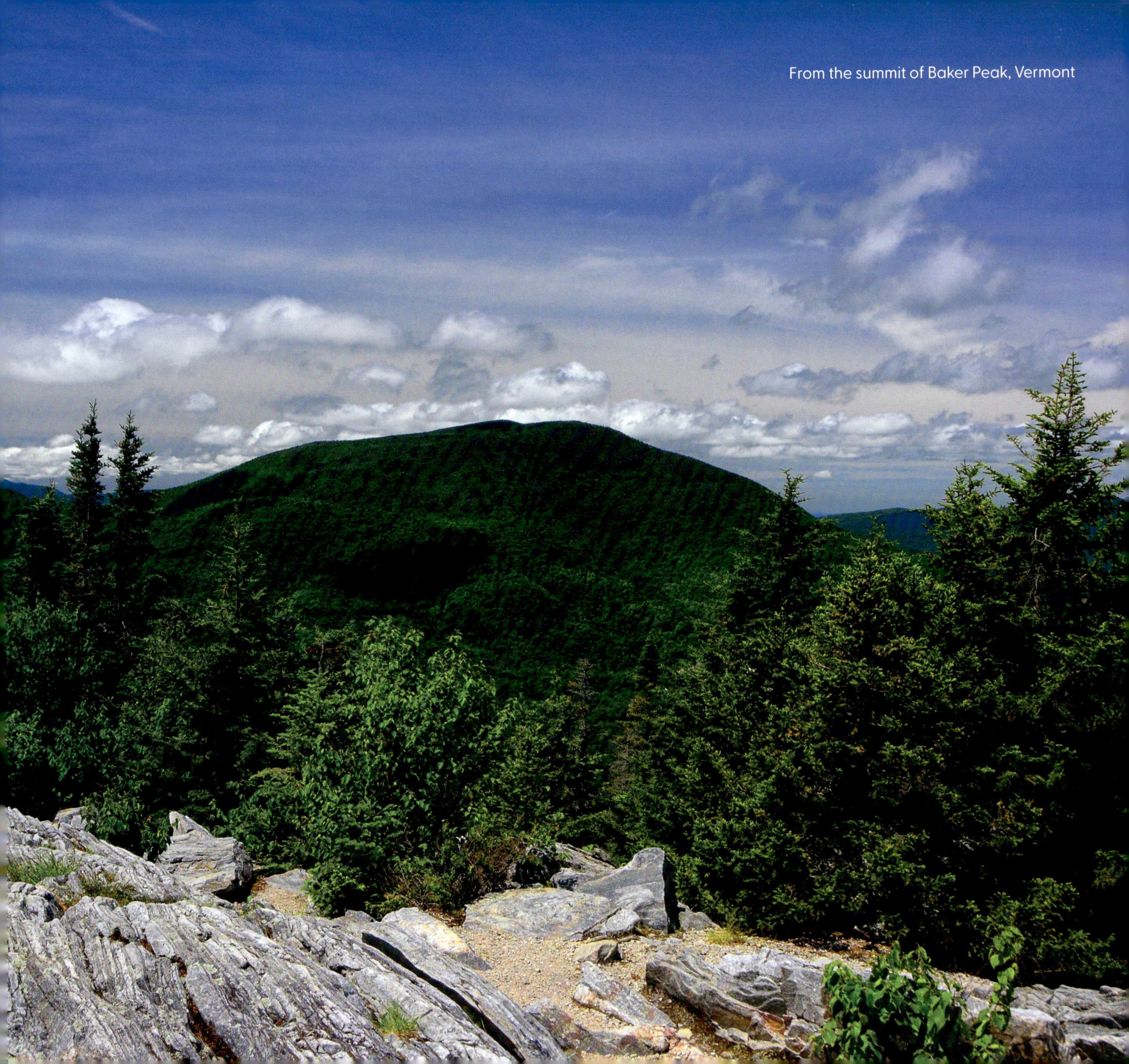

From the summit of Baker Peak, Vermont

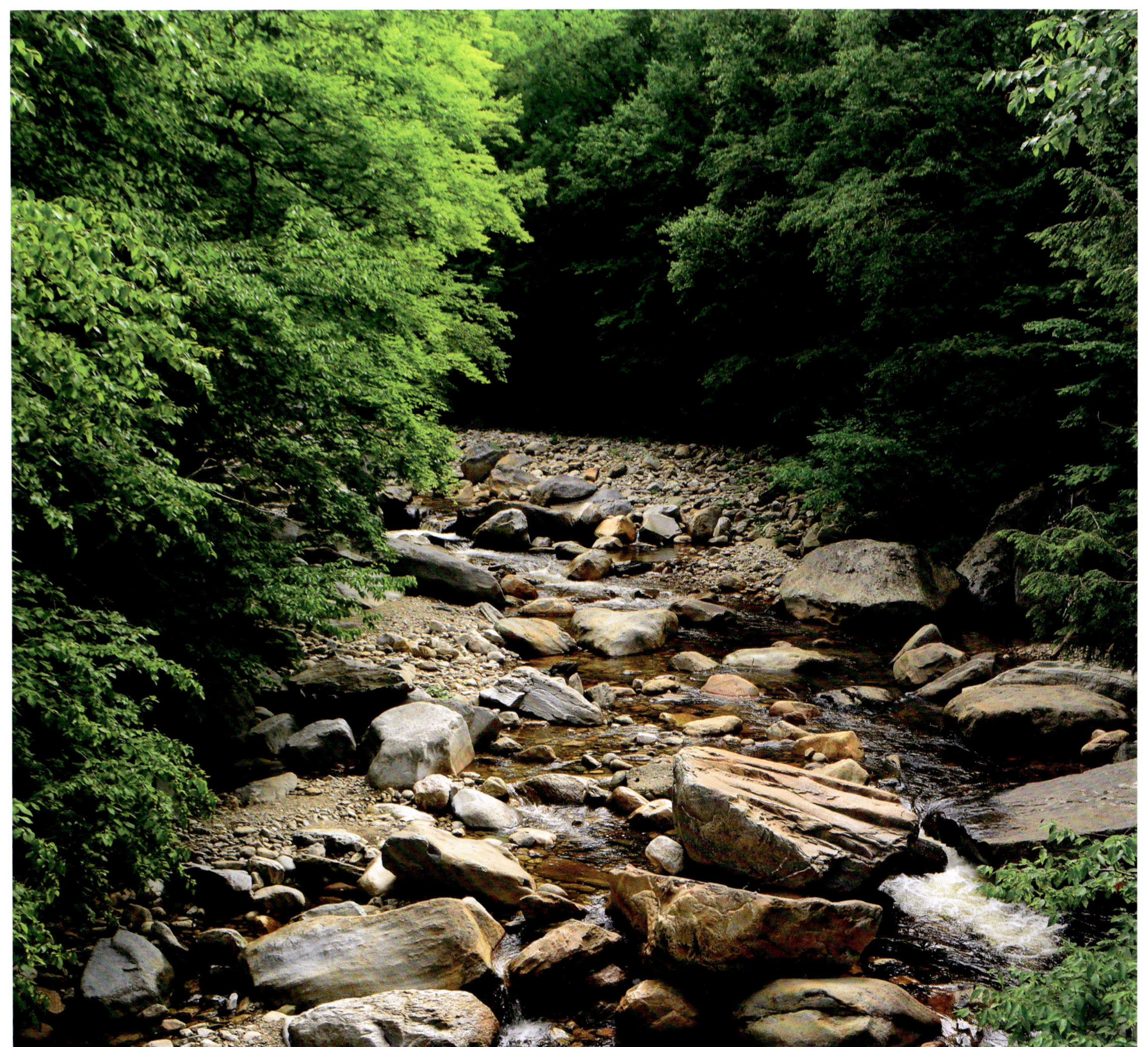

Branchbrook Creek, Vermont

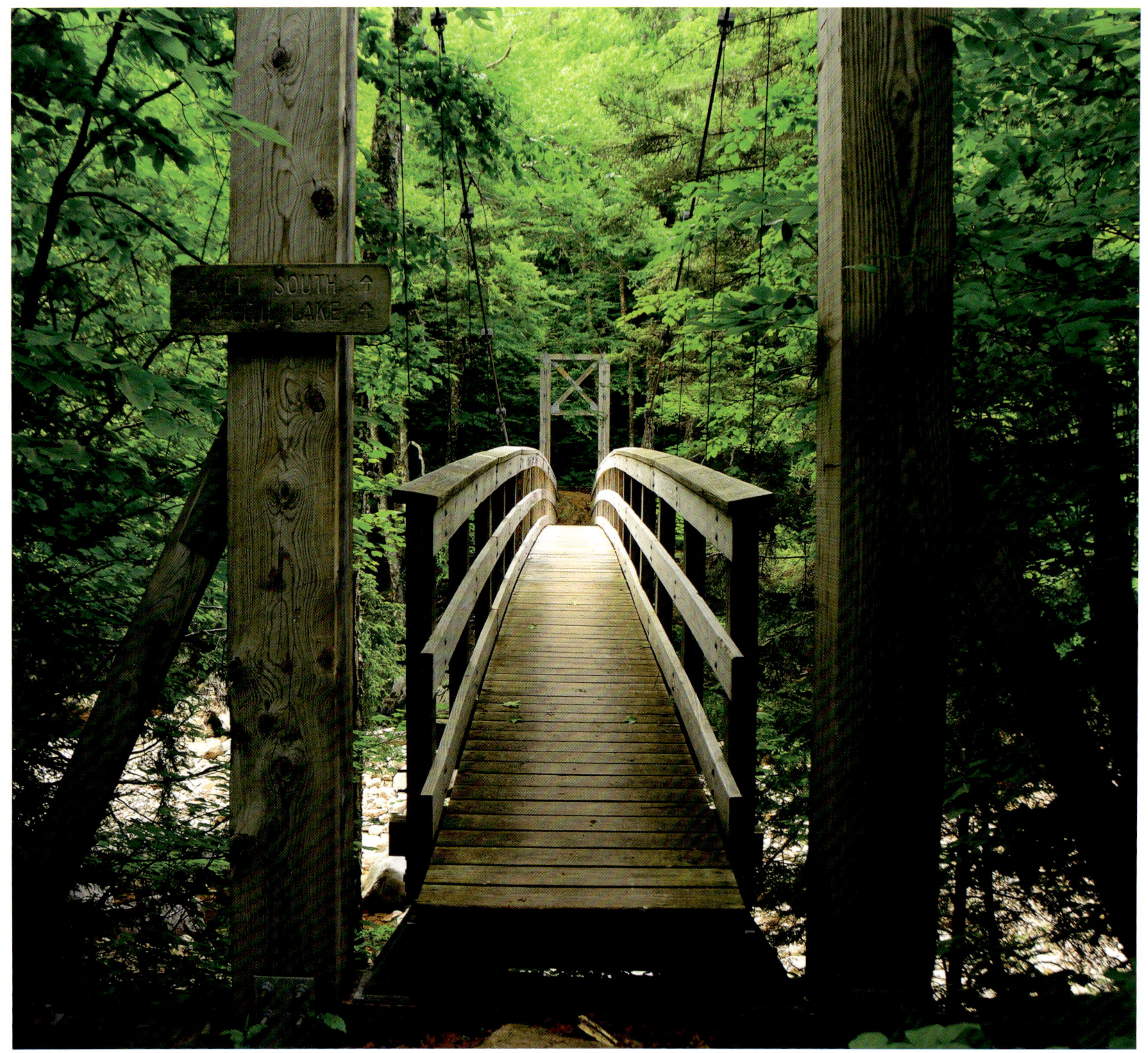

Branchbrook Creek crossing in Vermont

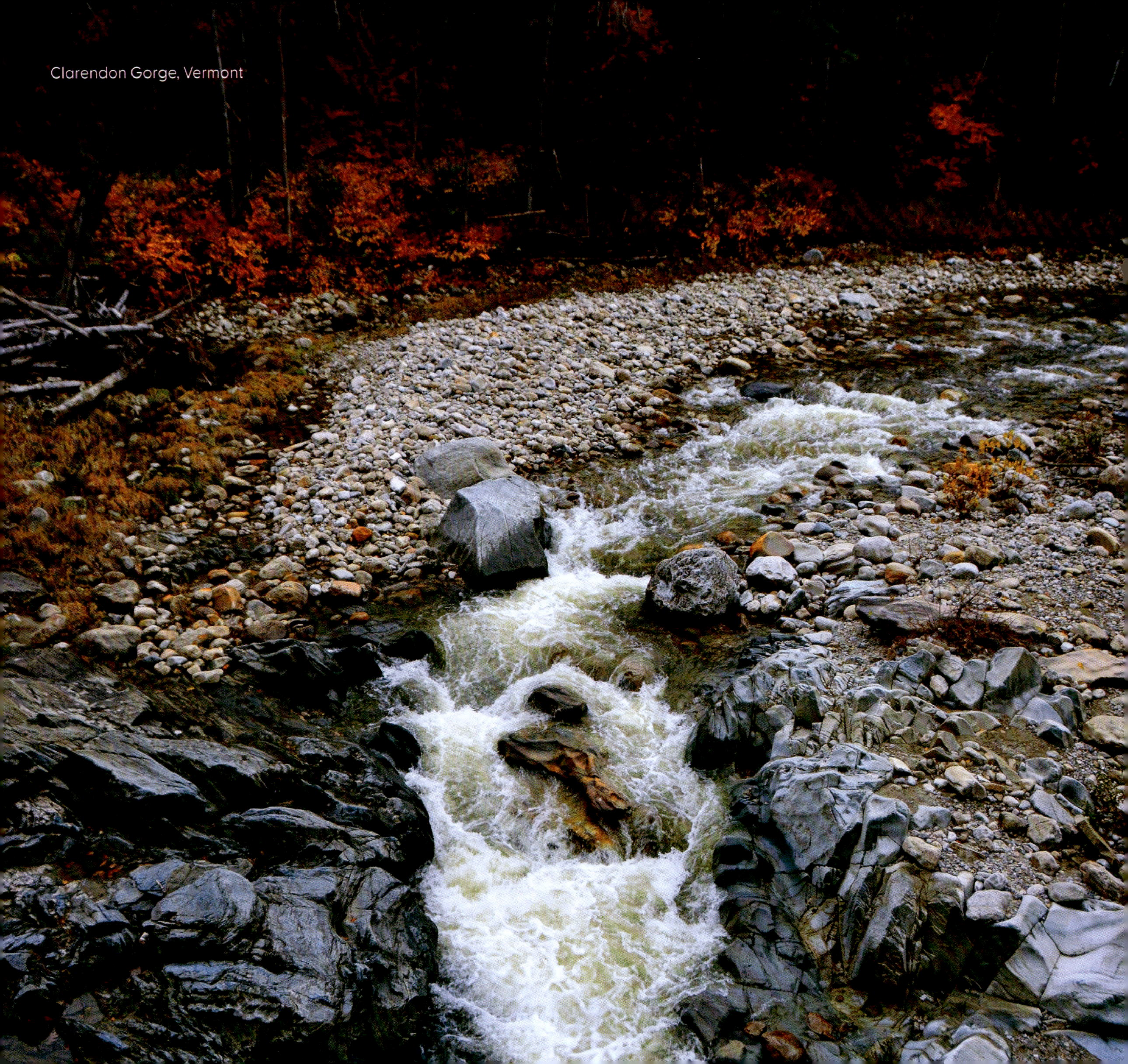

Clarendon Gorge, Vermont

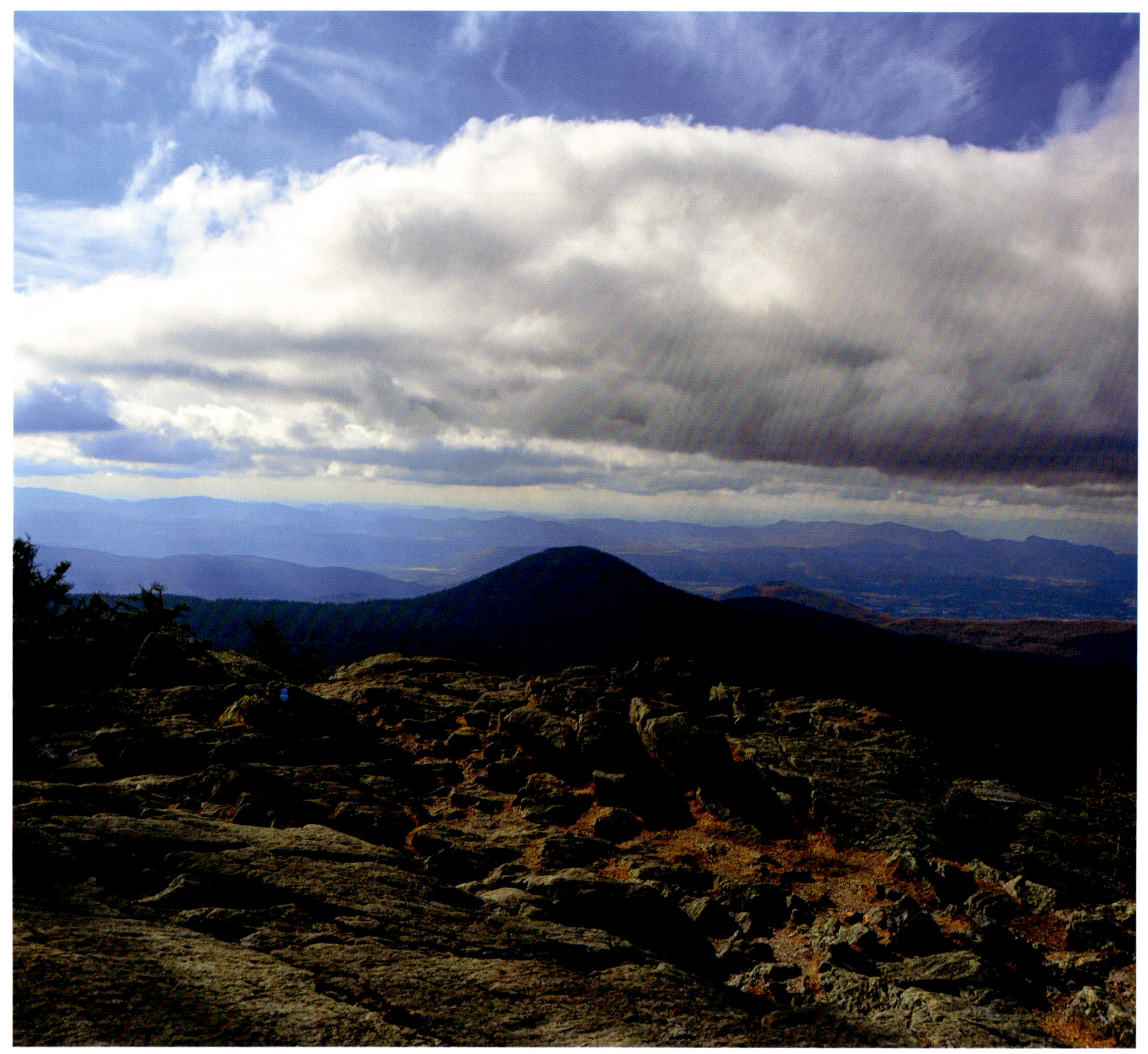

From the summit of Killington, looking west

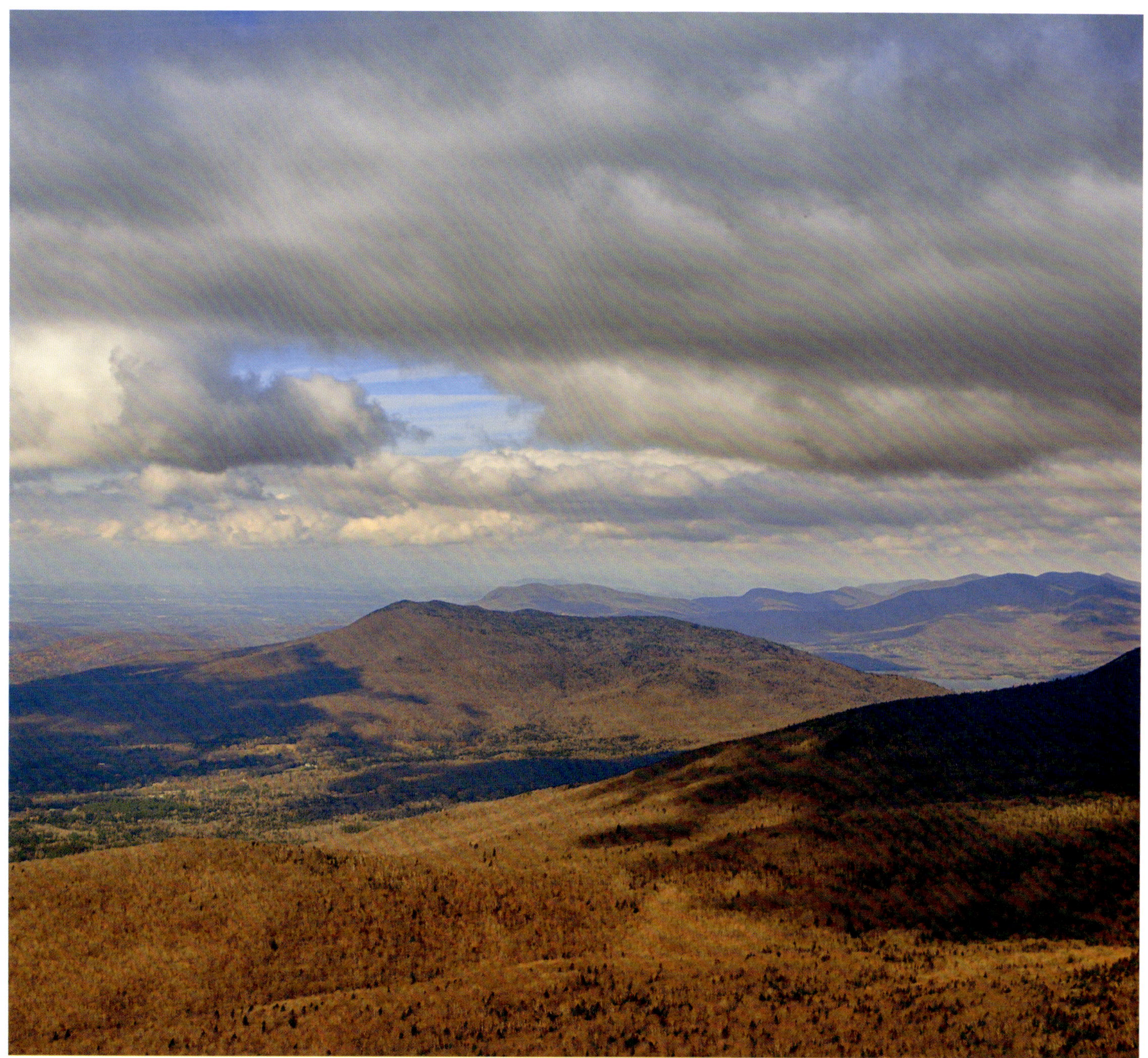

From the summit of Killington, Vermont

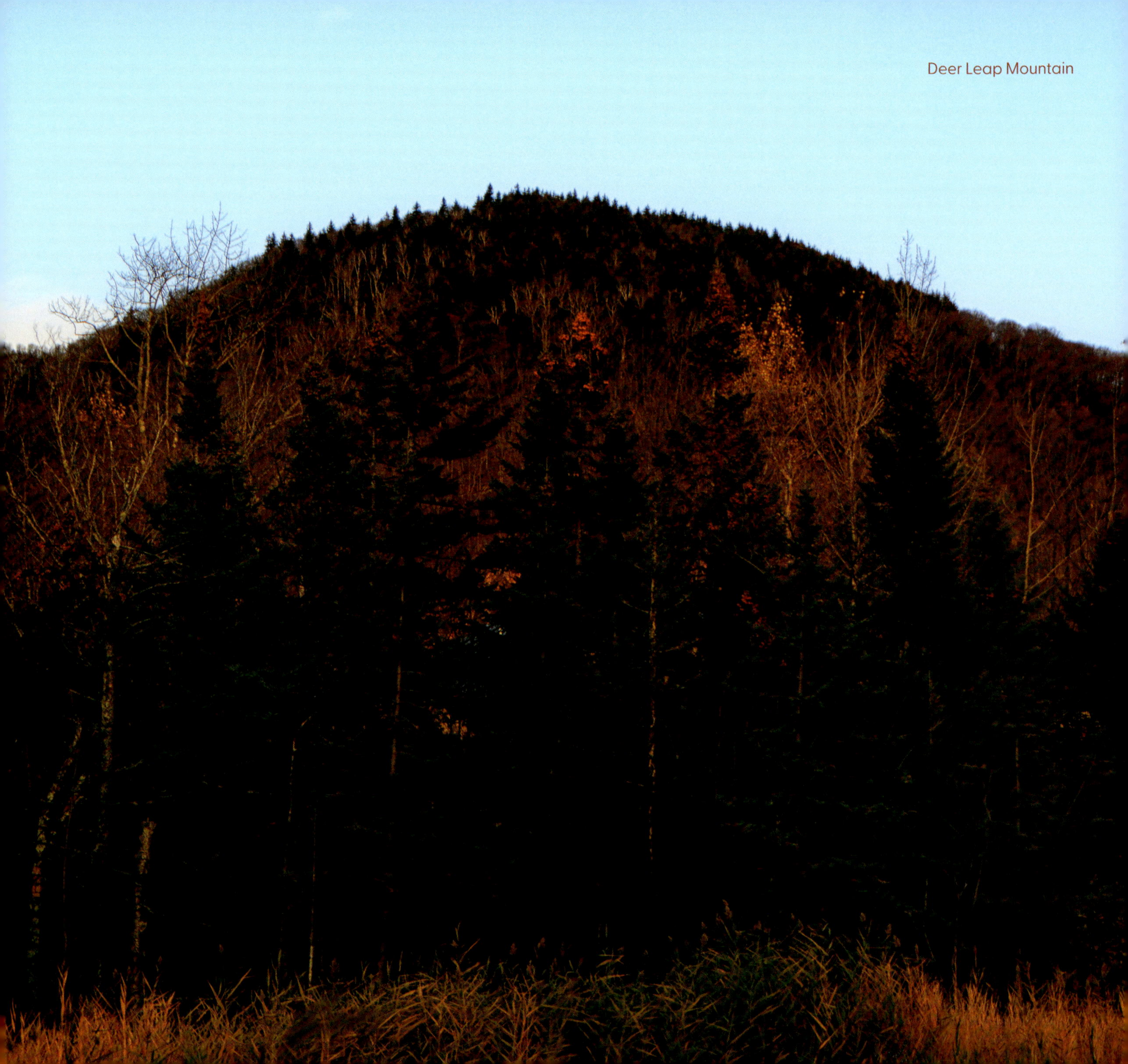
Deer Leap Mountain

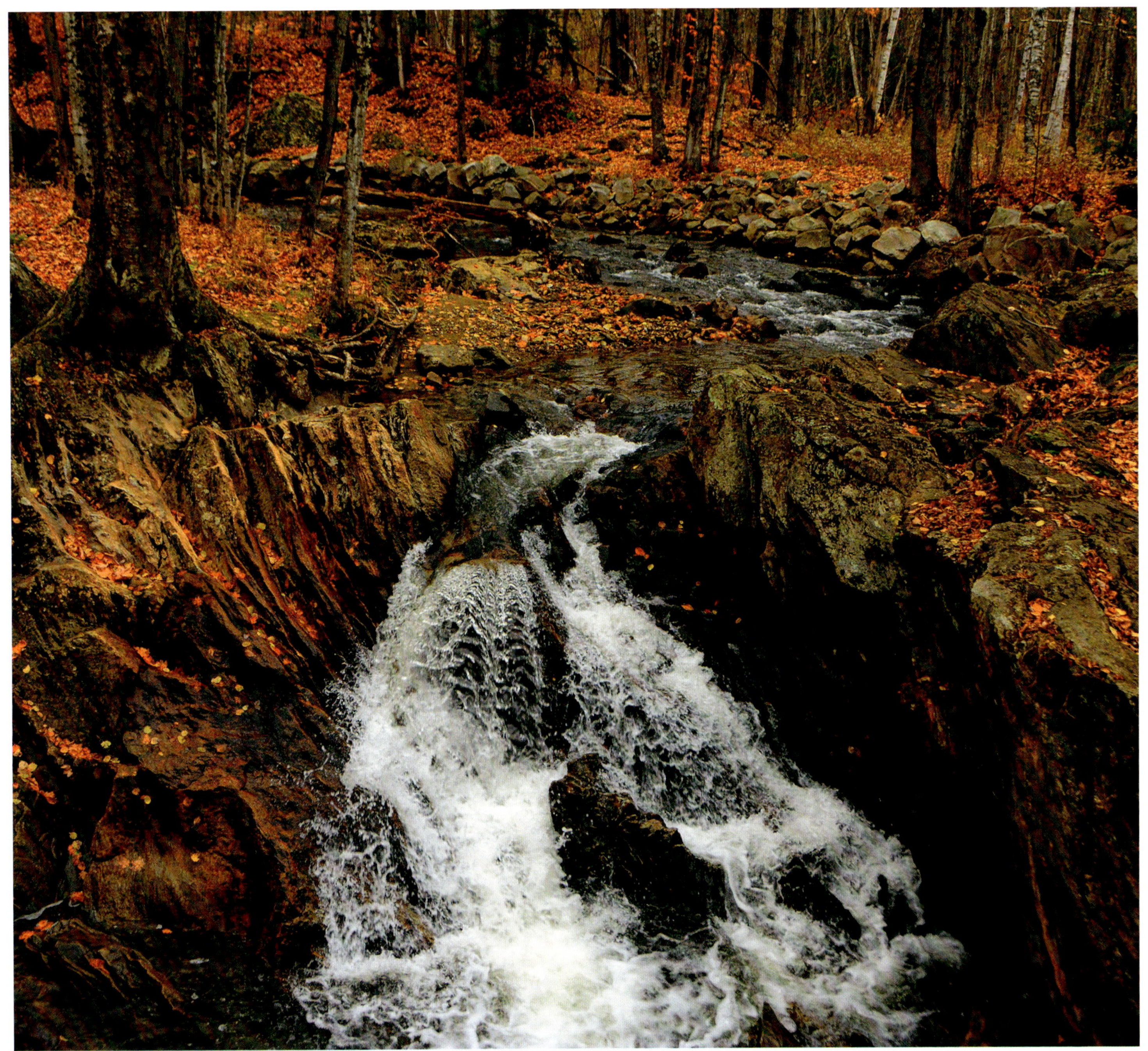

Vermont creek in autumn

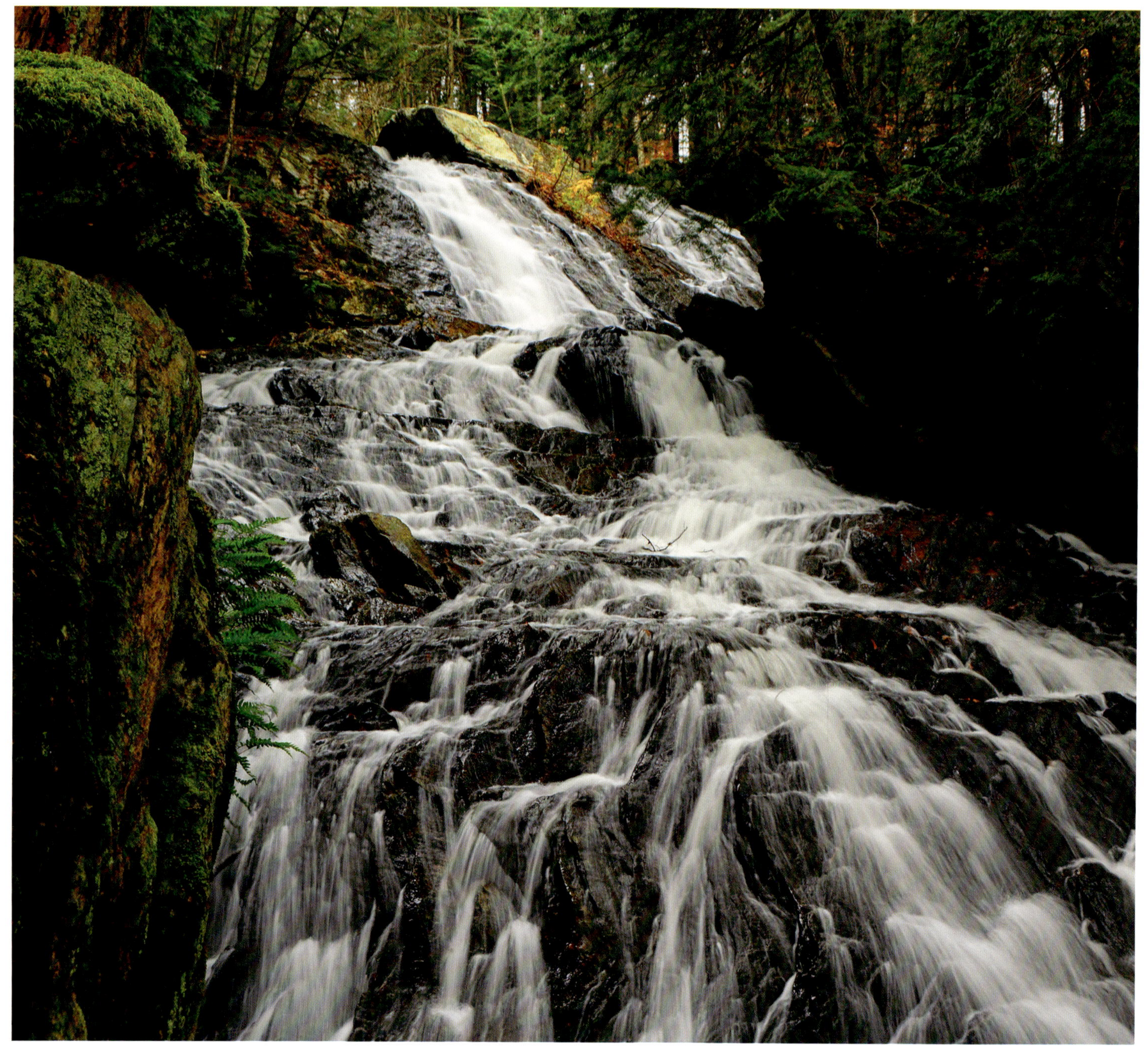

Thundering Brook Falls, Vermont

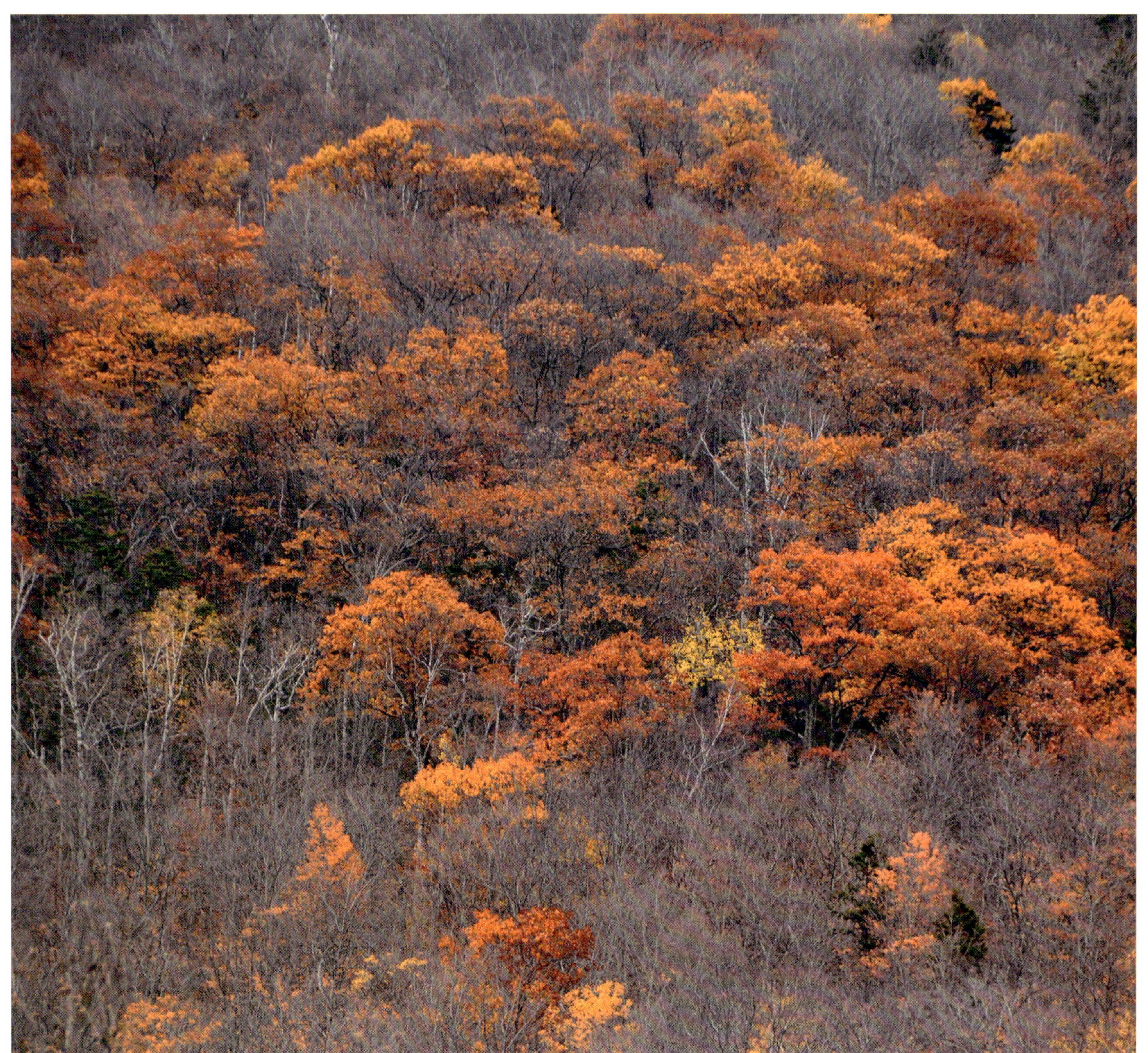

Foliage along the Appalachian Trail in Vermont

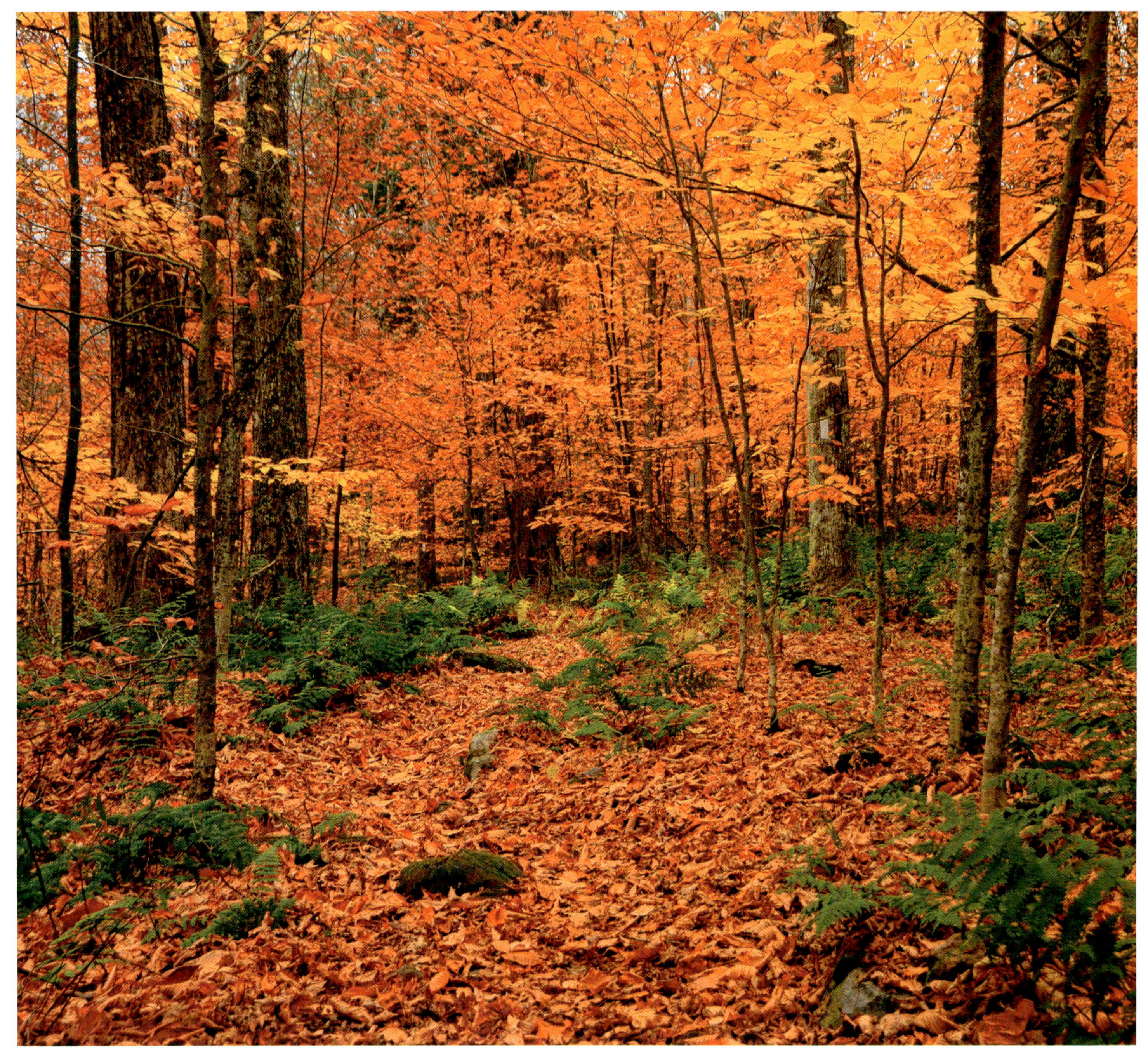

Autumn colors in Vermont along the Appalachian Trail

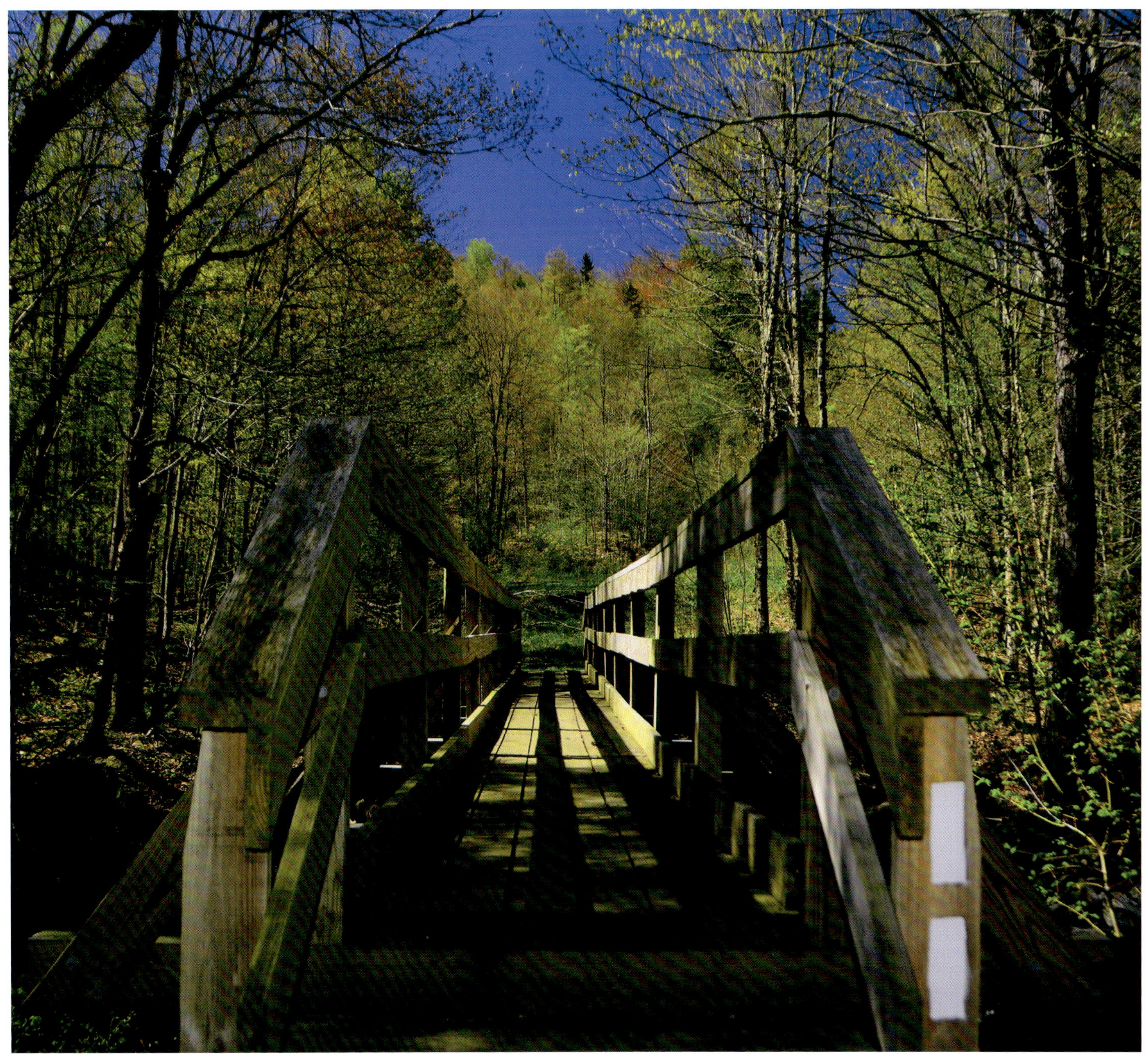

Stony Brook bridge crossing

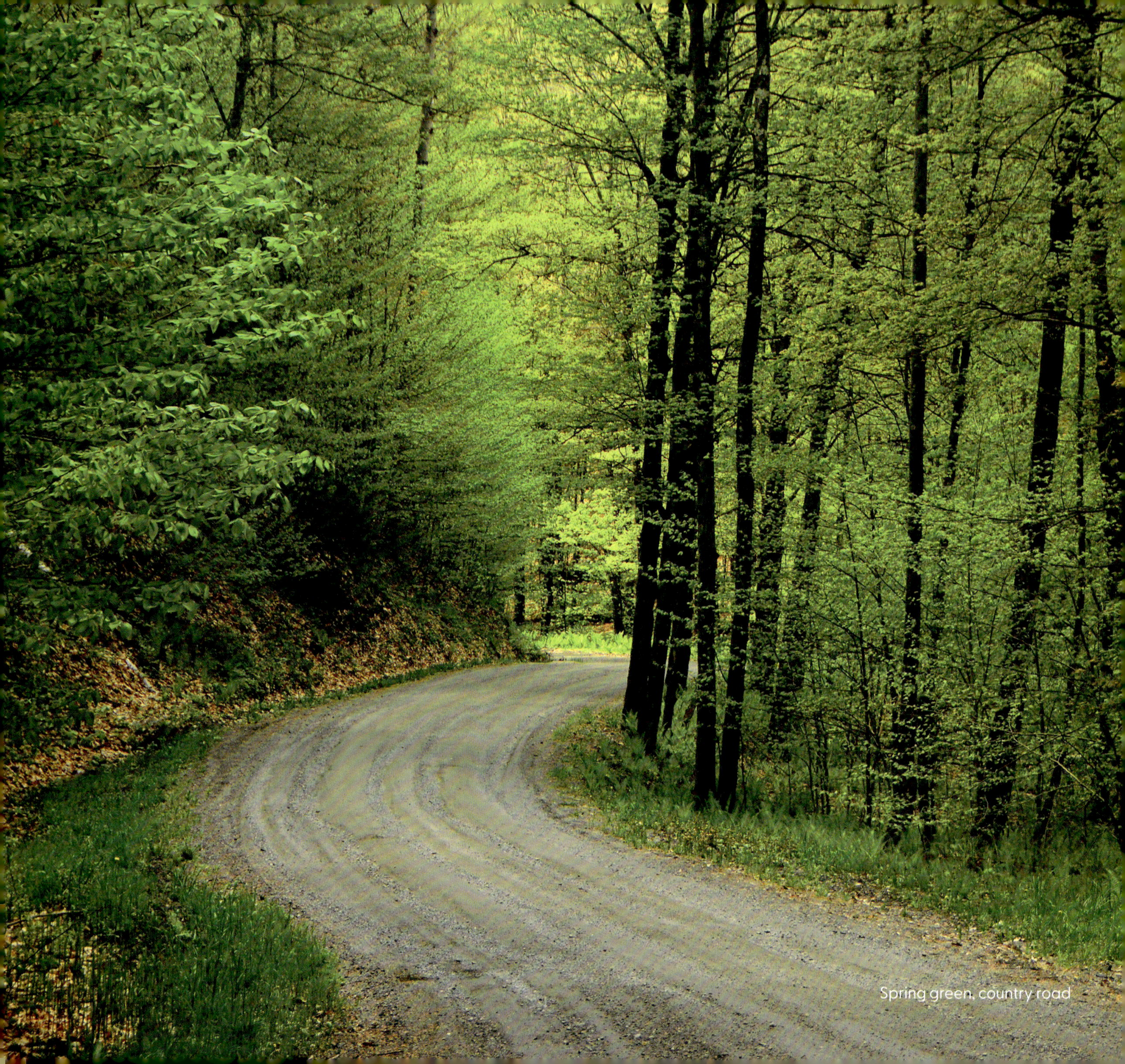

Spring green, country road

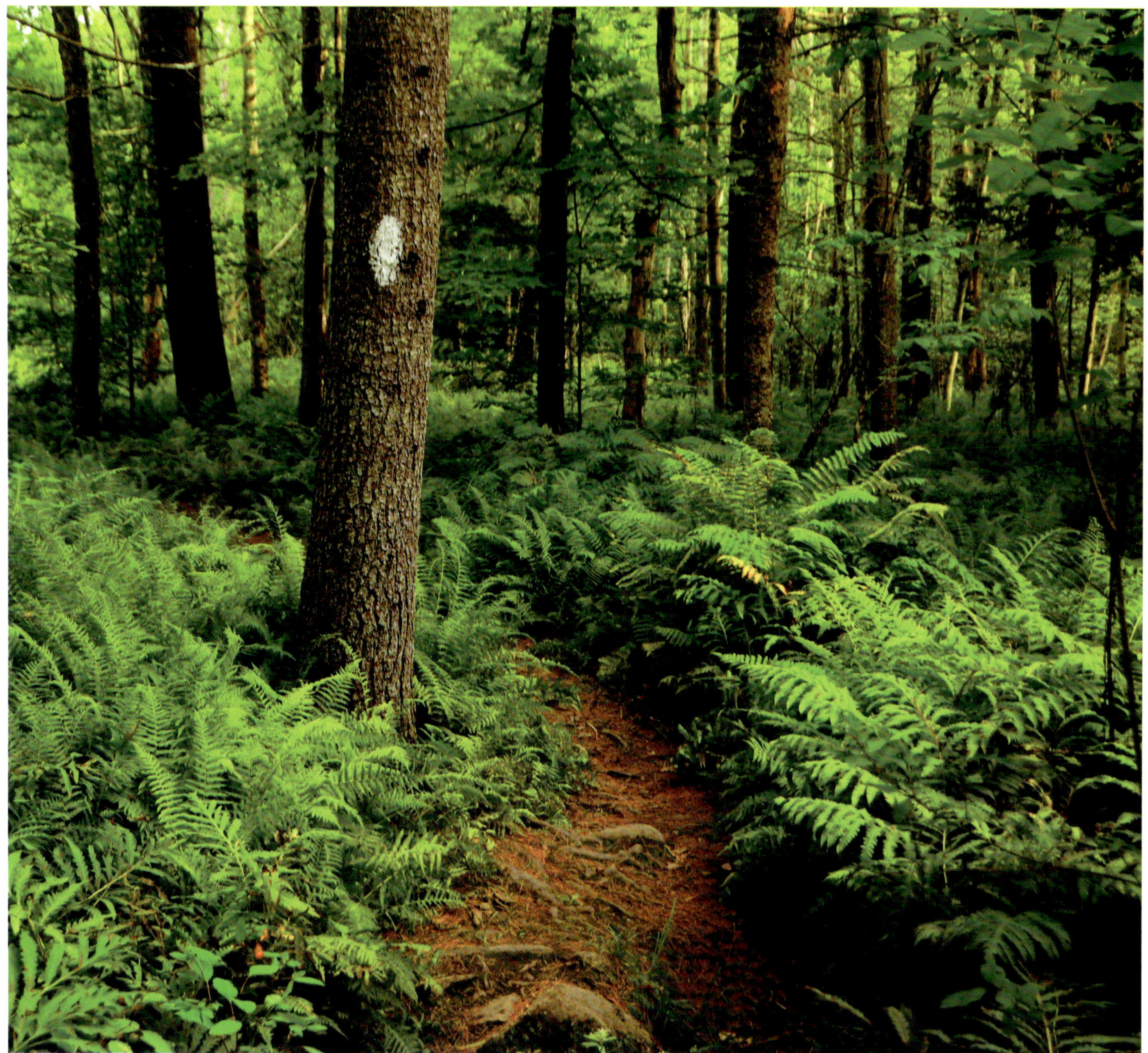

New Hampshire, the Appalachian Trail, ferns

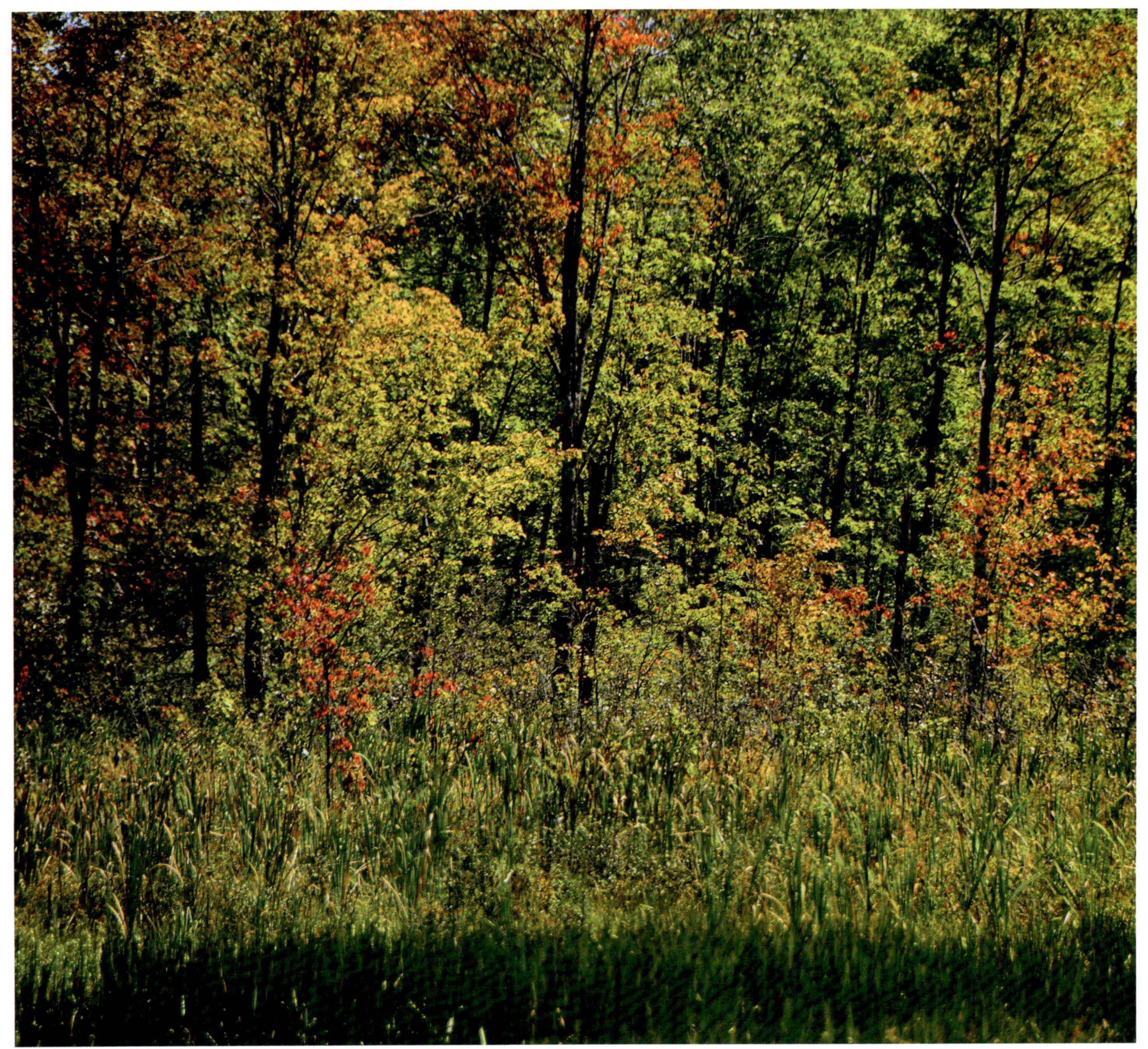

The Appalachian Trail in New Hampshire lowlands

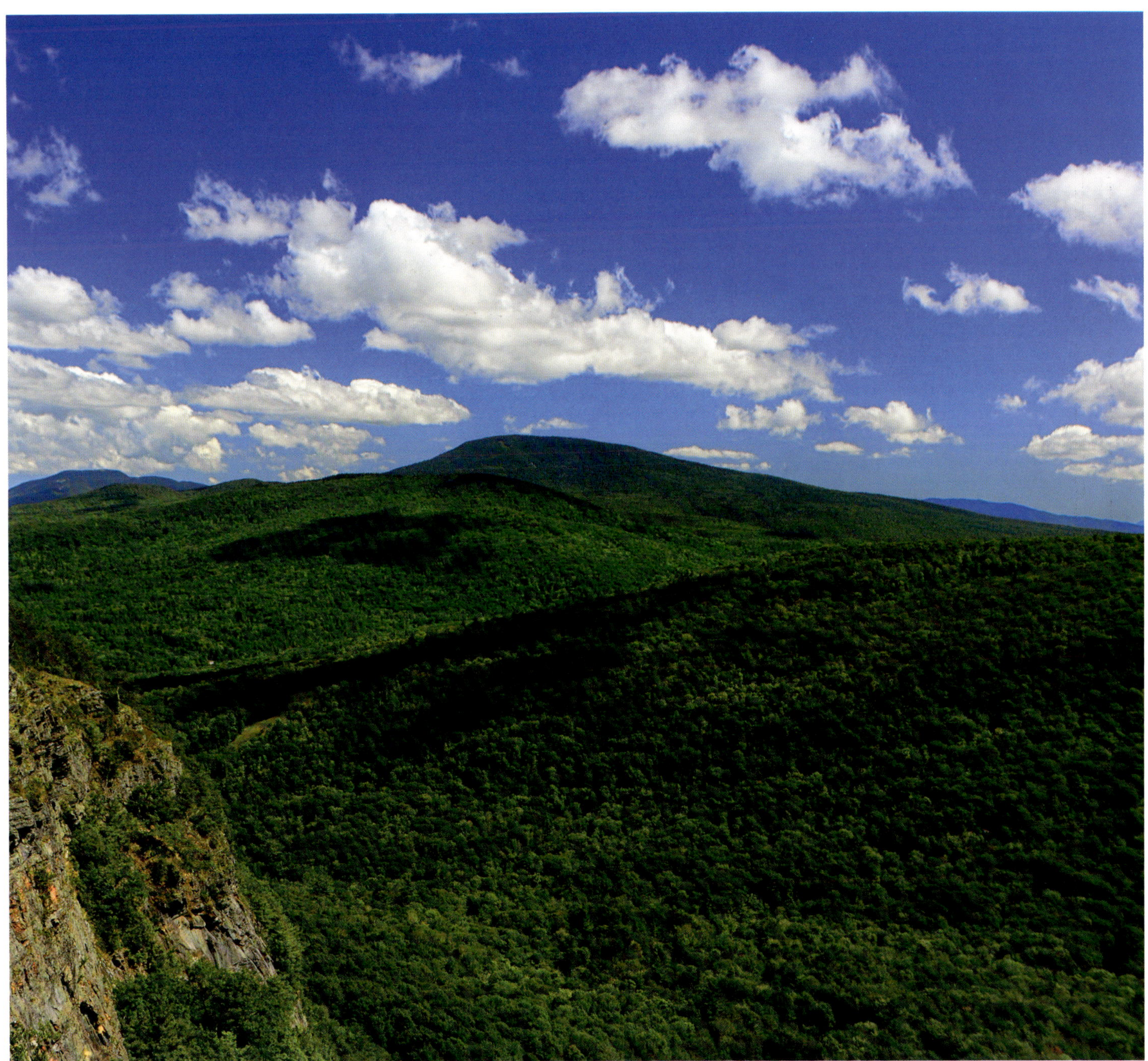

Smarts Mountain, New Hampshire

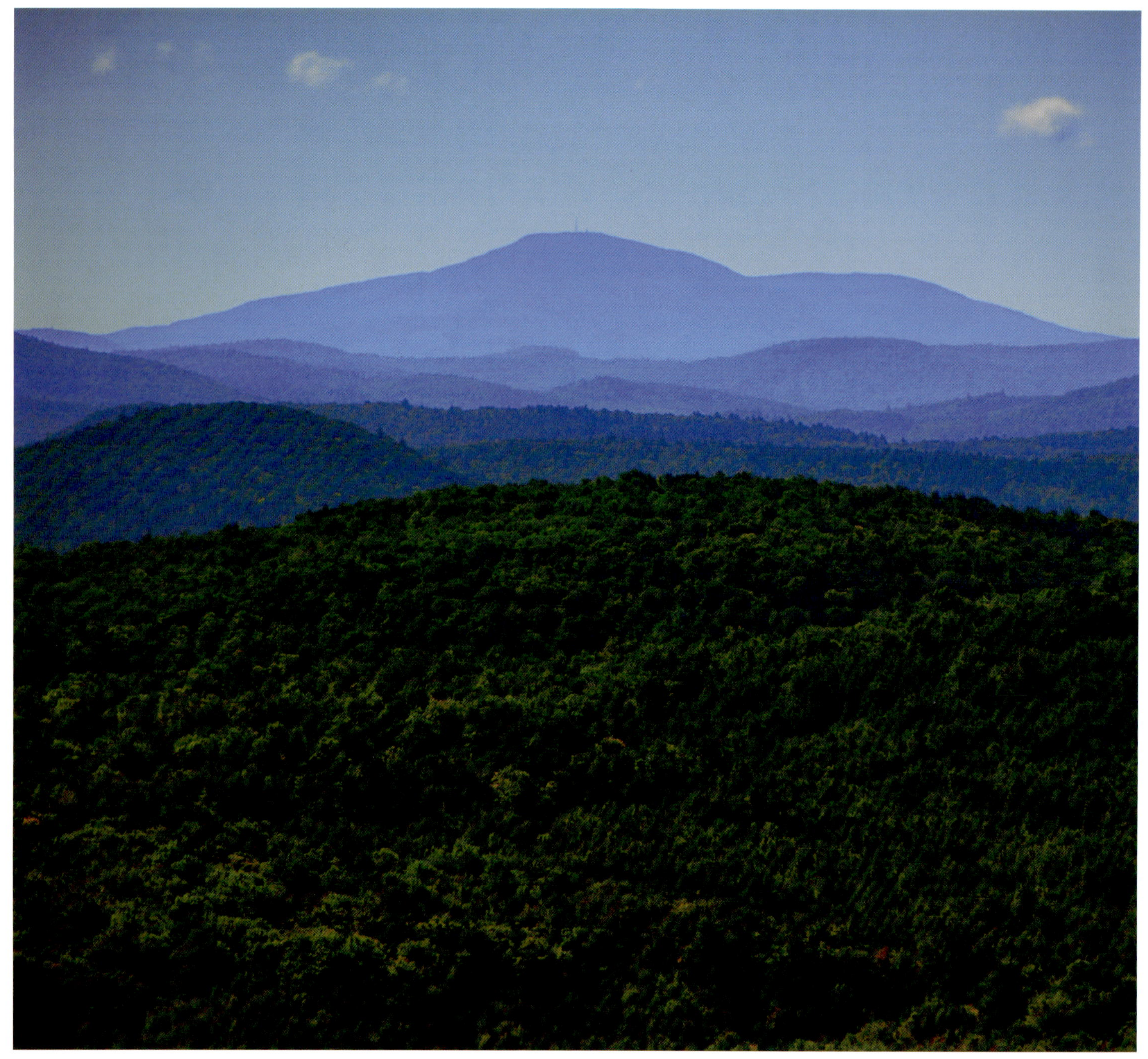

Lower New Hampshire peaks

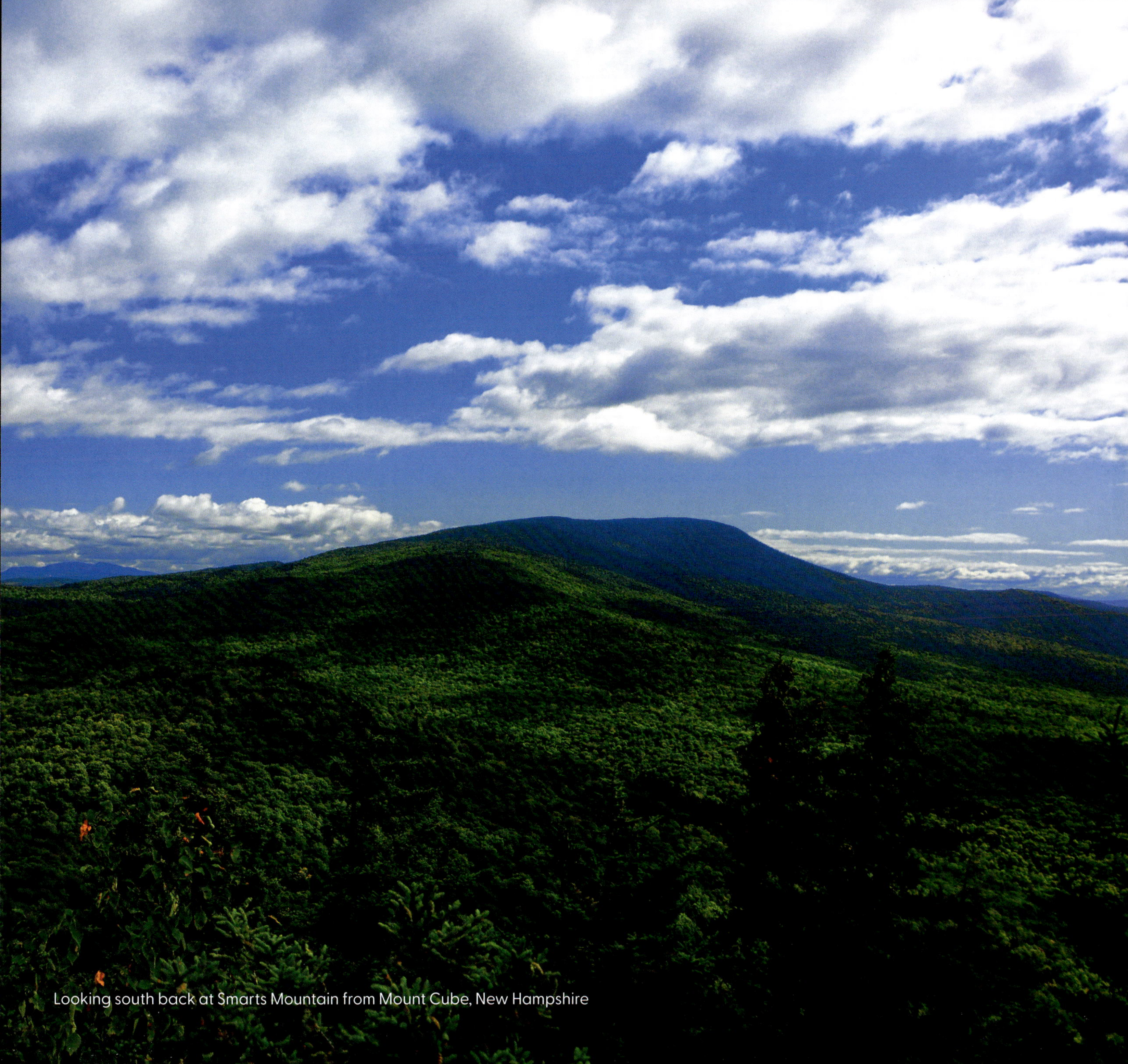

Looking south back at Smarts Mountain from Mount Cube, New Hampshire

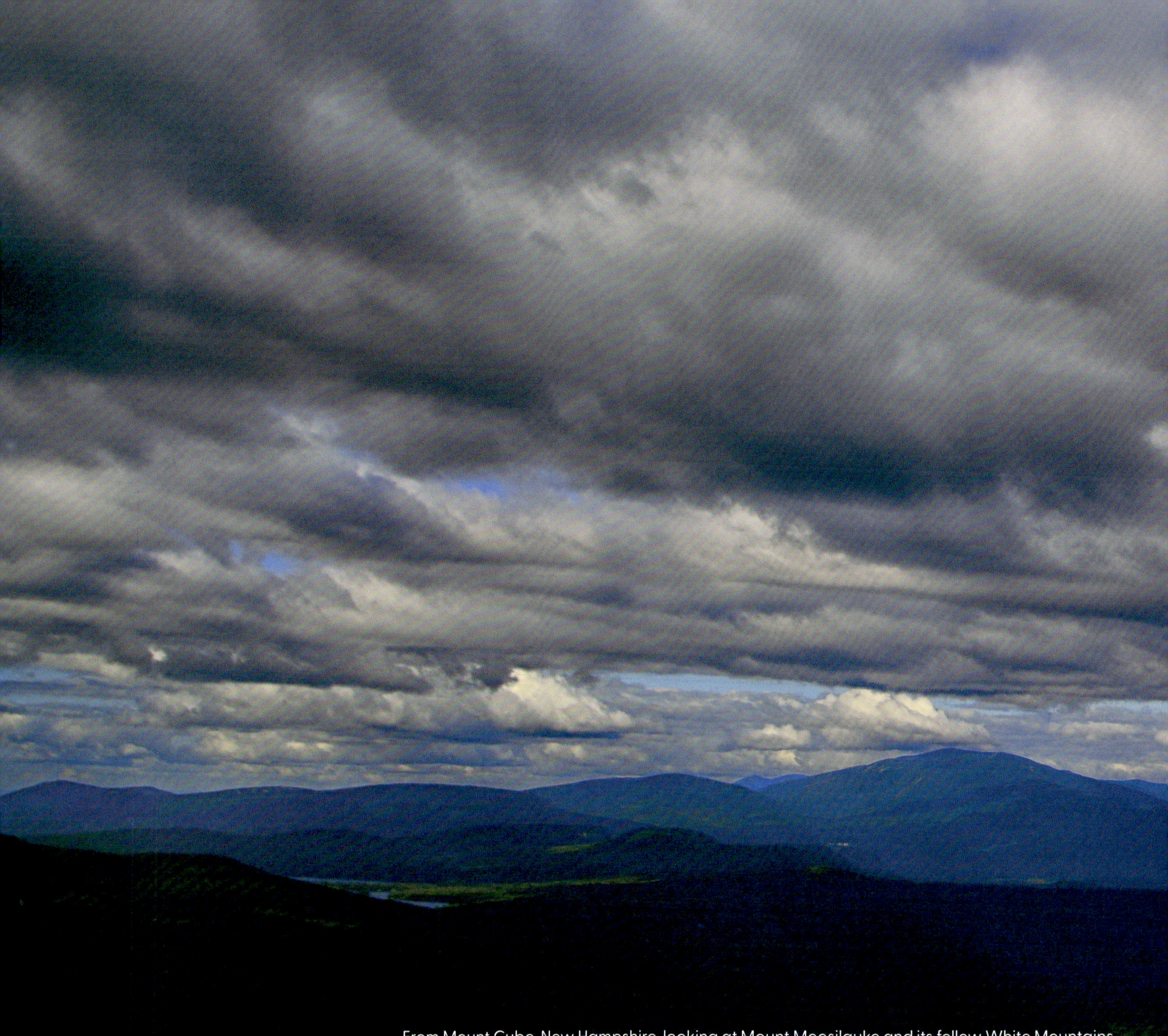

From Mount Cube, New Hampshire, looking at Mount Moosilauke and its fellow White Mountains

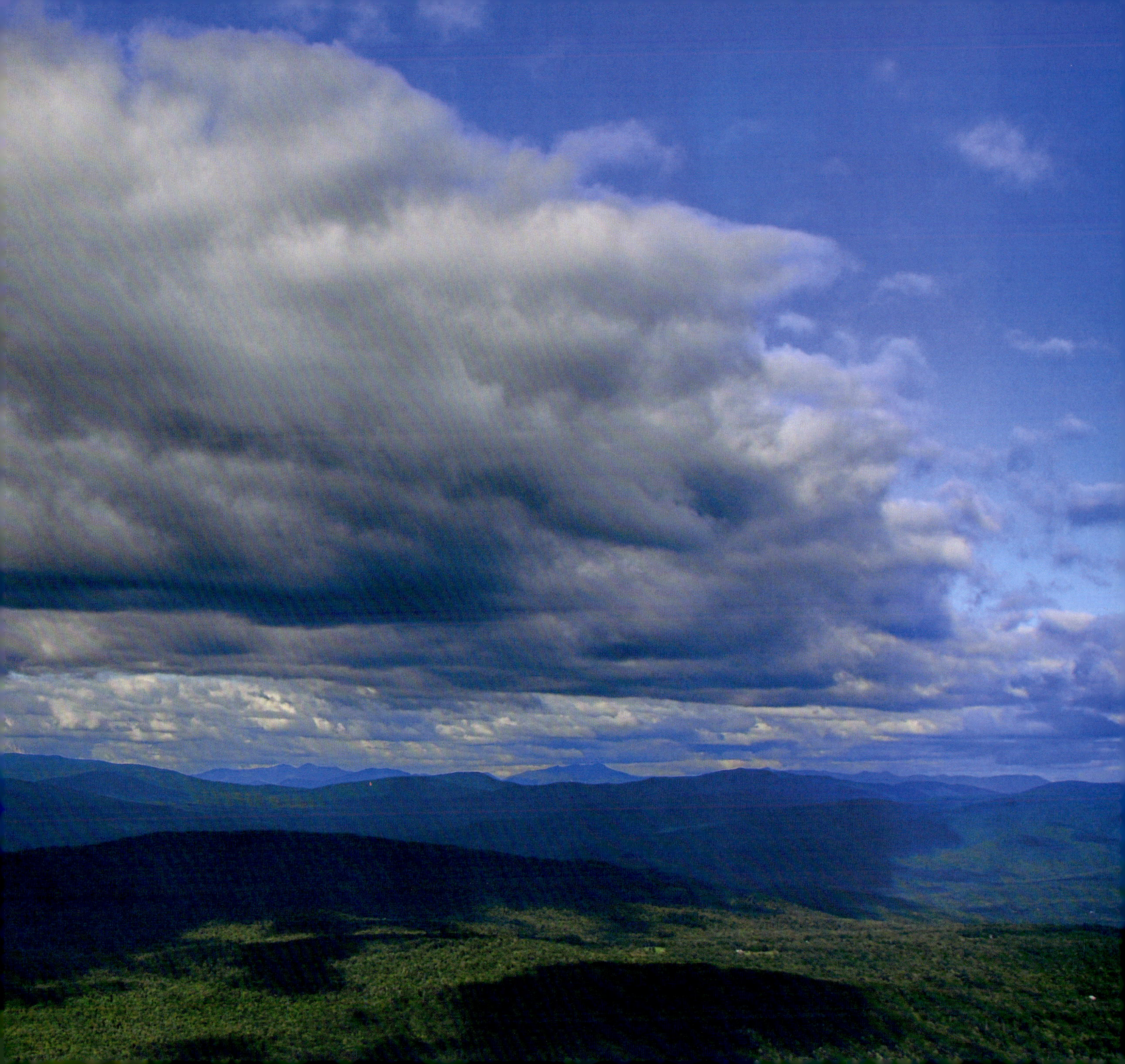

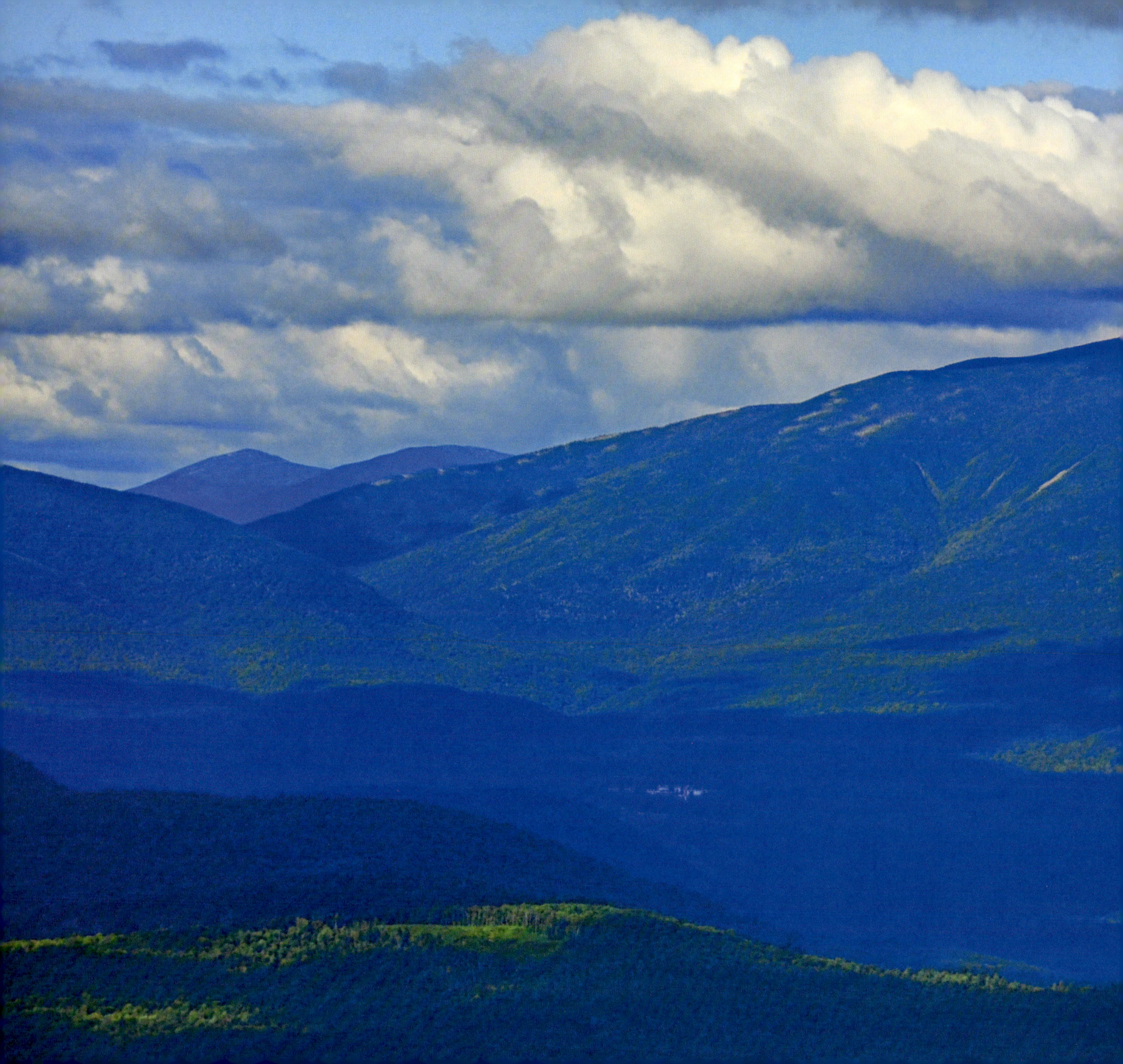

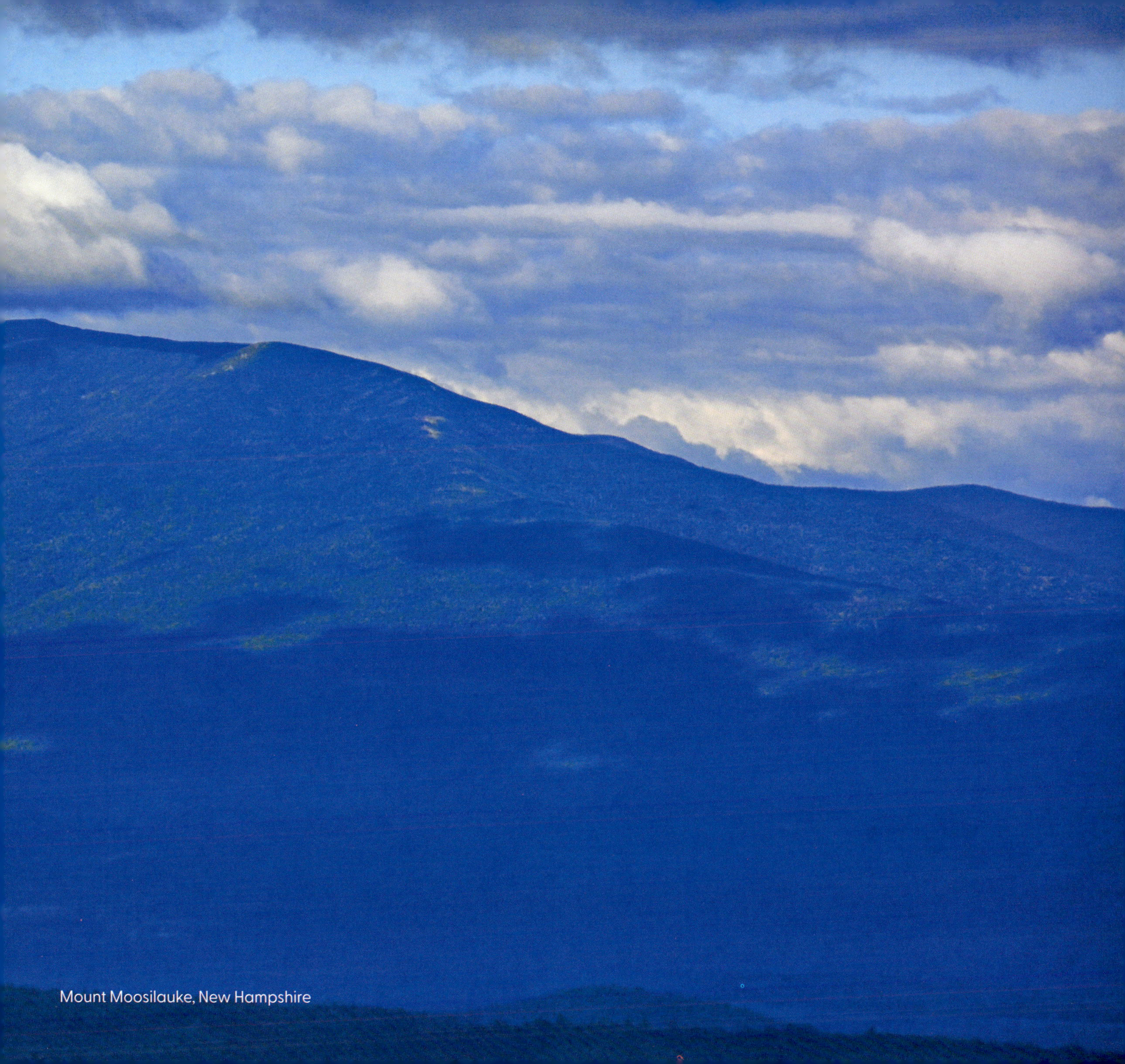

Mount Moosilauke, New Hampshire

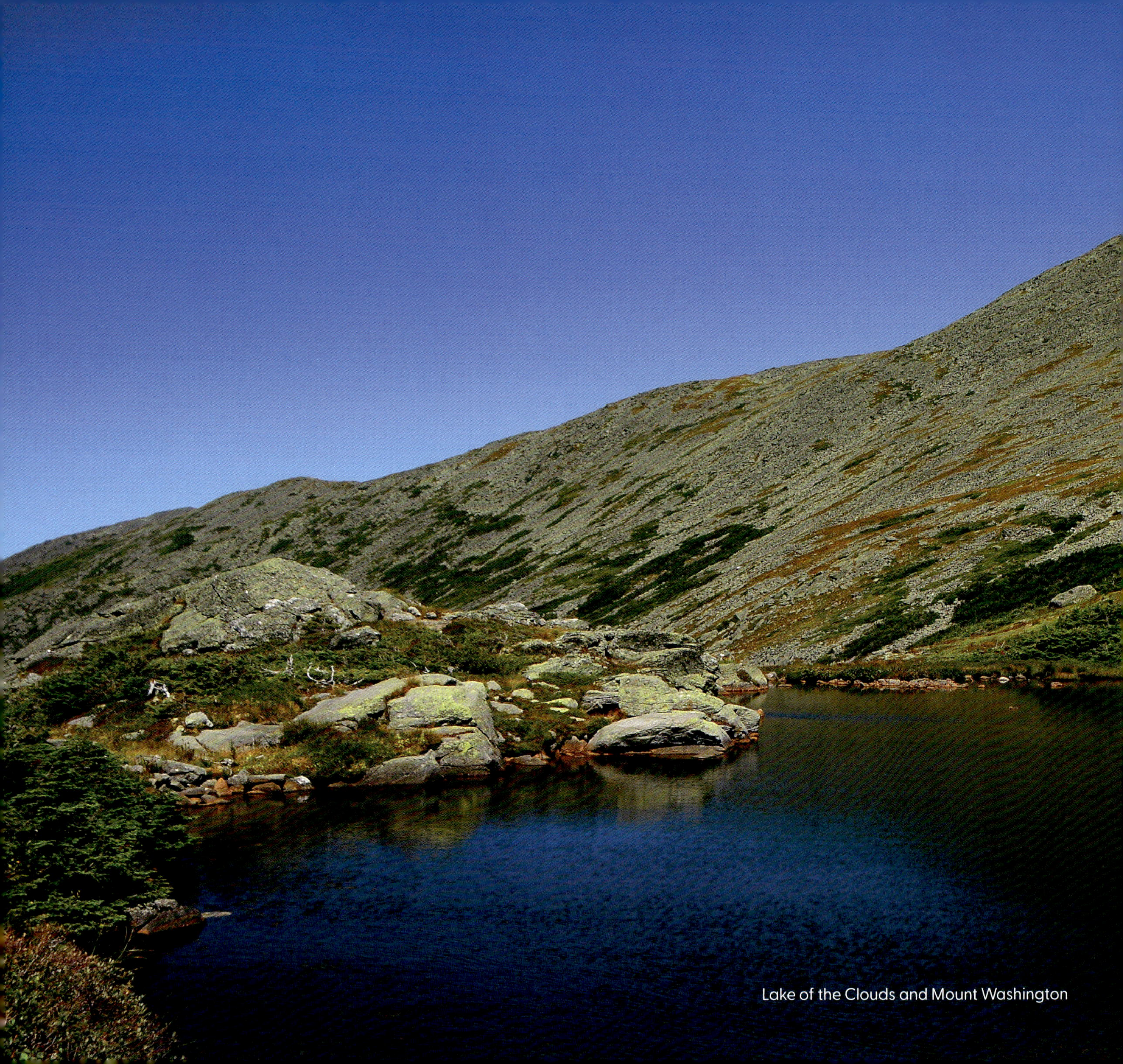

Lake of the Clouds and Mount Washington

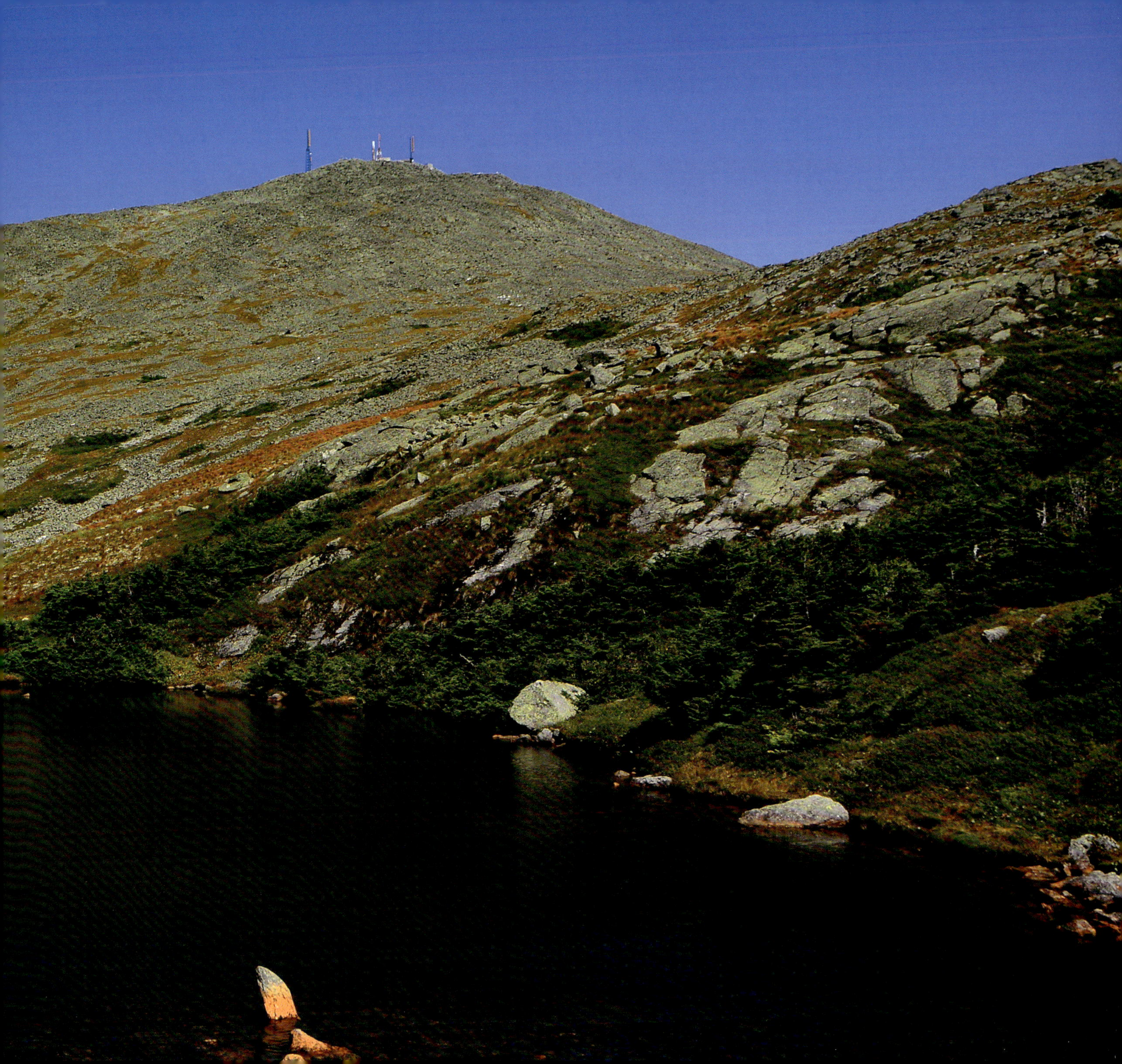

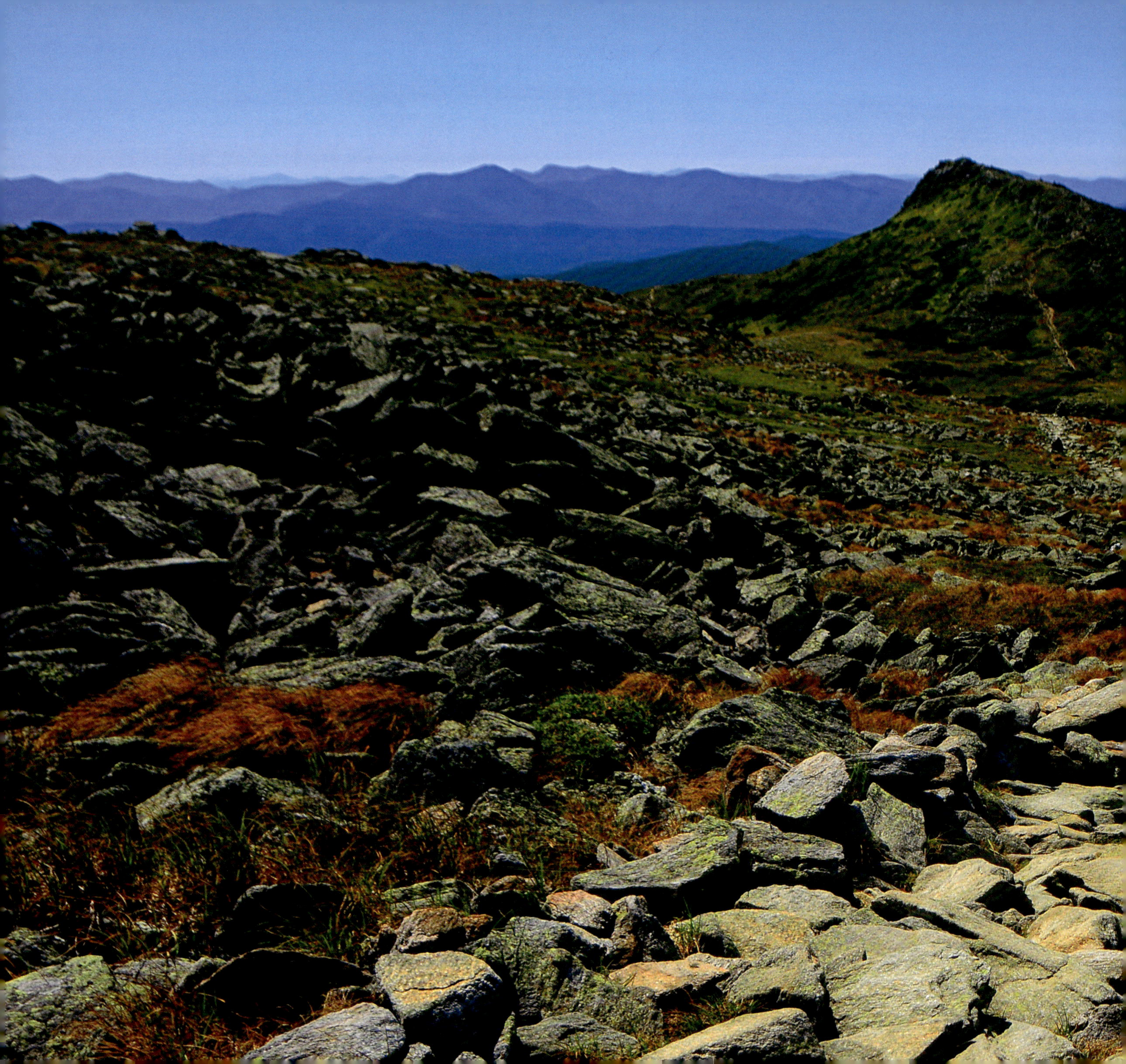

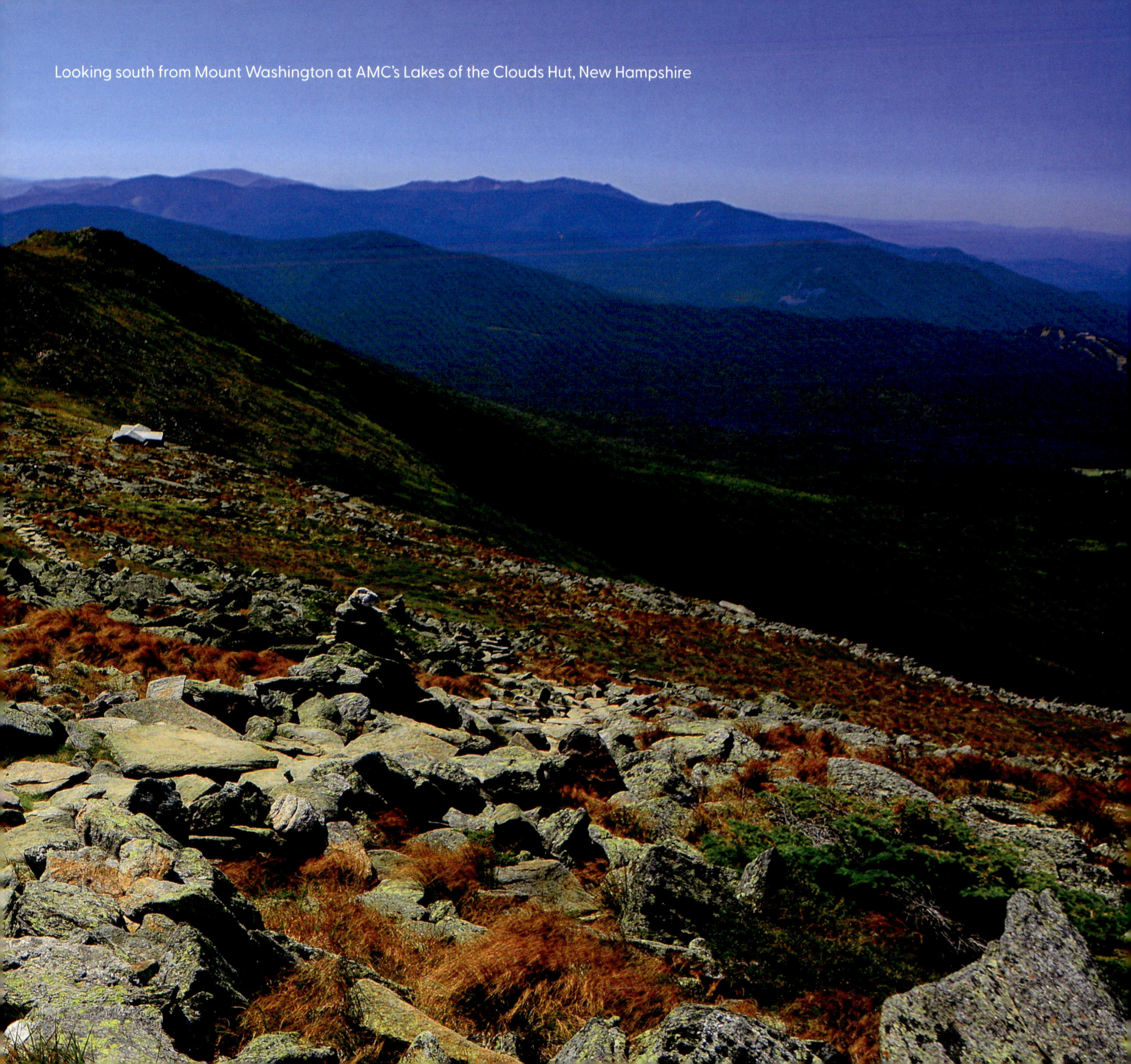

Looking south from Mount Washington at AMC's Lakes of the Clouds Hut, New Hampshire

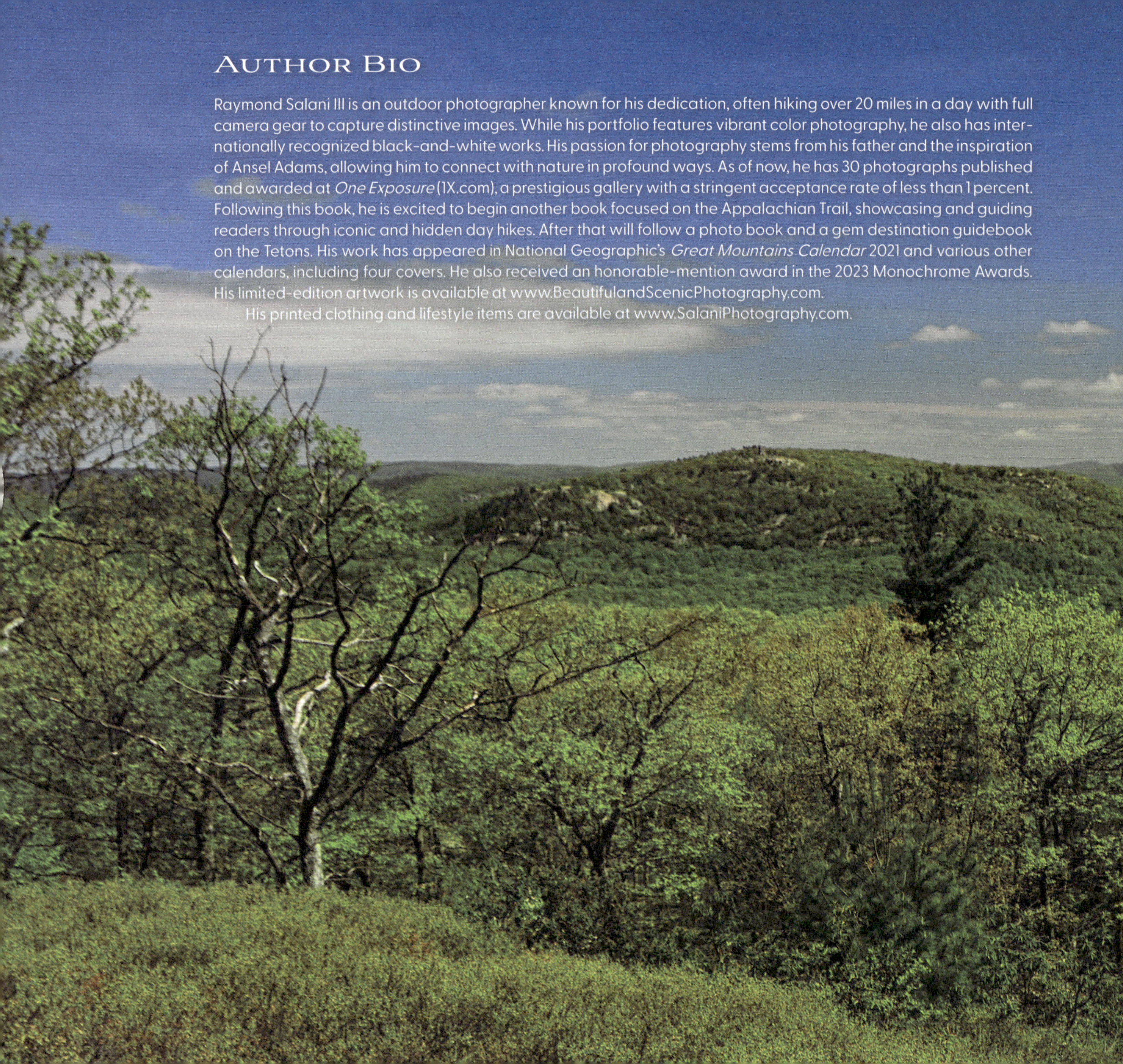

Author Bio

Raymond Salani III is an outdoor photographer known for his dedication, often hiking over 20 miles in a day with full camera gear to capture distinctive images. While his portfolio features vibrant color photography, he also has internationally recognized black-and-white works. His passion for photography stems from his father and the inspiration of Ansel Adams, allowing him to connect with nature in profound ways. As of now, he has 30 photographs published and awarded at *One Exposure* (1X.com), a prestigious gallery with a stringent acceptance rate of less than 1 percent. Following this book, he is excited to begin another book focused on the Appalachian Trail, showcasing and guiding readers through iconic and hidden day hikes. After that will follow a photo book and a gem destination guidebook on the Tetons. His work has appeared in National Geographic's *Great Mountains Calendar* 2021 and various other calendars, including four covers. He also received an honorable-mention award in the 2023 Monochrome Awards. His limited-edition artwork is available at www.BeautifulandScenicPhotography.com.

His printed clothing and lifestyle items are available at www.SalaniPhotography.com.